The Canadian Economic System

The Canadian Economic System

ANDRE RAYNAULD
Docteur (en sciences économiques) de l'Université de Paris
Professor and Head
Department of Economics
Université de Montréal

Translated from the French by
C. M. ROSS
Victoria College
University of Toronto

1967

THE MACMILLAN COMPANY OF CANADA LIMITED

TORONTO

Printed in Canada by Hignell Printing Limited

OUTLINE OF CONTENTS

DETAIL OF CONTENTS

Chapter 6. The Labour Market 111

Chapter 7.   Industrial Organization   133

Chapter 8.   The Anti-Combines Legislation   149

PART TWO: MONEY AND FINANCE

Chapter 9.   The Money Market   163

Chapter 10. The Capital Market 190

PART THREE: PUBLIC FINANCE

Chapter 11. Taxation   283

Chapter 12. Public Expenditures   308

Total expenditures by level of government; principal categories of expenditures; federal government expenditures; provincial government expenditures; municipal expenditures.

Chapter 13. Social Security   321

A. GENERAL CONSIDERATIONS 321

Chapter 16. The Balance of Payments and the Exchange Rate

PREFACE

Intended as a complement to any introductory work on economics, this book will, it is hoped, be read not only by students preparing for careers as economists, but by those of other university faculties who wish to know Canada better, and by all citizens who are concerned with public affairs.

The teaching of economics in Canada is based almost entirely on foreign texts; and, while this allows the student to make use of the best texts available, no matter where they originate, and helps to foster objective analysis, the disadvantage to the Canadian student is that he learns little about the economy of his own country from the examples or applications of economic theory that he finds in the texts he is generally using. It is the desire to make up for these omissions that prompted me to write this text on the Canadian economic system.

My original plan was simply to publish documents and statistical tables relating to the Canadian economy which research assistants, with the help of some members of the staff, had assembled and prepared for use in classes given by the Department of Economics at the University of Montreal. However, the demands of the subject proved to be such that I abandoned this original plan and turned to writing a whole book on the subject.

This book includes descriptive material whose choice has been dictated primarily by my concern with teaching elementary courses in economics. While it may also be looked on as a general study of the Canadian economy, it necessarily differs in emphasis from a work intended as a balanced picture of a country.

Since any textbook on a subject such as this is soon out of date, it has already been necessary to revise the statistical tables that appeared in the original French version. In addition to other less important changes which will be found throughout the text, such sections or chapters as those on the *caisses populaires*, the mortgage loan and the trust companies, the pension funds, and the consumer loan companies have been completely re-written, since in these particular fields the information brought out by the 1964 *Report of the Royal Commission on Banking and Finance* had to be taken into account. This English edition also contains an index; and a fairly extensive, annotated bibliography concludes each chapter.

In the suggested readings, titles of more general interest and relatively easy access are given first, followed by those of more specialized or restricted interest. At the end of some of the bibliographies, works on economic analysis are included.

I would like to express my deep gratitude to Professor Jean-Yves Rivard of the University of Montreal for preparing the readings and revising the statistical tables in this edition – a task which required several weeks of painstaking work – and to Professor C. M. Ross of Victoria College, the University of Toronto, who has done an excellent translation in spite of the many difficulties presented by the technical vocabulary.

I would also like to thank the College–Medical Books Department of the Macmillan Company of Canada Limited for the very exceptional care they have taken and the apparently unlimited time they have devoted to improving the manuscript and its presentation.

Part one

INCOME AND PRODUCTION

CHAPTER

1

THE NATIONAL ACCOUNTS

National accounting is one of the most useful tools of an economist, and frequently an indispensable one. It was defined in 1952 by the Organization for European Economic Co-operation (which has since become the Organization for Economic Co-operation and Development) as 'a technique which aims at presenting an over-all picture of a country's economy in quantitative terms'. The French economist Malinvaud offers an analogous but more detailed definition:

> National accounting is the presentation, based on a rigorous accounting framework, of the total of all the statistical data related to the economic activity of the country. It describes the fundamental phenomena of the production, distribution, division, and accumulation of wealth. It records the transactions among the major sectors that constitute the nation. Its results are presented in a form that facilitates comparisons and synthetic studies.[1]

National accounting is essentially economic and statistical; it differs in several important respects from business accounting. Its system of classifying the economic activities reflects the orientations and demands of economic theory. Similar considerations apply to the concepts and vocabulary that the national accounts

1. E. Malinvaud, *Initiation à la comptabilité nationale,* revised and updated edition, Paris, Presses Universitaires de France, 1960, p. 73.

make use of, so that these may be correctly referred to by the expression *descriptive economic models.*

In fact, although its origin goes quite far back, national accounting was developed as a result of the theoretical writings on national income that renewed the science of economics in the period between the two world wars and that will always be associated with the name of John Maynard Keynes. It was only in 1944 that the United States, England, and Canada adopted the essential rules of the present system, and only in 1947 that the United Nations proposed uniform international standards. National accounting is consequently something new.

Since 1947, remarkable progress has been made in the integration of statistical information. To the first national accounts set up, various elements have been progressively added, and today we have a clear picture of the complete and integrated system that most countries will adopt in the near future.

One cannot over-stress the use that economists make of national accounting. For them it is an item of daily consumption; this book will be filled with references to it. Malinvaud devotes part of the book from which we have already quoted to its various possible applications. His chapter titles show how important are the fields in which it is employed: studies in economic growth, international comparisons, structural analyses (exchanges between industries and changes in the composition of industries), business cycles, and economic forecasting.[1]

In addition to supplying the information necessary for economic analysis, the national accounts put this information in order and reconcile the estimates that have been made first on the many different particular categories and sub-categories. They are also an indispensable instrument for the elaboration of economic policy.

1. Malinvaud, *op. cit.*

A. The National Product

Through the national accounts we are primarily seeking as complete an evaluation as possible of the total economic activities of the country. *The over-all measure of this total is called the national product. It may be defined as the sum of all goods and services produced during a given period of time.* As one can well imagine, it is not easy to do this huge addition without making errors. Fortunately there are three different ways of measuring the national product so that the answers serve as a check for one another. These three methods are based on final output, expenditure, and income, as follows:

1. FINAL OUTPUT

Each product made and each service rendered has a price by means of which one can express them all, no matter how different, in the same terms: the value in dollars. The haircut can thus come into the national product in the same way as the automobile, paper, or potatoes. One must not, however, merely total up the value of the products of all the enterprises in the country, because then one would be counting the same thing several times over. A great number of products serve to manufacture other products, and in the selling price of each we find the accumulated value of the products that have been consumed in the course of transforming it into its present state.

We must therefore eliminate from our calculations all the intermediary products or services and retain only final output, that is, the products or the services that have reached the final stage in their transformation. A second way of resolving the difficulty consists of deducting from the total value of the production of all enterprises the sum of the intermediary purchases, a process which gives the value added. *Value added, then, is the difference between the value of the goods and services produced and the value of the goods and services consumed by this production over a certain period of time.* The following figure and example will make this clear:

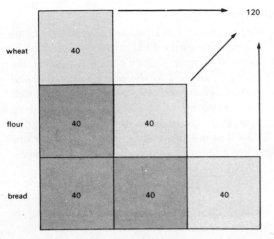

Final output: 120

Let us suppose three stages of production and three enterprises represented by wheat, flour, and bread. If we were to add the production of the three enterprises, let us say, 40 + 80 + 120 = 240, as in the figure, it is evident that we would be counting the wheat three times and the flour twice, for the price of the bread already includes the price of the flour that has been used to produce it. In order to establish the national product we may therefore retain only the final commodity, that of the bread in our example, or else we may deduct from the total product of each enterprise the use that it has made of the products of other enterprises.

In this example, the wheat producer hypothetically bought nothing, and the value of the wheat (40) consequently belongs to him in total; the miller bought for 40 and sells for 80 so that the transformation (the value added) of the wheat into the flour is of the value of 40. Finally, the baker bought for 80 and sells for 120: his services are worth 40. Whether we add the total of the values added or whether we count only the final product we obtain the same correct answer: 120.

TABLE 1:1

**Gross Domestic Product at Factor Cost,
by Industry, Canada 1963**

Value added by	*Millions of dollars*	*Percentage distribution*
1. Agriculture	2,401	6.3
2. Forestry	408	1.1
3. Fishing and trapping	114	0.3
4. Mining, quarrying, and oil wells	1,578	4.1
5. Manufacturing	9,811	25.6
6. Construction	1,991	5.2
7. Transportation	2,331	6.1
8. Storage	97	0.3
9. Communication	928	2.4
10. Electric-power, gas, and water utilities	1,260	3.3
11. Wholesale trade	1,737	4.5
12. Retail trade	3,373	8.8
13. Finance, insurance, and real estate	4,019	10.5
14. Public administration and defence	2,812	7.3
15. Services	5,431	14.2
16. *Gross domestic product at factor cost*	*38,291*	*100*
Indirect taxes, less subsidies	5,565	
Net income paid to non-residents	614	
Residual error of estimate	235	
Gross national product at market prices	*43,007*	

NOTE: Unless otherwise indicated, all the tables in this chapter are drawn from Dominion Bureau of Statistics, *National Accounts, Income and Expenditure*, 1963.

In order to be included in the national product every economic activity (every commodity) must have a price. Certain activities have none, such as agricultural produce that is consumed on the farm, the occupation of a house by its owner (the rent is not explicit), the services of the wife in the home. In the first two examples the commodities or the services are officially evaluated according to the prices that exist elsewhere for these same commodities. In the third, the activity is completely excluded from the national product.

The sum of the final products or the sum of the value added by each industry allows us to arrive at the national product through the domestic product at factor cost. We shall explain this last concept later; it may be forgotten at this stage.

The value added measures the real contribution of each industry or each industrial group to the whole economy. Table 1:1 supplies this information for Canada for the year 1963.

2. EXPENDITURE

A second way of measuring the national product consists of adding all the expenditures that have been made on final output. Instead of considering the products and services at the time they are being created, we consider their destination. What use is made of the goods and services that are not consumed by enterprises in the course of production? They may be used for personal consumption, they may be bought by governments, they may serve as investment, or they may be exported. These in fact are the usual categories of national expenditure: personal expenditure, government expenditure on goods and services, capital formation, and exports.

Consumption.

Consumption is the destruction of goods through use. The main consumption expenditure is on food, clothing, shelter, household operation, transportation, and personal services. The durable goods bought by families such as furniture, automobiles, and household equipment are not consumption in the strict sense of the term since they last for a long time, but for national accounts purposes they are treated as such. The purchase of real estate or of houses, however, is not considered a consumption expenditure.

Government Expenditure on Goods and Services.

Government expenditure on goods and services consist of the outlays of the federal, provincial, and municipal governments whether for purposes of consumption or of investment. The salaries paid, the office equipment, the new public buildings, the new highways, military pay and allowances, are all typical government expenditure. The goods and services are added in such a way as to exclude from all expenditure the transfer payments defined below. Capital expenditure and current expenditure by governments are generally kept separate.

Investment.

Investment is a central concept in economic analysis. In its general meaning it designates the additions to the real capital of the country: it includes residential, industrial, and commercial construction and the conversion of existing buildings, and the production of plant equipment, tools, machinery, trucks, and so on. The aggregate of these items is called either the investment in fixed capital or, more generally in Canada, fixed capital formation. Since public investment is included in the preceding paragraph, investment is here limited to business fixed capital formation.

Stocks.

Also attached to the concept of investment is the increase in stocks or inventories of all raw materials, goods in process, and finished but unsold goods. The national accounts record the value of the physical changes in inventories calculated on an average price (the profits realized or the losses incurred are irrelevant). The variations in inventories are taken into account in determining effective production for the year. If sales equal 100 and stocks have diminished by 20, production has only been 80.

Exports Less Imports.

In an open economy exports and imports must also be accounted for. Since it is a question of computing the country's total production, the products and services sold abroad must be added to the preceding categories. For the same reason expenditure on imported products or services must be deducted. Exports and imports are understood in a very broad sense and include all the items in the balance of international current account (not only those included in the trade balance).

The actual and relative importance of each of these components of the national product is indicated for the year 1963 in Table 1:2.

TABLE 1 : 2

Components of Gross National Expenditure, Canada 1963

	Millions of dollars	Percentage distribution
1. Personal expenditure on consumer goods and services	27,230	63.3
2. Government expenditure on goods and services	8,076	18.8
3. Business gross fixed capital formation	7,495	17.4
4. Value of physical change in inventories	459	1.1
5. Exports of goods and services	9,054	21.1
6. Imports of goods and services	−9,542	−22.2
7. Residual error of estimate	235	0.5
Gross national expenditure at market prices	*43,007*	*100*

Consumption expenditure amounts to almost two-thirds of the gross national product, government expenditure to 19 per cent, and capital formation to 17 per cent. The net balance on the international current account is negative. The gross national product is $43 billion.

3. THE GENERATION OF INCOME

The third method by which we can consider and arrive at the national product is to add all incomes generated in the course of production. *We are, of course, dealing with the same production as before and hence with final output. Now the value of this unduplicated output is necessarily equal to the total income of the factors of production (indirect taxes are neglected for the moment*). The factors of production are land, labour, capital, and entrepreneurship, which earn respectively rent, salaries and wages, interest, and profits. These are the categories of income into which the national product may be classified on this side of the coin. Salaries and wages are the labour income and the other components may be grouped under the term investment income.

Before going further with this third approach to the national product, it is necessary to introduce other closely related concepts.

4. TRANSFER PAYMENTS

The income and the expenditure with which we have dealt up to now are moneys expended by the producer in exchange for a service or for a contribution to production. *There are various other payments which are in no way related to production: for example, family allowances, unemployment benefits, old age pensions. These payments are called transfer payments, because, for the country as a whole, they are merely a redistribution of income: in these examples, the government has levied a tax on some in order to pass it on to others.* Hence the word *transfer*. An income approach consistent with the expenditure approach that we had before obviously requires that transfer payments be excluded from the calculations of the national product.

The above examples of transfer payments do not involve any ambiguity. There are others, however, that some readers may find difficulty in accepting as such. It should be noted, for example, that the profit realized from the sale of an existing building is a transfer payment, but that the real estate agent's commission is a return to a factor of production for services rendered; and that inheritances and gifts are transfer payments, as are subsidies and welfare assistance allowances. The profits realized on all trading by Canadian residents in existing securities, such as stocks or bonds, are also transfer payments from one individual or institution to another without change in the aggregate.

5. MARKET PRICES AND FACTOR COST

The national product can be evaluated according to the prices that the consumer pays, that is, the market prices. But these prices often include indirect taxes on the product. The price paid by the consumer, then, does not go entirely to the producer: part goes to the government. In other words there are both a consumer's price and a producer's price, the difference between the two being the indirect taxes. The producer's price is that which corresponds to the sum of the returns to the factors of production, as was explained previously. That is why the national accounts use the expression *at factor cost* to designate this price system. *By subtracting all the indirect taxes from the national product evaluated at market prices we thus obtain the national product at factor cost.*

6. GROSS NATIONAL PRODUCT AND NET NATIONAL PRODUCT

A building or a piece of equipment is not entirely consumed in the manufacture of one unit of a product, but it does depreciate. The wear and tear must be included in the cost of manufacture and in the selling price. Until the capital good is replaced, this price component is put aside as provisions or reserves for depreciation. At the national level, the concept of depreciation and the provision for it appears in the distinction that is made between gross investment and net investment.

gross investment = net investment + capital consumption allowances

Only the net investment represents a real addition to the capital stock of the country. The capital consumption allowances merely serve to compensate for the wear that existing capital has suffered in the course of production. The same concepts of 'gross' and 'net' are applied to the national product. *The gross national product includes the capital consumption allowances and the net national product does not.*

7. NATIONAL INCOME

The term national income is usually reserved for the sum of the factor incomes, corresponding to the net national product at factor cost, whereas the gross national product generally means the sum of the gross national expenditure at market prices.

The categories of national income used in the Canadian National Accounts are as follows:

1. Wages, salaries, and supplementary labour income;
2. Military pay and allowances;
3. Corporations profits before taxes (before the payment of direct taxes);
4. Rent, interest, and miscellaneous investment income;
5. Net income received by farm operators from farm production;
6. Net income of non-farm unincorporated businesses (including the net income of independent professional practitioners).

Since we are now acquainted with some additional concepts,

TABLE 1 : 3

National Income and Gross National Product, Canada 1963

	Millions of dollars	*Percentage distribution*
1. Wages, salaries, and supplementary labour income	21,550	66.2
2. Military pay and allowances	598	1.9
3. Corporation profits before taxes*	3,327	10.2
4. Rent, interest, and miscellaneous investment income	3,025	9.3
5. Accrued net income of farm operators from farm production	1,786	5.5
6. Net income of non-farm unincorporated businesses	2,451	7.5
7. Inventory valuation adjustment	−184	−0.6
8. *Net national income at factor cost*	*32,553*	*100*
9. Indirect taxes less subsidies	5,565	
10. Capital consumption allowances and miscellaneous valuation adjustments	5,124	
11. Residual error of estimate	−235	
Gross national product at market prices	*43,007*	

*Excluding dividends paid to non-residents.

TABLE 1 : 4

The Three Approaches to the National Product, Canada 1963, millions of dollars

Production		Expenditure		Income	
Primary industries	4,501	Personal expenditure on consumer goods and services		Wages, salaries, supplementary labour income, and military pay and allowances	22,148
Manufacturing	9,811		27,230	Investment income	6,352
Construction	1,991	Government expenditure on goods and services		Net income of unincorporated business	4,237
Trade	5,110		8,076	Inventory valuation adjustment	−184
Services	14,066	Business gross fixed capital formation (including physical change in inventories)			
Public administration	2,812		7,954		
		Balance of trade	−488	National income	32,553
Gross domestic product at factor cost	38,291				
				Indirect taxes less subsidies	5,565
Indirect taxes less subsidies	5,565			Capital consumption allowances	5,124
Net income paid to non-residents	−614			Residual error of estimate	−235
Residual error of estimate*	−235	Residual error of estimate	235		
Gross national product at market prices	43,007	Gross national product at market prices	43,007	Gross national product at market prices	43,007

we can state more precisely that if we add indirect taxes (less subsidies) and capital consumption allowances to the national income as defined above, we obtain the gross national product at market prices.

The sum of the incomes generated by production, then, gives us, as we have stated on page 5, a third method for evaluating the national product. The distribution of these incomes for the year 1963 is shown in Table 1:3.

8. NATIONAL AND DOMESTIC PRODUCT

The national product measures the production and the income that accrue to individuals and institutions normally resident in Canada. Residence status is therefore substituted for citizenship status. Canadian students and tourists abroad, and employees of Canadian embassies, are counted among residents of Canada, but Canadian citizens who usually live abroad are non-residents. *The national product as defined is clearly different from the domestic product which refers to the production carried on within the borders of the country.* The resident of Windsor who works in Detroit contributes to the *domestic product* of the United States but to the *national product* of Canada.

In practice the distinction between the national product and the domestic product takes into account only interest and dividends and travel expenditure. Payments of this kind to non-residents are subtracted from the *domestic* product and payments received from non-residents added to it, in order to get the *national* product.

---

*Concerning Table 1:4: an error of estimate will be found in all calculations. This error conceals no mystery. In Canada the national product is calculated by the income method and by the expenditure method. Since these are two largely independent estimates, two answers are found. Half of the difference between the two is subtracted from the higher figure and added to the lower figure, thereby finally giving us a single estimate of the national product. In 1963 the estimate based on income exceeded the estimate based on expenditure by 470 million dollars. Hence we find +235 on the expenditure side and —235 on the income side.

9. THE CONNECTIONS BETWEEN THE VARIOUS CONCEPTS OF THE
   NATIONAL PRODUCT

In order to understand the several connections between the three approaches from which we have considered the national product, it will perhaps be useful now to compare the three. In brief they are simply three different methods of breaking down the national product. Table 1:4 reproduces schematically the three previous tables.

Table 1:4 brings out the differences between National Income, Gross National Product, and Gross Domestic Product at Factor Cost. The reader should check to see that he can also find the Net Domestic Product at Factor Cost, the Gross Domestic Product at Market Prices, the Net National Product at Market Prices, the Gross National Product at Factor Cost. Each of these may easily be found from the table with the help of the previous explanations.

B. The Accounting Framework

In the first section of this chapter certain concepts relating to the aggregate of the economic activities of the country were defined. We have sought to learn about the whole. We shall now examine the sectors and the transactions between them. In the statistical framework the sectors are sub-totals that we try to make as homogeneous as possible so as to reduce the complexity and the number of the economic activities while at the same time stressing the significant and important group phenomena.

1. GENERAL RULES

Economic activity is classified according to the nature of the agents and the nature of the transactions. The agents (or *transactors*) are those responsible for the economic activity – for example, the entrepreneurs – and the transactions are the result of this activity – for example, the sale of a product.

Let us suppose that a consumer buys a commodity from a firm, paying for it in cash. We have two sectors and two goods. We can record the transaction in relation to each one of the sectors and in relation to each one of the goods as follows:

(a) Sectors Account.

	Personal sector			Business sector	
	Debit = *good* *received*	*Credit =* *good* *given*		*Debit =* *good* *received*	*Credit =* *good* *given*
Purchase of the commodity	10	–	Sale of the commodity	–	10
Money paid	–	10	Money received	10	–
Total	10	10	Total	10	10

(b) Transactions Account.

	Commodity			Money	
	Debit = *good* *received*	*Credit =* *good* *given*		*Debit =* *good* *received*	*Credit =* *good* *given*
Purchase of the commodity by the personal sector	10	–	Money paid by the personal sector	–	10
Sale of the commodity by the busi- ness sector	–	10	Money received by the business sector	10	–
Total	10	10	Total	10	10

As we can see, each transaction gives rise to four entries in each of the two accounts. National accounting is, so to speak, a quadruple-entry accounting system. The debit and the credit are necessarily equal in each account. In the transactions account, this is so because the purchase of one sector is the sale of the other. If the purchase is not paid for, the buyer contracts a debt and the seller grants a loan. Debt and loan then replace the entries for the transfer of the money. In the sectors account, the reason the debit also equals the credit is that we have made a double entry of the transaction concerned: one for what has been given and the other for what has been accepted in exchange. In a sectors account, the transactions are shown on the lines; in a transactions account, the sectors are shown on the lines.

The expressions *debit* and *credit* are always open to confusion. In the example given above, we must place on the debit side the good received and on the credit side the good offered. Fortunately these terms are increasingly being replaced by more descriptive words of which the main ones are as follows:

CREDIT		DEBIT
income	*and*	expenditure
revenue	*and*	expenditure
source	*and*	disposition
receipts	*and*	payments
origin	*and*	uses
debts	*and*	claims

(c) Economic Table.

The Canadian national accounts include four sectors accounts and two transactions accounts.

In practice no country has found it useful to set up separate transactions accounts for each of the sectors. (It is, moreover, often impossible because of the lack of information.) In France, however, it has been considered advisable to sum up the sectors accounts and the transactions accounts in an economic table which gives a useful over-all view such as is lacking in the Canadian system. The example on page 19 is much too simplified to bring out all the advantages and limitations of an economic table of this type, but it does show the principle of its construction. One goes about it in the following way:

	Debit = expenditure			Credit = income		
	Personal sector	Business sector	Total	Personal sector	Business sector	Total
Commodity	10	–	10	–	10	10
Money	–	10	10	10	–	10
Total	10	10	20	10	10	20

The columns reproduce the sectors accounts and the lines the various categories of transactions. We place the expenditure on the left and the income on the right, making sure that the entries are identical to those we had before. The economic table is undoubtedly more difficult to read than the sectors or transactions accounts. Instead of the purchase and sale of a commodity we have 'commodity' only, since, on the same line, we record the purchase under the expenditure column and the sale under the income column.

2. THE SECTORS

In the simplified Canadian accounts,[1] the economic sectors are limited to four: persons, businesses, governments, and non-residents:

(a) Persons.

The personal sector includes not only individuals as consumers but also the non-profit institutions and organizations such as universities and trade unions; private pension funds and various accounts related to insurance companies and to trust companies are also included.

---

1. By the simplified accounts reference is made to the national accounts published on a quarterly and annual basis. They are described in the publication *National Accounts, Income and Expenditure, 1926-1956.* By detailed accounts we shall be referring to the *National Transactions Accounts* which were drawn up for the years 1946 to 1954, then abandoned. These latter accounts are much more complete than the first. See further the paragraph on the development of the Canadian accounting system.

(b) Businesses.

This sector includes corporations, unincorporated business enterprises, independent professional practitioners, and government business enterprises. To this sector, then, belong all individuals and companies operating for profit.

(c) Governments.

The non-commercial activities of the federal, provincial, and municipal governments are placed in the government sector.

(d) Non-residents.

The non-resident sector includes all transactions carried on between residents and non-residents of Canada whether the parties be individuals, business enterprises, or governments.[1]

In the expanded national transactions accounts, there are eleven rather than four sectors. These are:

1. consumers
2. unincorporated businesses
3. non-financial corporations
4. government enterprises
5. banking
6. life insurance
7. other financial institutions
8. the federal government
9. provincial governments
10. municipal governments
11. rest of the world

In relation to the four preceding sectors, we can see that the original sectors 1 and 4 remain the same (except for the name) and that the business sector has been broken down into six and the government sector into three groups. Of the six groups under 'business', three are non-financial and three are financial enterprises.

---

1. The non-resident sector is not a group of homogeneous economic agents in the sense in which the preceding groups are.

The sector classification aims at constituting transacting groups whose behaviour and motivations are as homogeneous as possible. For example, consumers and producers must be clearly distinguished. Similarly, because investment is a basic function in an economy, statistics must seek to isolate it from the other functions and to group together all those who invest, in such a way that more may be learned about the subject.[1] In practice the application of this principle raises innumerable difficulties. Should we, for instance, class government business enterprises under the 'government' sector or the 'business' sector?

In the simplified national accounts the number of sectors – four – is clearly too much reduced to give homogeneous groups, no matter from what angle we may view them. The eleven sectors of the expanded system still present several problems. Thus the sector 'banking' includes the Bank of Canada, which is a government agency in charge of the monetary policy, the chartered banks, which are private enterprises, and the Exchange Fund, which is ultimately the responsibility of the Department of Finance.

In order to illustrate a sector account we reproduce in Table 1:5 the statistics relating to personal income and expenditure in Canada for the year 1963.

It should be pointed out that the sector accounts do not add up directly to the national income or the national product, because certain transactions between sectors cancel out in the process of consolidation. In Table 1:5 the transfer payments are entered at the sector level, but as we have said previously, they are excluded from the national income. The partial accounts do not produce the total accounts when added together.

---

1. In order to separate different functions, some sectors have to be broken up: the consumer becomes a business in the Canadian system when he builds a house, and the individual entrepreneur becomes a consumer in several respects. Jean Marchal, for one, in his *Nouveaux Eléments de comptabilité nationale française* (Cujas, 1962), rebels against this rule. In his eyes the unity of the economic agent takes precedence over the multiple activities in which he may engage. This question has led to sharp controversy.

TABLE 1 : 5

**Personal Income and Expenditure Account, Canada 1963,
millions of dollars**

Expenditure		*Income*	
Expenditure on goods and services	27,230	Wages, salaries, and supplementary labour income (less contributions)	20,712
Personal direct taxes	2,910	Military pay and allowances	598
Personal net saving	2,631	Net income of unincorporated business	4,101
		Rent, interest, and dividends paid out to persons	3,487
		Transfer payments	3,873
Total	32,771	Total	32,771

3. THE TRANSACTIONS

Economic activities are classified according to their nature. Four categories of activities are generally distinguished:

(a) transactions relating to goods and services
(b) transactions relating to factors of production
(c) transactions in securities and claims, such as stocks and bonds
(d) unilateral transactions: transfer payments. These payments are made with no direct service in return.

These transactions are organized without loss of identity into a certain number of transactions accounts which are set up for each one of the sectors previously identified. In principle, a complete accounting system[1] would include four different transactions accounts for each sector, of which the components and interconnections would be those of Table 1:6 (for the business sector), namely:

> a production account
> an income and expenditure account
> a financial transactions account
> a capital account

(a) The Production Account.

The production account consists of an economic table of inter-industry flows of goods and services. Only France, to the writer's knowledge, incorporates these transactions in its annual national accounts. In Canada such a table was constructed for the year 1949 and another is in preparation for the year 1961. Although the concepts of the inter-industry flow table are consistent with those of the traditional accounts, the content of each sector (notably the government and business sectors) is not the same, so that the inter-industry flow table is in fact kept separate from the national accounts.[2] It is, however, without doubt an integral part of the national accounts.

As the expression indicates, the inter-industry flows show the technical relations that link industries to one another. The flow tables show the purchases and sales of current goods and services that a particular industry carries out with other industries: for

---

1. A complete accounting system should record not only the flows or the changes which take place in the course of a year (which is what we are limiting ourselves to here) but also the assets, liabilities, and net worth of the country. This has not yet been accomplished on a regular (yearly) basis in any country.

2. The inter-industry flow table is an *alternative* set of production accounts, because in this table the economy is divided according to industries whereas it is divided according to sectors in the present sector accounts. Both classification systems are needed to take care properly of all the categories of transactions. The industry classification is preferable in the production account, but the sector classification is indispensable in some of the others.

TABLE 1 : 6

Outline of the National Transactions Accounts of the Business Sector

Expenditure	*Income*

(a) Production Account

Expenditure	Income
Intermediary purchases	Total production
BALANCE: GROSS VALUE ADDED AT FACTOR COST	

(b) Income and Expenditure Account

Expenditure	Income
	GROSS VALUE ADDED AT FACTOR COST
Factor incomes paid (wages, interest, dividends)	Factor incomes received from non-residents
Transfers to other sectors (direct taxes and other)	Transfers from other sectors
BALANCE: GROSS UNDISTRIBUTED PROFIT = GROSS SAVING OF THE SECTOR	

(c) Financial Transactions Account

Changes in assets	*Changes in liabilities*
Cash and deposits	Net new issues of securities
Purchase of securities	
BALANCE: NET INDEBTEDNESS	

(d) The Capital Account

Expenditure	Income
Net fixed capital formation	
	GROSS UNDISTRIBUTED PROFIT
Capital consumption allowances	
	NET INDEBTEDNESS
Purchase of existing real assets	

example, the tobacco, paper, and power that the cigarette industry consumes. Note, however, that a production account records only transactions related to current operations. It does not include, for instance, the purchase of a piece of equipment.

The main interest of each of the transactions accounts is in the balancing item that is carried over from one account to another. The difference between total production and the intermediary purchases is the value added (or final output). While it is a debit entry in the production account, the value added becomes a credit entry in the income and expenditure account.

(b) The Income and Expenditure Account.

This account is more familiar to us since it is concerned with the transactions that enter into the national product. As income (on the credit side) we have the sale of the products and as expenditure (on the debit side) the distribution of the earnings of the factors of production to the sectors to which they belong – wages and salaries, rent, interest, dividends, and so on. In addition to these items, transfer payments must be included on both sides.

The balance is what remains finally to the business sector, namely, the gross undistributed profits, or the saving of the sector. The profits are said to be 'gross' because capital consumption allowances are included.

The nomenclature of these accounts applies, of course, to the business sector that we have taken as our example. The personal sector for Canada has no production account, but the most casual reader will undoubtedly have noticed an income and expenditure account in Table 1:5. The balancing item is the personal net saving.[1] The balance of the government sector, for the same transactions, is the budgetary surplus or deficit, and the balance for the non-residents sector is the surplus or deficit for Canada on international current account.[2] These balances step

---

1. By definition in the personal sector, there is no capital formation and therefore there are no capital consumption allowances.

2. The income and expenditure account as defined above is in conformity with Canadian practice. In the French edition of this book the same account does not cover as much. There is an 'appropriation account' in between, which in the business sector distributes profits as dividends and direct taxes.

over the next account and go directly to the capital account.

(c) The Financial Transaction Account.

The financial transactions account describes the financial networks throughout the economy. The purpose of these operations is to transfer funds from the lending to the borrowing sectors. As a result there are changes in assets and liabilities, which appear on the debit side and the credit side respectively. The balance is equal to the net borrowing or net lending of the sector. The balance is carried over to the capital account.

The expanded Canadian framework has nine categories of financial transactions and fourteen sub-categories. The list of the categories is as follows:

1. currency and deposits
2. charge accounts and instalment credit
3. loans
4. claims on associated enterprises
5. mortgages
6. bonds
7. stocks
8. insurance and pensions
9. foreign inheritances and migrants' funds

The classification of financial transactions is based upon the liquidity of the securities. This list, in principle, follows an order of decreasing liquidity. The demanding reader, however, will quickly discover several anomalies in the application of the rule. Mortgages are certainly not any more liquid than the Treasury bills that are included with the bonds. It is also regrettable that loans and bonds have been classed according to institutional characteristics rather than according to the length of their term.[1]

---

1. We shall return to the financial transactions account in chapter 10.

(d) The Capital Account.[1]

In this account are classed the investment transactions of each sector. The resources of the account (on the credit side) consist of the saving from the income and expenditure account and of the net indebtedness from the financial transactions account. These financial resources are used for fixed capital formation, for capital consumption allowances, and for the purchase of existing real assets.

It should be noted that the fixed capital formation transactions deal with goods and services that are included in the national product, but that from the standpoint of the economy as a whole the transactions on existing real assets are no more than a particular kind of transfer between sectors. It is obviously necessary that total lending should be equal to total borrowing (do not forget that the rest of the world is a sector). For this reason the financial transactions do not appear as such in the national product.

The nature of each of these transactions accounts shows clearly that the estimate of the national product, sophisticated as it is, is only a part of the economic accounts of the country. We

Regular Canadian Accounts

	Consumers	Business	Governments	Non-residents
Production account				
Income and expenditure account				
Capital account				

1. The name of this account is a slight departure from Canadian practice. The author's preference is too strong to abide by usage. It is more than a *saving account* since there are borrowing and lending, and the other name suggested, *investment transactions account*, describes only one of the two sides of the account.

can better understand at this stage, perhaps, what is meant by *final* output: in fact the concept of final output leaves aside both the production account and the financial transactions account.

In the simplified Canadian accounts we have four sectors and few transactions accounts.

Six accounts only have been established in a regular way: a business production account, four income and expenditure accounts,[1] and a consolidated capital account for the whole economy.

In the expanded national transactions system, the production account has been eliminated. The income and expenditure account applies to six sectors, and the financial transactions account, as well as the capital account, has been set up for each of the eleven sectors.

4. THE ECONOMIC NETWORK

One of the fundamental principles of economic life is the interdependence existing between all sectors and markets. National accounting illustrates this principle very clearly. Figures will now follow that serve as a check on our understanding of national accounting and of the relationships between the various parts of the system.

Table 1:7 reproduces the current transactions that took place in Canada in 1963. *Current transactions, it should be remembered, are just another name for the income and expenditure transactions.* Part (a) of the table consists of the account of each of the four sectors of the simplified Canadian national accounts. The arrangements are such that we can establish the transactions between sectors while preserving the necessary interconnections and indicating the balances proper to each account. Part (b) is an economic table dividing the transactions of each sector in accordance with their nature. Both the sectors and the categories of transactions are in balance.

---

1. The business income and expenditure account is represented by a dotted line because in fact it is a transactions account (rather than a sector account) concerned with the investment income of business and of non-residents.

Table 1:7 has been constructed using the National Transactions Accounts as a basis; the adjustments are indicated on pages 482 to 488 in W. C. Hood, *Financing of Economic Activity in Canada*.

The investment income is not distributed among the sectors because the accounts are not set up explicitly for this category of transactions.[1]

As for the balances, they represent the savings of each sector. In total they are by definition equal to investment, as we have shown in part (b) of the table (taking into account the error of estimate).

1. Persons. The total exceeds that of the national accounts (N.A.) by the social insurance contributions ($838 million).

2. Business. The total is lower than that of the N.A. by the value of the imports, which are subtracted from the exports rather than counted among the expenditure of the sector. This procedure is designed to show that it is not only business firms that import from abroad even if imports have been arbitrarily included in this sector. The residual error of estimate is also imputed entirely to the business sector.

3. Governments. The total is that of the national accounts.[2] The balance is obviously the budgetary deficit.

4. Non-residents. The total is that of the national accounts plus the Canadian deficit on current account ($488 million).

Finally, part (c) of the table is a diagram illustrating intersectoral exchanges.

1. It should be possible to derive the sectors distribution from the available figures but the attempt was not made.

2. It will be noted that taxes less subsidies on the debit side of business amount to $7.52 billion and that 'taxes' coming from business are $7.50 billion on the credit side for government. Similarly the transfers to the credit of consumers amount to $3.97 billion, and the transfers debited to government are $3.83 billion. The difference in the two is a transfer of business to the persons, or a private transfer amounting to $44 million. Remaining discrepancies are due to rounding.

TABLE 1 : 7a

Inter-sectoral Transactions, Canada 1963, billions of dollars

1. Persons — Expenditure		1. Persons — Income		2. Businesses — Expenditure		2. Businesses — Income	
1. Direct services	1.09	Wages and salaries	1.09	1. Wages, salaries and income of unincorporated businesses	21.02	Sales to residents	25.42
2. Purchases of goods	25.42	Wages and salaries and income of unincorporated businesses	21.02				
3. Direct taxes	3.75	Income from governments	4.14	3. Taxes less subsidies	7.52	Sales to governments	3.93
		Transfer payments	3.87				
4. Imports of services	0.72	Rent, interest, and dividends	3.49	4. Investment income paid out	4.04	Exports	8.83
				Residual error of estimate	−0.23	Imports	−7.97
						Gross capital formation	7.95
BALANCE: SAVING	2.63			BALANCE: GROSS SAVING	6.04	Residual error of estimate	0.23
Total	33.61	Total	33.61	Total	38.39	Total	38.39

TABLE 1 : 7a (Continued)

| 3. Governments | | 4. Non-residents | |
Expenditure	Income	Expenditure	Income
1. Wages and salaries 4.14	Direct taxes and contributions 3.75	1.	Travel expenditure and other receipts 0.73
Transfer pay-¹ ments 3.83			
2. Purchases of goods and services 3.93	Taxes less subsidies 7.50	2. Exports 8.83	Imports 7.97
Interest on the public debt 1.41	Investment income 1.33	Interest and dividends 0.23	Interest and dividends 0.84
BALANCE: DEFICIT ON TRANSACTIONS RELATING TO NATIONAL ACCOUNTS −0.73		BALANCE: DEFICIT ON CURRENT ACCOUNT 0.48	
Total 12.58	Total 12.58	Total 9.54	Total 9.54

TABLE 1 : 7b

Inter-sectoral Transactions, Canada 1963, billions of dollars

	Expenditure					Income				
	P	B	G	N-R	Total	P	B	G	N-R	Total
Wages, salaries, and income of unincorporated businesses	1.09	21.02	4.14	—	26.25	26.25	—	—	—	26.25
Goods and services (including capital formation)	26.14	—	3.93	8.83	38.90	—	38.16 (7.95)	—	8.70	46.86 (7.95)
Investment income	—	4.04	1.41	0.23	5.68	3.49	—	1.33	0.84	5.66
Transfer payments and taxes	3.75	7.52	3.83	—	15.10	3.87	—	11.25	—	15.12
Gross saving	2.63	6.04	-0.73	0.48	8.42		0.23			0.23
Residual error of estimate		-0.23			-0.23					
Total	33.61	38.39	12.58	9.54	94.12	33.61	38.39	12.58	9.54	94.12

P = Persons
B = Businesses
G = Governments
N-R = Non-residents

TABLE 1:7c

Inter-sectoral Transactions, Canada 1963, billions of dollars

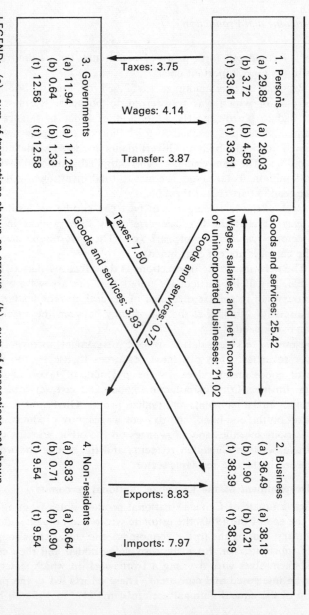

1. Persons
(a) 29.89 (b) 3.72 (t) 33.61
(a) 29.03 (b) 4.58 (t) 33.61

3. Governments
(a) 11.94 (a) 11.25
(b) 0.64   (b) 1.33
(t) 12.58 (t) 12.58

2. Business
(a) 36.49 (a) 38.18
(b) 1.90   (b) 0.21
(t) 38.39 (t) 38.39

4. Non-residents
(a) 8.83   (a) 8.64
(b) 0.71   (b) 0.90
(t) 9.54   (t) 9.54

Taxes: 3.75

Wages: 4.14

Transfer: 3.87

Goods and services: 25.42

Wages, salaries, and net income of unincorporated businesses: 21.02

Taxes: 7.50

Goods and services: 0.72

Goods and services: 3.93

Exports: 8.83

Imports: 7.97

LEGEND: (a) sum of transactions shown on arrows (b) sum of transactions not shown

(t) total of the sector according to Table 1:7a

Table 1:7 could call forth pages of comments. Let us limit ourselves to the most important ones:

1. Personal savings amounted to $2,631 million in 1963, the major part of which was transferred to business. Business, in effect, had to borrow nearly $2 billion in order to finance its investment, since this reached $7.95 billion and business savings amounted to $6.04 billion. Governments incurred a deficit of $735 million. The non-residents sector supplied additional savings of $488 million. Total saving is equal to total investment. All this may be read in part (b) of the table.

2. Each of the five categories of part (b) can be reconstituted from part (a). Of the five categories only three appear in the inter-sectoral transactions of part (c). The investment income and the balances are not distributed.

3. The network of the transactions is described by part (c) of the table. It will be particularly noted that the arrows are less numerous than in similar diagrams of several current textbooks. The reason for this is that the consistency between the accounts is often overlooked.

Consumers receive salaries, wages, investment income, and transfer revenues. They put these resources to use by the purchase of goods and services, by the payment of taxes, and by savings. Business firms manufacture goods and give services, for which they make payments and realize profits. Governments collect taxes on the one hand, and pay out wages, buy products, and grant various subsidies and allowances on the other. Finally, current trade between Canadian residents and the rest of the world is recorded in the non-residents sector.

C. Development of the Canadian National Accounts

The first estimate of Canada's national product dates from 1919. Until the end of the 1930s the estimate was based on value added by industry. During the forties economists and statisticians sought to find substitutes for this method of value added and then concerned themselves with devising a framework in which statistics would be integrated and consistent. These efforts led to the publication of the annual national accounts in 1947. In 1951 an historical series appeared, going back to 1926. Then the latter was revised in an important publication, *National Accounts: Income and Expenditure, 1926-1956* (1958).[1] This publication contains not only the statistical series but also a complete description of the methods and sources. No important modification has been made in it since that time. It is this accounting system that has been described in this chapter.

As indicated already these accounts are not complete: inter-industry and financial transactions are still missing.

In the field of inter-industry statistics, a table of forty-two sectors was constructed for the year 1949 which was published in 1956 at consumer's prices and in 1960 at producer's prices. At the time of writing an enlarged table is being prepared for 1961.[2]

The task in respect of financial transactions is somewhat more advanced. It was begun sooner. After the war various economists concerned themselves with financial flows, and in 1955 the Bank of Canada published direct estimates of personal saving, using the method of variations in assets and liabilities. These estimates applied to the years 1939-1954. Also in 1955, the research personnel of the Royal Commission on Canada's Economic Prospects began to work on a full financial transactions system. In 1956 the Dominion Bureau of Statistics set up, within the framework of the balance of payments, the financial statistics relating to foreign trade. Thus in 1959 the Royal Commission was able to complete its national transactions accounts for the years 1946-1954. These accounts are the most comprehensive of all. It is highly regrettable, however, that this work has not been continued. At the present time we have no systematic information concerning financial transactions beyond 1954.

1. Ottawa, Queen's Printer.

2. The author constructed a table of inter-industry flows of goods and services for the year 1949 for the province of Quebec. See A. Raynauld, *Croissance et structure économiques de la province de Québec,* Ministère de l'Industrie et du Commerce de la Province de Québec, 1961, pp. 111-65. A table for Quebec 1961 is being prepared by the Provincial Bureau of Statistics. Professor Kari Levitt has done a similar work for the Maritime Provinces (unpublished at the time of writing).

SUGGESTED READINGS

DOMINION BUREAU OF STATISTICS: *National Accounts: Income and Expenditure, 1926-1956*, Ottawa, Queen's Printer, 1958.
The basic document concerning the Canadian National Accounts. It presents the data from 1926 to 1956, the conceptual framework of the accounts, and the sources and methods. The data for recent years are found in annual and quarterly publications.

N. AND R. RUGGLES: *National Income Accounts and Income Analysis*, second edition, New York, McGraw-Hill, 1956.
Attempts to build up the national income concepts from the basic accounts of individual units. The purpose is to bridge the gap between micro- and macro-economic concepts.

R. STONE AND G. CROFT-MURRAY: *Social Accounting and Economic Models*, London, Bowes & Bowes, 1959.
Presents a brief description of social accounting, including input-output.

A Critique of the United States Income and Product Accounts, National Bureau of Economic Research, Conference on Research in Income and Wealth, Vol. 22, Princeton University Press, 1958.
A systematic and critical analysis of the United States Accounts. See especially the paper by G. Jaszi, which re-examines the conceptual basis of the accounts.

J. R. HICKS AND A. G. HART: *The Social Framework of the American Economy*, Oxford University Press, 1945.
An early analysis of social accounting, its methods and underlying assumptions. See especially chapters XI to XVI.

L. M. READ: 'The Development of National Transactions Accounts', *Canadian Journal of Economics and Political Science*, February 1957, pp. 42-57.
An introduction to the Canadian National Transactions Accounts.

DOMINION BUREAU OF STATISTICS: *The Inter-Industry Flow of Goods and Services, Canada, 1949,* Supplement, Ottawa, Queen's Printer, 1960.
An application to Canada of an inter-industry flow table developed for the United States by V. Leontieff.

R. STONE: *Input-Output and National Accounts,* Paris, Organization for Economic Co-operation and Development, 1961.
Deals with the subdivision of the national accounts on an industry basis so as to provide a detailed picture of the industrial structure. A clear presentation of the input-output tables and their uses.

The Flow-of-funds Approach to Social Accounting, National Bureau of Economic Research, Conference on Research in Income and Wealth, Vol. 26, Princeton University Press, 1962.
Series of technical papers discussing the integration of the flow of funds and the national income and product accounts. The system developed in Canada is discussed, pp. 103-32.

R. FRISCH: *A Generalized Form of the REFI Interflow Table* and *The Oslo REFI Interflow Table,* memoranda from the Institute of Economics, University of Oslo, November 17, 1959, and June 27, 1960.
Presents the frame of the REFI table (RE = real, FI = financial), that is, a table exhibiting how real and financial flows gear into each other to form an integrated system. Such a table is the latest refinement in national accounting.

Further readings on the national accounts are suggested in chapter 10.

CHAPTER

2

ECONOMIC GROWTH

A. General Concepts

Economic growth, in its most general sense, means the increase in total production over time. We also use the term for the increase in output per capita. This latter is a much more restrictive notion, implying an idea of progress. If production is increasing at a slower rate than population, the standard of living falls even though economic growth still exists in a general sense. With output per capita as an index of economic growth we can say that a country is in a period of growth only when the increase in production is more rapid than the increase in population.

The notion of economic development differs from the concept of growth, although it is closely linked to it. Economic development evokes the idea of a threshold beyond which the country is developed, and short of which the country is underdeveloped. The concept of development is very close to the concept of industrial revolution and implies major transformations in the economic and social structures of a country.

Applying this distinction, we would use the term economic growth for the evolution that has taken place in the last hundred years in the United States and in England, but we would describe as economic development the changes now under way in most of the countries of Latin America and Asia. The distinction having been made, however, it must be admitted that growth and development are often used with the same meaning.

The process of economic development is very complex and

may be indicated by a great variety of phenomena. We know, for example, that growth is accompanied by industrialization, urbanization, changes in the make-up of the total demand and in the structure of industries, and so forth. Leibenstein[1] has drawn up a list of thirty-five characteristics of development (or of underdevelopment), divided into four classes: economic, demographic, cultural and political, technological and other. This way of envisaging development satisfies our curiosity, but it is of little use for analysis because it confuses causes, effects, and special institutional features. From the standpoint of Leibenstein's characteristics, moreover, no country could ever be regarded as either developed or underdeveloped. Canada, for instance, could be considered an underdeveloped country in several respects because it is primarily an exporter of raw materials, because it imports capital, because the manufacturing sector is relatively less important to the national product than in the United States, and finally because the entrepreneurs are for the most part foreigners.

It is better to restrict the number of criteria by which to judge a country's degree of development. This writer would propose two indices only: national income per capita and the proportion of investment in the national income.

National income per capita is the most generally used index. *Since (in a closed economy) real income is equal to production, income per capita measures the quantity of goods and services that the economic system offers per person during a given period of time.* An increase in the index from one year to the next indicates that a greater quantity of goods and services is available for each person, on the average, whether immediately, in the form of consumer goods, or for the future, in the form of capital goods; this is not only economic progress, as we have noted, but also social progress, if these goods and services are widely distributed. Since the index of per-capita income relates the production

1. Harvey Leibenstein, *Economic Backwardness and Economic Growth,* New York, Wiley and Sons, Inc., 1957, pp. 40-1.

of goods to population, it is a highly significant measurement, for these two key variables appear in all explanations – or should we say all models – of economic growth.

National income per capita is not only a measurement, but also a concept, of economic growth. Unfortunately, almost insurmountable difficulties arise if it is used for making comparisons between countries: since monetary units, consumption habits, and price levels differ between countries, such an index has almost no statistical value.

The proportion of investment in the national income appears to be superior to income per capita as a means of comparing the rates of growth of different countries, though not, of course, the stages of development they have already reached. The development level of the U.S.S.R., for example, is much lower than that of the United States, but since the U.S.S.R. devotes 25 to 30 per cent of its national income to investment and the United States 16 to 17 per cent, we know that the U.S.S.R. is progressively making up for lost time. It has been proposed[1] that a country be considered as developed if it succeeds in devoting at least 10 to 12 per cent of its national income to saving and investment. Finally, as we shall see later, investment is an indispensable condition for economic growth, and so this measurement is useful in explaining economic conditions.

If we confine ourselves to the most general concept of economic growth, that given at the beginning of this chapter, we can calculate the increases in national product (gross or net) from year to year. To do this, values are usually corrected in order to eliminate price variations. Rates of growth of real output are thereby obtained.

B. Strategic Variables

An unusual unanimity exists among economists regarding the factors that control or explain economic growth. In a first category let us place what philosophers would call the remote causes and what the historian Rostow[1] has defined by the term *propensities. They include the whole of the reactions of a society to motivations of an economic order; from the point of view of the individual they include the social and historical setting of his activities, affected as it is by the predominating system of values, by political, legal, and other institutions and the efficiency with which these institutions fulfil their functions; they also include the attitudes to new technological and scientific knowledge and the national temperament. Finally, they include the personal character of individuals, such things as the spirit of initiative and innovation, and the zeal for work – what Joseph Schumpeter called the 'social climate' and Alfred Marshall the 'spirit of the people'.*

In a second category of determinants of growth are the variables that are properly economic. We shall discuss three, examining the contribution of each to economic growth. *They are* (1) *the increase in the labour force,* (2) *the increase in the stock of real capital, that is, industrial, commercial, and residential buildings, and equipment in the form of machines and tools, and* (3) *the total factor productivity in the economy.* Our statistics on this subject apply to the United States, but there is every reason to believe that they are equally applicable in Canada. (See, however, page 47.)

1. THE LABOUR FORCE

A country's production increases mainly because of an increase in the number of workers. If wages make up about 65 per cent of the national income, an increase of 10 per cent in the labour force at the same average wage will increase the national income by 6.5 per cent. A study made in the United States by E. F. Denison shows that between 1929 and 1957 the increase in the size of the labour force contributed 31 per cent of the total increase of the national income.[2]

---

1. W. W. Rostow, *The Process of Economic Growth*, New York, Norton, 1962.

2. E. F. Denison, *The Sources of Economic Growth in the United States and the Alternatives Before Us,* Committee for Economic Development, Paper no. 13, 1962.

Allowance has been made for the fact that working hours per week and per year decreased by 18 per cent in the same period and that obviously this represents, in part, a decrease in production. Denison's estimate (p. 40) is that the 18 per cent reduction in working hours diminished production by only 6 per cent, because a reduction in working hours has resulted in an increase in the productivity of labour. Also it was found possible to measure the importance of the educational level of the labour force; no other study known to this writer paints such a clear picture of the contribution of education to economic growth. The quality of the labour force in the United States improved by 30 per cent between 1929 and 1957. This improvement represents a contribution of 23 per cent to the growth of the national income, or a contribution of 42 per cent to the increase in productivity (or the national income per capita). If we take into account both its increase in quantity and its improvement in quality, the labour factor accounts for 54 per cent of the growth rate.

2. CAPITAL FORMATION

For two centuries the increase in the stock of real capital has been very rapid in developed economies, much more rapid in fact than the population increase. Nevertheless, according to statistics, its contribution to economic growth has been a minor one. U.S. statistics show that not more than 15 per cent of the growth rate can be attributed to investment in capital equipment. This observation seems to contradict the insistence on capital accumulation that is found in all theoretical studies. This writer believes, however, that the insistence is well founded and that statistical measurement and even theory under-estimate the real importance of capital. The reason for this is that several categories of expenditures are treated in the statistics as consumption rather than investment – notably investment in people, such as education and public health. We might perhaps better include education and health in the category of capital rather than in that of labour, where they now are, and therefore consider that a portion of all salaries and wages represents a return on investment rather than simply remuneration for work done.[1]

In an underdeveloped country the labour force is generally very large but the level of production remains low. If the labour force were all that is needed for economic growth, China would be the richest country in the world. *Thus it is the relative scarcity of capital and the absence of 'know-how' that check economic growth; it is the material and human equipment that is lacking.* In other words, capital does not increase sufficiently quickly, and the investment is too small to accumulate wealth or to increase the country's productive capacity. Let us take a further step and ask ourselves how it is possible, then, to bring about the accumulation of capital. A moment's reflection will provide the answer: We must not spend all of our current production. We must save part of it and invest it in capital goods, in the human and material equipment that we have just mentioned. In this way future income will in turn be increased.

Thus we arrive at the conclusion that in the underdeveloped countries it is savings that are insufficient in relation to the increase in population. Such a conclusion may seem rather old-fashioned at first glance, since, in order to combat a depression and unemployment, we are now advised to spend more money, even to dig holes and fill them if we cannot think of anything better to do, and to resort to bank credit if necessary. The essential difference, of course, is that in a depression savings exist but no one is willing to invest them, whereas in underdevelopment they simply do not exist.

One may with good reason wonder where natural resources fit in among the growth factors. Going back to the example given above for labour, we realize that the contribution of a factor of production to the growth of the national income is measured by

1. This type of analysis calls for an extended notion of capital to cover not only the material capital, which is adequately accounted for in current growth models, but also the human capital in such forms as education, training, and health. For a brief look at such an approach, see Harry G. Johnson, *The Canadian Quandary,* Toronto, McGraw-Hill, 1963, chapter 14.

the earnings of that factor multiplied by the increase over time in the quantity of the factor. The specific earnings of the natural resources are called rents; rents amounted to 3 per cent of the national income in the United States in 1954-8. However, the quantity of the factor – that is, the quantity of the agricultural and mineral land available for use – is fixed or constant. As a result, the contribution of natural resources to the growth of the national income is zero (rents of 3 per cent multiplied by a zero increase in the quantity of land gives zero).

In order for this arithmetic to make sense, it is necessary to understand that the benefits derived from natural resources are and must be imputed to capital investment or labour rather than to the natural resources themselves because without capital investment or labour the natural resource would be producing nothing. And of course there is in this approach no denial that natural resources are important. If the soil is very fertile, for instance, the return on capital invested will be high; if the soil is poor, the return will be low. If the specific contribution of natural resources to economic growth is nil it is largely because that contribution is already accounted for under labour or capital.

To sum up, capital contributes 15 per cent of the growth rate and the labour force (quantity and quality) 54 per cent. The source of the remaining 32 per cent remains to be stated.[1] *In a word, this is productivity – not the productivity of labour or of capital taken separately, but the output per unit of all factors together or, in other words, total factor productivity.*

3. TOTAL FACTOR PRODUCTIVITY

This third factor may be referred to as efficiency. Efficiency, thus defined, is therefore related to the increases in production that are ascribed not to labour or to capital but to more general phenomena.

The most widely known example is economies of scale. Canadian industries often complain about the small size of the

1. See Table 2:1 for exact figures.

market. Certain economists claim that this is the main reason for the relative inefficiency of business firms compared with United States firms. In spite of several years of effort, however, it has not been possible to find evidence with sufficient generality to carry the day. Nor have statistical studies in other countries revealed any significant relationship between the size of the market and the productivity levels of the manufacturing establishments, except in a very limited degree. The well-documented studies of Marvin Frankel,[1] L. Rostas,[2] and others tend to show that the importance of market size has been exaggerated. In Canada, the studies of the Royal Commission on Canada's Economic Prospects, on the other hand, attach considerable significance to it, but again, only on the evidence of special cases.[3] The general conclusion to the effect that three-quarters of the difference in manufacturing productivity between the United States and Canada is attributable to the difference in the scale of their industries is not justified, in this writer's opinion. It is now generally agreed that the contribution of the size of the market to general economic growth should be fixed at about 9 per cent. Kuznets, Kendrick, and Denison in the United States[4] use this figure in their estimates.

All the other influences that can be measured and that may affect productivity, such as disguised unemployment and the speed of adaptation of the labour force to changes in employment, have been considered in Denison's study, but together would scarcely contribute to more than 6 or 7 per cent of the

---

1. Marvin Frankel, *British and American Manufacturing Productivity*, University of Illinois Bulletin no. 81, 1937, pp. 64-80.

2. L. Rostas, *Comparative Productivity in British and American Industry*, Cambridge University Press, 1948, p. 59.

3. D. H. Fullerton and H. A. Hampson, *Canadian Secondary Manufacturing Industry*, Royal Commission on Canada's Economic Prospects, Ottawa, Queen's Printer, 1957, chapter 4.

4. Kendrick and Kuznets apparently use 10 per cent. See Denison, *op. cit.*, p. 266.

general growth; certain of them reduce, rather than increase, productivity.

We have said that after capital and labour are taken into account, about 32 per cent of the growth rate still remains to be accounted for, the causes of which we group under efficiency, or total factor productivity. Almost two-thirds of this – that is, 20 per cent of the total growth rate – cannot be attributed to any identifiable and measurable phenomenon. This residue is called the contribution of the general advancement of knowledge, or of

TABLE 2 : 1

Contribution of Several Factors to Economic Growth, United States 1929-57

	Annual rate of growth	Percentage of total
Over-all growth	2.93	100
1. LABOUR	1.57	54
Number of workers and reduction in working hours	0.80	27
Changes in the age structure and sex of the labour force	0.10	4
Education	0.67	23
2. CAPITAL	0.43	15
Increase in labour and capital inputs	2.00	68
3. EFFICIENCY	0.93	32
(a) Economies of scale	0.27	9
(b) Non-optimal distribution of resources	−0.07	−2
(c) Other sources identified and measured	0.15	5
(d) Remainder: technical progress	0.58	20

NOTE: The errors are due to rounding.

SOURCE: E. F. Denison, *The Sources of Economic Growth in the United States and the Alternatives before Us, op. cit.*, p. 266.

technical progress. Viewed from another angle, it is 'the measure of our ignorance', as Abramovitz has remarked.[1] One can place within this 20 per cent anything that one desires. The Americans generally include in it technical progress and advancements in knowledge; certain European writers include either the contribution of the state or the efficiency of the capitalist system, depending on the ideology to which they subscribe. A. Lewis and W. W. Rostow, quoted above, would certainly see in it the 'spirit of the people' that we mentioned previously.

Table 2:1 summarizes the statistical measurements that indicate the contribution of each of the factors to the general economic growth.

C. Canada's Economic Growth

Only a very brief sketch of the economic growth of Canada will be given in this section, for all the chapters of this book study a particular aspect of this general picture.

While factors making for growth are everywhere the same, their relative importance may vary from country to country and from time to time. On the whole, however, Canada differs little from the United States in this respect, although according to recent studies the contribution of the residual 'factor' would be much more important in Canada than the previous figures show it to be in the United States. Total factor productivity, of which technical change is a major component, would account on a comparable basis between the two countries for 58 per cent of the growth rate in the United States and 70 per cent in Canada. Although the rate of growth of labour in Canada has been higher than in the United States when adjustments are made for quality changes and hours worked, the contribution of Canadian labour to the over-all growth rate is comparatively lower by a rather wide margin. The relative importance of material capital is similar, but in Canada education does not show up as a major factor as it does in the United States. It appears that improvements in

---

1. M. Abramovitz, *Capital Formation and Economic Growth*, National Bureau of Economic Research, Princeton University Press, 1955, Introduction.

the educational level are too recent to bear visible fruit as yet. The situation should be different in the future.[1]

1. POPULATION

In 1867 Canada's population was approaching three and a half million. In 1961 it reached 18.2 million. It doubled in forty years twice: from 1881 to 1921 and again from 1921 to 1961. The long-term rate of growth was 1.67 per cent per year,[2] which is a relatively high rate for the near-century under consideration. Immigration has been responsible for a high proportion of population increase, and consequently changes in the economic conditions of the country have affected the rate of increase. More people want to come to Canada when times are good than when they are bad. Population increases are substantial in periods of prosperity and slight during periods of stagnation or depression: between 1870 and 1890, and again in the 1930s, they were relatively slow, but the most rapid increase occurred between 1890 and 1910, a period of most intense economic activity, and another rapid increase came during the expansionary years 1946-1956. The figures can be seen in Table 2:2.

2. NATIONAL PRODUCT PER CAPITA

It would be long and tiresome to describe all the economic changes that have taken place in Canada since Confederation. They are the same as have occurred in all countries that have become industrialized and have known a long period of prosperity. Let us limit ourselves to a few main points.

In current dollars the annual gross national product of Canada has multiplied a hundredfold since 1867, growing from $419 million to $43 billion in 1963. Because of the rise in prices, however, this multiplication may be misleading. When corrected for

1. These observations are based upon the findings in N. H. Lithwick, 'Economic Growth in Canada: A Quantitative Analysis', unpublished Ph.D. dissertation, Harvard University, 1963, and in chapter 4, also by Lithwick, of *Growth and the Canadian Economy*, Ottawa, Carleton University, March 1965.

2. O. J. Firestone, *Canada's Economic Development*, London, Bowes & Bowes, 1955. A compound rate of increase of 1.67 per cent means a doubling every 41.9 years.

TABLE 2 : 2

Population, Canada and the Provinces, 1871-1961, in thousands

	1871	1901	1911	1921	1931	1941	1951	1956	1961
Newfoundland							361.4	415.0	458.0
Prince Edward Island	94	103.2	93.7	88.6	88.0	95.0	98.4	99.2	105.0
Nova Scotia	388	459.5	492.3	523.8	512.8	577.9	642.5	694.7	737.0
New Brunswick	286	331.1	351.8	387.8	408.2	457.4	515.6	554.6	598.0
Quebec	1,192	1,648.8	2,005.7	2,360.5	2,874.6	3,331.8	4,055.6	4,628.3	5,259.0
Ontario	1,621	2,182.9	2,527.2	2,933.6	3,431.6	3,787.6	4,597.5	5,404.9	6,236.0
Manitoba	25	255.2	461.3	610.1	700.1	729.7	776.5	850.0	922.0
Saskatchewan		91.2	492.4	757.5	921.7	895.9	831.7	880.6	925.0
Alberta		73.0	374.2	588.4	731.6	796.1	939.5	1,123.1	1,332.0
British Columbia	36	178.6	392.4	524.5	694.2	817.8	1,165.2	1,398.4	1,629.0
Yukon		27.2	8.5	4.1	4.2	4.9	9.0	12.1	14.0
Northwest Territories	48	20.1	6.5	8.1	9.3	12.0	16.0	19.3	23.0
Canada	3,700	5,371.3	7,206.6	8,787.9	10,376.7	11,506.6	14,009.4	16,080.7	18,238.0
Average annual rate of growth (%)		1.5	3.4	2.1	1.8	1.08	2.1	2.9	2.68

SOURCE: *The Canada Year Book*, 1961, p. 146, and Census Bulletins.

differences in price levels, the increase in the G.N.P. is still very impressive. It is 3.39 per cent per annum for the period 1867 to 1953. For the shorter period 1929 to 1957 it is 3.55 per cent per annum, compared with 2.93 per cent in the United States as shown in Table 2:1. For the post-war period, 1946 to 1957, the annual increase was 4.25 per cent in Canada and 3.4 per cent in the United States. Thus it can be seen that since 1929 the economic growth of Canada has been slightly more rapid than that of the United States. It must be remembered, however, that here we are speaking of the absolute rate of growth (of the G.N.P.), not to be confused with the rate of growth *per capita*, which in that period was lower in Canada than in the United States because of a more rapid increase in population.

We stated earlier that Canadian population has doubled about every forty years since Confederation. Now we observe that production has doubled every twenty years in the same period. (This is roughly what 3.39 per cent per annum means.) It follows clearly from this that the Canadian citizen has improved his standard of living and that he is much better off today than formerly. In fact, the G.N.P. per capita has increased by 1.65 per cent per annum during the whole of this period. An increase in income of 1.65 per cent per annum may not seem impressive, until one realizes that it represents a doubling every 42.4 years. If this tendency continues, as there is every reason to believe that it will, Canadians in the year 2000 will earn twice as much as now. It must be emphasized that this doubling is *real*: it actually means twice as many goods and services at the disposition of everyone. When we think of it, looking back on the thousands of years of history that the world has known, this progress is extraordinary in the strongest sense of the word, so extraordinary that we can scarcely imagine its being continued indefinitely into the future. We can always imagine catastrophe more easily than wealth or happiness.

In the past men were never able to conceive of a world of abundance. Those who attempt to do so today are still the exceptions.[1] If it is so difficult to have the vision of 'opulence', it is largely because progress in the past has never been continuous. On the contrary, economic evolution has been highly unstable. In all the developed countries, the periods of famine that characterized the pre-industrial era have been succeeded since the industrial revolution by economic depressions, which have occurred with disconcerting regularity.

So it has been in Canada. The period of prosperity from 1896 to 1913 (the G.N.P. increasing by 5.3 per cent per annum from 1900 to 1910) was followed by a long depression during the thirties. If we take the level of the G.N.P. in 1929 as 100, then in 1933 it had fallen to 70 and as a result Canadians on the average had lost almost a third of their incomes. It was only in 1939 that the G.N.P. regained the 1929 level, even though the population had increased considerably during the intervening ten years. (In fact, in 1939 the G.N.P. per capita was still lower by 6 per cent than in 1929.)

To come closer to the present, a post-war period of great prosperity, during which the rate of growth was 4.25 per cent per annum up to 1956, was followed by five years of stagnation during which the G.N.P. per capita *decreased* (in 1949 prices) from $1,480 in 1956 to $1,431 in 1961. 1962 was marked by a strong recovery: the G.N.P. increased by 6 per cent in real terms.[2]

3. CAPITAL FORMATION

The second of the two indices of economic growth referred to on pages 39 and 40, annual investment expressed as a percentage of

1. But Keynes, farsightedly, was able to write in 1930: 'Yet there is no country and no people, I think, who can look forward to the age of leisure and of abundance without a dread. For we have been trained too long to strive and not to enjoy.' 'Economic Possibilities for Our Grandchildren' in *Essays in Persuasion*, Macmillan & Co, 1931, p. 368. A leading exponent of the long view is John Kenneth Galbraith, *The Affluent Society*, Boston, Houghton Mifflin Co., 1958.

2. The economic fluctuations are described in chapter 4.

the gross national product, is widely used. Canada has excellent statistics available for this index for the years since 1926, but for the previous years the estimates leave much to be desired.

In any event it appears that from the time of Confederation Canada devoted a high percentage of its resources to investment. A very marked increase also occurred in the decade of 1900-1910, and this increase serves as a basis, among other observations, for Rostow's thesis according to which Canada, before the First World War, went through a period of rapid 'take-off' in the race for growth and economic expansion.[1] O. J. Firestone gives two statistical investment series which are reproduced in Table 2:3.[2]

TABLE 2 : 3

Gross Investment as a Percentage of the G.N.P., 1870-1920

	Private investment including changes in inventories	*Private investment excluding changes in inventories*
1870-1900	14.6	12.9
1910-1920	24.8	18.2

SOURCE: O. J. Firestone, *Canada's Economic Development*. The first column is taken from p. 72, the second from p. 100.

So far as the period since 1926 is concerned, it is sufficient to note in Table 2:4 that investment varies according to economic conditions, as everyone knows already, and that, generally speaking, it has contributed a high percentage of the total resources. Certain writers go so far as to say that expenditures on overhead capital were for a long time excessive in Canada and that they

1. Rostow, *op. cit.,* and *The Stages of Economic Growth*, Cambridge University Press, 1960, chapter 4.

2. A third series may be quoted – net investment as a percentage of the net national product in constant dollars: 1870, 4.7 per cent; 1890, 6.3 per cent; 1900, 3.2 per cent; 1910, 9.5 per cent; 1920, 10.9 per cent. *Canada's Economic Development,* p. 112.

have been so until recently. In support of this thesis the two railway lines crossing the country have often been cited. But in economic life there is no use lamenting over the past.

Table 2:4 includes two different sets of figures illustrating the importance of investment in the national product. But these are not equivalent to the two sets in Table 2:3. This time we are dealing with private investment in the one set and private plus public investment in the other.

TABLE 2 : 4

Gross Investment as a Percentage of the G.N.P., 1926-1963

	Private investment	*Private and public investment*
1926	16.3	18.2
1933	4.1	6.4
1946	14.5	17.1
1956	25.7	29.8
1961	17.3	21.4
1962	18.6	23.0
1963	18.5	22.7

NOTE: Investment includes the value of physical change in inventories.

SOURCES: *National Accounts, 1926-1956*, for 1926 to 1946; *National Accounts, 1962*, for 1956 to 1962; *National Accounts, 1963*, for 1963.

Table 2:5 gives the industrial distribution of the investment in fixed capital. The main expenditures are residential construction, manufacturing industries, and government departments. A comparison over the years reveals that by 1961 the manufacturing sector had considerably reduced its investments, both in millions of dollars and as a proportion of the total, and that government departments made up for the difference. In 1964, manufacturing recovered fully and the proportion contributed by governments was lower (although in terms of dollars the government contribution had increased slightly). This phenomenon of compensation affords an excellent example of the Keynesian doctrine,

TABLE 2 : 5

Public and Private Gross Investment

	1956 As a percentage of the total	1961 As a percentage of the total	1964 In millions of dollars	1964 As a percentage of the total
1. Agriculture, fishing	6.07	6.42	820	7.57
2. Forestry	0.90	0.60	73	0.67
3. Mining, quarrying, oil wells	6.70	5.56	633	5.85
4. Manufacturing	17.30	12.62	1,815	16.76
5. Electric power, gas, water transport, water systems	11.37	9.51	936	8.65
6. Construction	2.48	1.62	151	1.39
7. Transport, warehousing, communications	10.12	11.00	1,141	10.54
8. Trade, wholesale and retail	4.04	4.05	351	3.24
9. Finance, insurance, real estate	1.54	3.78	328	3.03
10. Institutional services	5.00	7.58	766	7.07
11. Housing	19.60	18.09	2,028	18.74
12. Government departments	12.60	16.38	1,468	13.56
13. Commercial services	2.01	2.72	317	2.93
14. Total gross investment	99.73	99.93	10,827	100
15. Gross investments as a percentage of gross national expenditure	26.3	21.7		23.2

NOTE: The data include capital expenditures only. In 1964, the figures represent the preliminary actual data. On line 15, the 1964 G.N.E. is the 'third quarter seasonally adjusted at annual rates' figure. On the same line, the 1961 percentage differs from that of Table 2:4, column 2, by the amount of inventories.

SOURCE: *Private and Public Investment in Canada, Outlook*

according to which public expenditures maintain the over-all demand and compensate for reductions in the private sector. The year 1956 was one of rapid if not excessive expansion, 1961 a year of stagnation and unemployment, and 1964 a year of renewed expansion.

4. REGIONAL ECONOMIC STRUCTURE

The most elaborate thesis existing on the economic development of Canada is the staple-product theory.[1] To explain its economic development Canada is considered in this theory as a particular and peripheral region within a wide international economic system which may be called the Atlantic area (to include the United States, Great Britain, and France).[2] To this vast market Canada has been essentially a supplier of raw materials which have changed in nature in the course of time in response to the 'Atlantic' demand and in accordance with the resources available in the region. Only one aspect of it need be stressed here: since the natural resources are the main source of expansion for the economy, and since these resources are in quite specific places in the national territory, Canada's economic development has been characterized at each stage by the exploitation of new frontier areas. *Growth has been accomplished by territorial extension.* So it has been with furs, lumber, grain, mining products, and oil.

This type of development is of course characteristic of countries with vast territory and low population density. It results initially in a national economy wide open to foreign trade and lacking in internal integration and cohesion. This phase lasts as long as the bases of the economic development remain the same – that is, as long as there are resources and new territories to be exploited and as long as the population is too small for domestic demand to replace foreign demand as a main source of expansion.

1. See the suggested readings.

2. For important statistical illustrations of this approach, see Kenneth A. H. Buckley, *Population, Labour Force and Economic Growth,* Vol. 2, Working Paper prepared for the Banff Business Policies Conference on Canadian Economic Survival, 1963. Mimeo.

No doubt the Canadian economy has already attained a certain level of integration; it has progressively equipped itself with supporting overhead capital and productive capacity, especially in the central part of the country, in Ontario and Quebec. To the extent that this development has taken place, the initial pattern of economic development is now less applicable to Canada. Since 1926 the importance of foreign trade to the national income has declined, while the rate of expansion has been relatively high.[1] It follows that this expansion cannot be attributed exclusively to world demand for Canadian resources. Nevertheless, in the author's belief the Canadian economy in the main still retains its original structure, that is, one linked very closely to the exploitation of natural resources for the world market. The most striking development in the last thirty years is not so much the increased importance of the domestic market as the shrinking of the foreign one. The Atlantic market of former days has become the American market. Also, while there has been progressive integration internally, it is still easy to see differences in regional economic structures resulting from differences in natural resources.

It is with the regional economic structure that we shall deal here, since foreign trade will be examined in the final part of the book. The best way to measure the degree of integration in an economy is to compare the level of internal trade with that of foreign trade. Unfortunately we do not have figures on interregional trade in Canada. What we can show by statistics is merely that the economic structure is still dominated by the natural resources of each region (with the exception of a narrow band extending from Hamilton to Montreal). With this in mind Tables 2:6 and 2:7 were drawn up. Canada is divided in these tables into five regions: the Atlantic provinces, Quebec, Ontario, the prairie provinces, and British Columbia. In Table 2:6 the economic structure is represented by seven sectors of activity covering the production of goods but excluding services. Table 2:7 deals with the structure of the manufacturing industry only,

1. This is the emphasis in W. C. Hood and A. S. Scott, *Output, Labour and Capital in the Canadian Economy*, listed in the Suggested Readings.

TABLE 2 : 6

Industrial Production

Value Added as a Percentage of the Total for Each Region, Canada 1961

	Atlantic Provinces	Quebec	Ontario	Prairie Provinces	British Columbia	Canada
1. Agriculture	5.9	5.4	6.8	22.0	4.9	8.7
2. Forestry	6.4	3.5	1.4	0.8	15.0	3.5
3. Fishing and trapping	5.3	0.1	0.1	0.3	2.0	0.6
4. Mining	10.3	5.1	5.1	20.7	5.0	8.1
5. Electric power	5.7	4.8	3.9	3.9	5.2	4.4
6. Manufacturing	38.1	63.8	67.6	24.4	45.5	55.5
7. Construction	28.3	17.3	15.1	27.9	22.4	19.2
Total	100	100	100	100	100	100
8. Industrial production in millions of dollars	1,043.8	5,033.0	8,039.5	3,203.9	1,898.3	19,218.5
9. Industrial production per capita in dollars	550	957	1,289	1,008	1,165	1,055
10. Index of industrial production per capita	52	90	122	95	110	100

SOURCE: Dominion Bureau of Statistics, *Survey of Production, 1961.*

TABLE 2 : 7

Manufacturing Industries

Value Added as a Percentage of the Total for Each Region, Canada 1961

	Atlantic Provinces	Quebec	Ontario	Prairie Provinces	British Columbia	Canada
1. Food and beverage industries	28.5	14.5	14.0	28.8	16.4	15.9
2. Tobacco, rubber, leather	0.2	6.1	4.3	0.3	0.2	4.1
3. Textiles, knitting mills, clothing	2.5	16.0	5.4	4.7	1.2	8.1
4. Wood and paper products	37.4	21.8	15.3	18.1	52.5	21.3
5. Primary metal industries	—	6.8	13.7	8.6	7.7	10.5
6. Metal fabricating, machinery, transportation equipment	11.0	13.8	22.3	13.8	10.2	17.7
7. Non-metallic mineral products, petroleum, and coal	2.6	6.0	5.0	11.3	2.0	6.3
8. Electrical and chemical products	1.2	12.3	16.0	6.4	5.6	12.9
9. Miscellaneous and industries for which no data are published	16.6	2.7	4.0	8.0	4.2	3.2
Total	100	100	100	100	100	100
10. Manufacturing production in millions of dollars	397.3	3,207.9	5,429.9	782.9	863.4	10,682.1
11. Manufacturing production per capita in dollars	209	610	871	246	530	586
12. Index of manufacturing production	35	104	148	42	90	100

NOTE: Discrepancies are due to rounding.

SOURCE: Dominion Bureau of Statistics, *Manufacturing Industries of Canada, 1961*, by province.

that is, giving in more detail one of the lines of Table 2:6. The comparison is made on the basis of the value added by each of the productive sectors. In the following remarks we shall add other information that will help to interpret the tables. What picture, then, can we draw of the economic structures of the five regions we have distinguished?

(a) Atlantic Provinces.

The primary sector accounts for one-third of industrial production in the Atlantic provinces. Among the manufacturing industries wood and paper products predominate with 37 per cent of the total; next is fish processing (included in foods and beverages). In Newfoundland manufacturing is centred on wood and fish products (65 per cent of the total). In Prince Edward Island agriculture and fishing predominate. In Nova Scotia the economy is more diversified: to relatively rich natural resources such as farmland, forests, fish, and coal mines, several secondary industries have been added. However, 40 per cent of the manufacturing industry is still based on the processing of staple products. In New Brunswick pulp-and-paper mills and sawmills alone supply 40 per cent of manufacturing production.

Such an economic structure is generally unproductive. Industrial production per capita is only half that of the national average. As for the manufacturing industries proper, the output per capita is only a third of the national average and a little less than a quarter of that of Ontario.

(b) and (c) Quebec and Ontario.

In industrial composition Quebec and Ontario are two rather similar regions. Their manufacturing accounts for nearly two-thirds of the industrial production and for 80 per cent of the manufactures of the country as a whole. Their economic structures differ considerably from a staple-product structure. Mineral extraction, agriculture, and forestry are less important to them than are numerous transformation industries. However, a closer examination reveals, first, quite marked differences between the two provinces, and second, a manufacturing structure in each – but particularly in Quebec – that remains, in effect, a projection of the natural resources of the region. The two principal manufacturing industries of Quebec are the pulp-and-paper industry and the non-ferrous metals refining industry. Groups 4, 5, and 7 of Table 2:7 account for a third of total manufacturing. Agriculture gives rise to other important industries such as meat-packing and the processing of dairy products. On the other hand the development of a great number of light industries in Quebec that produce consumer goods is accounted for not by foreign demand but by the progressive enlargement of the domestic market (and by tariffs). Such are the industries of groups 2 and 3, and to a lesser extent the industries of groups 6 and 8.

In Ontario, the structure of the manufacturing industries is still more diversified. In this province capital and technical knowledge on the one hand, and the size of the market on the other, account better for the industrial structure than do the nature and abundance of the natural resources. The place occupied by sectors 6 and 8 (38.3 per cent of the total) illustrates this fact. To be more specific, Ontario is the site of more than 80 per cent of Canadian production in a large number of industries including the manufacture of automobiles, heavy electrical equipment, agricultural implements, several types of household furniture, tools, bicycles, office furniture. Natural resources are not far behind, however, in the line-up of the important industries; after automobile manufacturing there follow immediately primary iron and steel mills, non-ferrous metals refining, pulp-and-paper manufacturing, and slaughtering and meat-packing. Ontario is by far the most highly industrialized province. Manufacturing production per capita attains the index of 148 (Canada = 100). Quebec follows with 104.

(d) Prairie Provinces.

In the three prairie provinces we again find a large-scale exploitation of the natural resources. Foremost, of course, is wheat. Combined with the cultivation of this and other cereal crops are cattle-raising and dairy farming: hence the importance of the manufacturing industries of slaughtering and meat-packing, and butter- and cheese-making. In Alberta and Saskatchewan agriculture is now being reinforced by the oil industry. Grain, live-stock, dairy products, and petroleum are the mainstays of prairie economic activity. The manufacturing industry is still largely dominated by the natural resources. Almost half of industrial production is based on the region's primary products, compared with 17 per cent in Ontario and 19 per cent in Quebec (see Table 2:6). The four leading manufacturing industries are, in order of importance, slaughtering and meat-packing, oil-refining, butter- and cheese-making, flour-milling. These contribute 43 per cent of the total manufacturing production. Unlike the Atlantic provinces, this region is prosperous. The industrial production per capita is very close to the national level in spite of low manufacturing production.

(e) British Columbia.

People generally compare British Columbia with Ontario because average personal income in the two provinces is about the same. In the structure of their economies, however, they are not at all comparable. The economy of Ontario is the most diversified in Canada. That of British Columbia is based essentially on exploitation of the forests. Nowhere else does one find such a concentration: 52.5 per cent of the manufacturing production of British Columbia is composed of wood and paper products (Table 2:7, group 4) and 15 per cent of the industrial production comes from logging (Table 2:7, forestry).

If the true picture has not been too much distorted by this brief examination of the dominant features of the economic structures of the five regions of the country, we ought by now to expect a definite predominance of natural resources in Canada's exports. If adequate statistics were available, we would also expect to find that the exported products indicate the lines along which certain clearly defined regions have specialized. This part of the story will be told in chapter 15.

SUGGESTED READINGS

W. A. MACKINTOSH: 'Economic Factors in Canadian History', *Canadian Historical Review*, March 1923, pp. 12-25; also 'Some Aspects of a Pioneer Economy', *Canadian Journal of Economics and Political Science*, November 1936, pp. 457-63. Two early discussions of the staple-products theory.

H. A. INNIS: *The Fur Trade in Canada: An Introduction to Canadian Economic History*, revised edition, University of Toronto Press, 1956.
It is, along with other books by the same author, a classic presentation of the role of a staple industry in economic development.

K. BUCKLEY: 'The Role of Staple Industries in Canada's Economic Development', *Journal of Economic History*, Vol. XVIII, 1958.
The author argues that, according to his interpretation, the staple-products theory of Canada's economic development breaks down after 1820.

M. H. WATKINS: 'A Staple Theory of Economic Growth', *Canadian Journal of Economics and Political Science*, May 1963.
A restatement of the staple-products theory and its relevance to the Canadian case.

G. W. BERTRAM: 'Economic Growth in Canadian Industry, 1870-1915: The Staple Model and the Take-off Hypothesis', *Canadian Journal of Economics and Political Science*, May 1963.
Examines Rostow's 'take-off' hypothesis in a Canadian context. Concludes that in Canada a stage analysis is not illuminating and evidence of a take-off cannot be found.

JOHN H. DALES: 'Some Historical and Theoretical Comment on Canada's National Policies', *Queen's Quarterly*, Vol. LXXI, No. 3, 1964, pp. 299-316.

A very remarkable paper which questions in strongest possible terms the accepted doctrine on the Canadian 'National Policy'. Also a piece of outstanding literature in the field.

K. BUCKLEY: *Capital Formation in Canada, 1896-1930*, University of Toronto Press, 1955.
Presents new statistical series which establish the trend and pattern of real investment in Canada for the early period covered.

O. J. FIRESTONE: *Canada's Economic Development, 1867-1953*, Income and Wealth, Series VII, London, Bowes & Bowes, 1958.
A statistical analysis of Canadian economic development since Confederation.

W. C. HOOD AND A. S. SCOTT: *Output, Labour and Capital in the Canadian Economy*, Royal Commission on Canada's Economic Prospects, Ottawa, Queen's Printer, 1957.
A review of past trends in the growth of significant variables in the Canadian economy along with projections extending to 1980. Includes also a theoretical discussion on economic growth.

R. E. CAVES AND R. H. HOLTON: *The Canadian Economy, Prospect and Retrospect*, Cambridge, Harvard University Press, 1961.
Isolates the strategic factors in Canadian development; projections are made for 1970.

R. D. HOWLAND: *Some Regional Aspects of Canada's Economic Development*, Royal Commission on Canada's Economic Prospects, Ottawa, Queen's Printer, 1957.
A study of past growth and future trends in Canada, divided according to six regions: the Atlantic provinces, Quebec, Ontario, the prairie provinces, British Columbia and Yukon, and the Northwest Territories.

CHAPTER

3

THE INDUSTRIALIZATION
OF QUEBEC[1]

There was a time when Quebec (then New France) was all of Canada. It was from the cities of Quebec and Montreal that expeditions set forth to explore and conquer the interior. It was not until around 1840, some eighty years after the end of French rule, that the population of Ontario (Upper Canada) equalled and then began to exceed the population of Quebec (Lower Canada). At that time the economy of Quebec was predominantly based on agriculture and small crafts. Until 1850, indeed, the development of the country was based on an economy of colonial exploitation. For a long time, Canada exported furs and lumber, mainly to England. Shipbuilding also flourished. Then, under the influence of major changes in technology and as a result of the industrial revolution in England, foreign demand for Canada's 'staple products' gradually dwindled.

From 1870 to 1890 there was a world-wide decline in economic conditions; a period of more or less pronounced stagnation was experienced. Canadians, rightly or wrongly, turned towards the domestic market. They sought to create a vast hinterland to absorb the products of the central provinces, Ontario and Quebec. Because of the grandiose political design of Confederation they were able to achieve this objective by means of an

1. Originally published as an article in *La Revue française,* August 1961. Revised.

active and successful land-settlement policy, enormous investments in transportation, and finally high tariffs to protect industry against foreign competition. (The policies in respect of land
settlement, transportation, and tariffs are known as the 'national
policy', and the tariff policy alone is called the 'National Policy'.)

All these measures, which were as much political as economic,
prepared the scene for the great expansion to come. Not all the
components of the economic policies of the time – especially of
the tariff policy – could be described as necessary for economic
growth, but it can be said in general terms that the conditions for
economic growth were now assembled. Beginning in 1896 and
extending to 1920 a first upsurge of industrialization took place.
The period 1896-1913 in Canada is a significant illustration of
Rostow's 'take-off' concept. In Quebec, for example, an increase
in volume of 76 per cent in manufacturing production occurred
between 1900 and 1910; since the population increased by only
21 per cent, production per capita increased by 4.2 per cent per
annum, more than double the average long-term growth rate for
Canada as a whole (1.65 per cent). For the whole country the
proportion of investment to the gross national product increased
from an average 12.6 per cent per annum in current dollars during the period 1870 to 1900, to 18.2 per cent in 1910. The
income per capita in Canada in 1910 was already as high as the
average income per capita was to be in 1953 for fifty-five countries of the world. This means that since before World War I
Quebec has belonged to the category of developed and industrialized countries or regions.

In addition to the spectacular settlement of Western Canada
that resulted from the preparatory measures mentioned above,
the considerable import of foreign capital helped to make the
Canadian take-off possible. The total population of the five main
cities of the prairie provinces grew from 51,720 to 238,978
between 1901 and 1911; Winnipeg alone increased its population
from 42,340 to 128,157. The central provinces, notably Quebec,
supplied the necessary equipment and part of the savings. Furthermore, under the pressure of internal demand and protected

against foreign competition, the industrialization of this period was marked by a very noticeable predominance of light manufacturing industries. In its essentials this type of structure has endured right down to the present day. In 1910, the most important manufacturing industries of the province of Quebec were those making wood products and railway equipment. Next in importance were the industries that are the best examples of tariff protection: manufacture of clothing, footwear, textiles, and tobacco products. Finally, there were two important industries based upon agriculture – flour-milling and butter- and cheese-making. These industries together contributed more than half of the manufacturing production.

Since World War I a second wave of industrialization can be observed in Quebec, the high point of which, measured by the rate of growth, appears to be 1956. Since 1935 particularly, the economy of Quebec has undergone profound transformations in structure. Light manufacturing, although still very important, has marked time, and the expanding industries are those that exploit the natural resources of the region on a world scale and for world markets. *Whereas the early phase of development was centred on the domestic market, the second phase is directed at the foreign market; while the first phase favoured labour-intensive industries in order to absorb the considerable surpluses in the labour force, the second is based on capital-intensive industries. This change in long-term trends is explained to a large extent by the evolution in technology.* The beginning of the century saw the triumph of coal, which is not found in Quebec; but today the sources of energy have become diversified, and electric power, abundant in Quebec, is widely employed in the province's industries, in aluminum industries especially. Similarly, substitutes for steel have been discovered which allow the province to exploit as never before the wealth of its subsoil – for example, asbestos, nickel and copper, and iron ore. Finally, the pulp-and-paper industry has provided the necessary basis for large-scale exploitation of the forests. In brief, modern technology favours the province of Quebec because it requires certain natural resources that are found there in abundance, notably water power, minerals, and forests.[1]

It is not surprising then that in Quebec, where the cost of electricity is among the lowest in the world, the two leading manufacturing industries are pulp-and-paper making and the smelting and refining of non-ferrous metals. These alone account for almost 20 per cent of the total manufacturing production. Moreover, because of the multiple trading networks that these two industries have built up and maintained, they have become centres of vigorous and sustained growth for the entire province.

An island of French language and culture on the American continent, the province of Quebec is often represented as being an economic enclave, a frontier territory that is relatively self-sufficient and undeveloped. The historical and 'continental' perspective that we have just outlined is sufficient to show that the facts are quite different, but the additional statistical information in the following pages will be of interest.

Let us turn to Colin Clark's well-known classification.[2] The primary resource industries in Canada contributed 45 per cent of the national product in 1870, but scarcely 11 per cent in 1963; the secondary sector (manufacturing and construction) rose from 22 per cent to 31 per cent in the same period; and the contribution of the tertiary sector (trade and services) increased from a third to more than half. Quebec's development has been similar to that of Canada as a whole, and both have been similar to that of the great industrial countries of the world. In all cases the transformation of the economy has been marked by a decrease in the relative importance of the primary sector, a slow advance in the secondary sector (slow in terms of employment

1. M. Lamontagne and A. Faucher, 'History of Industrial Development', in J.-C. Falardeau, ed., *Essais sur le Québec contemporain,* Quebec, Presses Universitaires Laval, 1953, pp. 23-54.

2. Colin Clark, *The Conditions of Economic Progress,* New York, St. Martin's Press, 1957. The classification has serious limitations into which it is not possible to enter here.

especially, as a result of the increase in productivity), and a rapid advance in the tertiary sector.

Table 3:1 provides illustrative figures for Canada for selected years.

TABLE 3 : 1

Gross Domestic Product at Factor Cost by Sector, Canada 1870-1963

	Primary *(per cent)*	Secondary *(per cent)*	Tertiary *(per cent)*
1870	45	22	33
1926	23	26	51
1950	17	34	49
1960	11	33	56
1963	11	31	58

SOURCES: O. J. Firestone, *Canada's Economic Development*, London, Bowes & Bowes, p.189, for the year 1870. (All adjustments have been carried over to the tertiary sector.) For the other years, *National Accounts*.

The main difference in production structure between Quebec and the rest of the country probably consists in the narrowness of its agricultural base. Few people realize that Quebec stands with British Columbia as the least agricultural province. This fact emerges clearly from the calculations, whether we use the figures on employment or those on the value of output. In 1962 the value added by agriculture as a percentage of the gross domestic product at market prices was 2.1 per cent for Quebec, 5.3 per cent for Canada without Quebec.[1] Only 7.7 per cent of Quebec's labour force was employed in agriculture in 1962; for Canada without Quebec this figure was 10.7 per cent. Quebec since the war has become so little agricultural, and its people have turned away from agriculture at such a rate, that the rest of the econ-

1. Estimates

omy has had many difficulties in making the necessary adjustments. For the time being the abandonment of farms has certainly much to do with the persistence of surplus labour in Quebec. In the future, however, this movement off the land will provide scope for increased agricultural productivity and income, benefiting farmers and consumers alike.

Table 3:2 completes the examination of the economic structure. The importance of agriculture is measured here on the basis of value added as a percentage of the industrial production (rather than the domestic product). Table 2:6 gives comparable figures for the other regions of the country. Of particular interest here, however, are the changes since 1935. Part A of Table 3:2 shows that the relative declines in agriculture and in electric-power production have been compensated for by the increased importance of mining, manufacturing, and construction. Part B refers to the structure of the manufacturing industry. The most important groups of manufactures are wood and paper products and those made from non-ferrous metals and non-metallic minerals, followed closely by food and beverages. Textiles and clothing come next, followed by metal products and transportation equipment, chemical and electrical products, and in last place tobacco, rubber, and leather products. The manufacturing structure has undergone striking changes since the war. The first three groups in Part B of the table, which formerly accounted for more than half of the manufacturing production, have declined in importance. The change is particularly noticeable in textiles and clothing. These are light industries producing non-durable consumer goods; their expansion dates from the end of the last century. The second wave of industrialization is reflected in the figures for groups 5, 6, and 7; these have been expanding since 1935. Wood and paper products (group 4), important for a long time, have maintained their position. It becomes clear from these figures that Quebec manufacturing has turned more and more to industries producing durable consumer goods and production goods, much of the change being directed to the transformation, the treatment, or the increased utilization of the natural resources of the province.

TABLE 3 : 2

**Evolution of Quebec's Economic Structure 1935-1961
as a Percentage of the Total in Each Category**

	1935	1961	Variations
A. INDUSTRIAL PRODUCTION (VALUE ADDED)			
1. Agriculture	12.4	5.4	−7.0
2. Forestry	3.8	3.5	−0.3
3. Fishing and trapping	0.5	0.1	−0.4
4. Mining	3.0	5.1	+2.1
5. Electric power	8.0	4.8	−3.2
6. Manufacturing	57.8	63.8	+6.0
7. Construction	14.3	17.3	+3.0
Total	99.8	100	
B. MANUFACTURING (SELLING VALUE OF FACTORY SHIPMENTS)			
1. Foods and beverages	20.4	17.8	−2.6
2. Tobacco, rubber, and leather	9.3	5.5	−3.8
3. Textiles, knitwear, and clothing	23.9	15.6	−8.3
4. Wood and paper products	18.1	18.6	+0.5
5. Metal products, machinery, transportation equipment	8.4	11.8	+3.4
6. Primary metal, non-metallic mineral products, petroleum, and coal products	13.0	18.6	+5.6
7. Electrical and chemical products	6.2	10.0	+3.8
8. Miscellaneous	0.7	2.1	+1.4
Total	100	100	

NOTE: Figures for value added in manufacturing are not available for 1935; part B of the table thus measures selling value rather than value added. Changes in the classification of manufacturing industries in 1960 make the figures for 1935 and 1961 not strictly comparable; a check, however, was made by comparing both classifications for the year 1959, and the picture does not change materially for this reason.

SOURCES: Dominion Bureau of Statistics, *Survey of Production*, 1926-1956 and 1961; Dominion Bureau of Statistics, *Manufacturing Industries of Canada, Province of Quebec*, 1961.

On the whole, industrialization has proceeded rapidly. Manufacturing production has increased at an average annual rate of
5.58 per cent since 1870, mineral production at a rate of 8.2 per
cent since 1899. Real income has increased by an average of 3.39
per cent per annum since 1870 and real income per capita by
1.65 per cent, so that the standard of living of Quebec citizens
more than tripled in ninety years.[1] From 1957 to 1961 the rate
of expansion slowed down, but this deceleration followed a
period of extremely rapid acceleration extending from 1935 to
1956, during which period the rate of increase of the national
product in constant prices exceeded 4 per cent per annum. Since
1961, expansion has resumed.

The social consequences of industrialization have been the
same in the province of Quebec as everywhere else. The measurements change but the phenomena remain the same. *Among
the changes which generally accompany transition from an agricultural and pre-capitalist economy to an industrial economy are
a rise in the standards of living, expansion of the cities and
desertion of the countryside, a rise in the standards demanded
by consumers in matters of education and social security, and a
lowering of the birth-rate which is more or less compensated for
by a lowering of the death-rate.* Quebec has experienced all of
these.

However clear one may be about the fundamental changes in
the society, it is often difficult to avoid imputing to industrialization in its strict sense social changes of which the origins lie elsewhere. So it is that industrialization is generally confused with
the increase in real income, and all the consequences of a rise in
income are attributed, falsely, in this writer's opinion, to industrialization. However this may be, in the present work we shall
limit the significance of the concept by equating it to a transfer

---

1. Statistics on real income are for Canada as a whole. They apply to the province of Quebec as well because the long-term rate of growth is the same since
1870, for Ontario, Quebec, and Canada as a whole, as is shown in A. Raynauld, *Croissance et structure économiques de la Province de Québec,* Quebec,
Ministère de l'Industrie et du Commerce, 1961, chapter 1.

to industry of the economic activities of agriculture and small crafts. Such a change in economic activity undoubtedly causes people to move to cities, where it is more profitable to bring factories together. Moreover, it makes a considerable difference in the size of the production units; the manufacturing plants operate on a much larger scale than the farms or the former workshops. In turn, urban living has everywhere caused a lowering of the birth-rate and consequently has modified the age structure of the population. Let us examine briefly these different points.

In 1961 the population of Quebec reached 5.2 million, about 29 per cent of the Canadian population of 18.2 million. Quebec's long-term rate of increase is 1.67 per cent per annum, but between 1940 and 1956 the growth has been much more rapid. In the ten years 1946-1956 the population of Quebec increased by more than 27 per cent, as did that of Canada. The Canadian population is now among the most rapidly increasing in the world – in 1961 its rate of increase was the sixth highest. Natural increase and immigration contribute much to this remarkable increase in population, but among French Canadians the very high birth-rates have clearly been the predominating influence. In 1926, for example, the birth-rate of French Canadians was 34 per 1,000 and that of other Canadians of British descent 19.7 per 1,000. These differences have been progressively diminishing, however: in 1951 the rates were 31.9 and 24.1 respectively.

In Quebec as elsewhere, industrialization exerts a significant influence on several other demographic characteristics. In 1951, in the agricultural regions of the province the ratio representing the number of children of under five years to the number of married women of 15 to 44 years was 154; in the urban regions it was only 87.

As we noted earlier, the urbanization movement has been very rapid. Table 3:3 shows that in ninety years the proportion of urban population to total population almost completely reversed. In this respect Quebec has changed as rapidly as the rest of Canada, if not more rapidly. In 1961 its cities accounted for 74 per cent of its population and in the whole of Canada the cities

TABLE 3 : 3

**Rural Population as a Percentage of the Total Population,
Quebec and Canada**

	Quebec	*Canada*
1870	77	80
1901	62	63
1911	54	56
1921	48	52
1931	40	46
1941	38	43
1951	33	37
1956	30	33
1961	26	30

NOTE: The figure for 1870 is not strictly comparable to those of the following years as its definition of rural population is different.

SOURCE: Dominion Bureau of Statistics, Census of Canada.

accounted for 70 per cent; 40 per cent of the population of the province is concentrated in the metropolitan area of Montreal alone.

Closely linked to the phenomenon of industrialization is that of the growing size of manufacturing establishments. Since 1917 the average plant has become six times larger, if we are going by the value of production. Today the average Quebec manufacturing establishment produces annually goods to the value of $600,000.

SUGGESTED READINGS

A. RAYNAULD: 'The Economic Problems of Quebec', in *Economics: Canada*, ed. M. H. Watkins and D. F. Forster, Toronto, McGraw-Hill, 1963, pp. 325-30.
A short introductory statement on the question.

M. LAMONTAGNE AND A. FAUCHER: 'History of Industrial Development', in *Essais sur le Québec contemporain*, ed. J.-C. Falardeau, Quebec, Presses Universitaires Laval, 1953, pp. 23-54.
The first essay to challenge the view that Quebec's economic development is explained by cultural factors. An alternative model is developed in strict economic terms. A basic text.

J. H. DALES: 'A Comparison of Manufacturing Industry in Quebec and Ontario', in *Canadian Dualism*, ed. M. Wade, University of Toronto Press, 1960, pp. 203-22.
An original approach to Quebec's industrial structure which questions the empirical and theoretical basis of the Lamontagne-Faucher model.

Hydroelectricity and Industrial Development: Quebec 1898-1940, Cambridge, Harvard University Press, 1957.
A study of the relationship between hydro-electric developments and the growth of secondary manufacturing industry in Quebec.

A. RAYNAULD: *Croissance et structure économiques de la Province de Québec*, Quebec, Ministère de l'Industrie et du Commerce, 1961.
An analysis of Quebec's economic structure, industrial growth, and comparative advantage, along with a comparison of Quebec's and Ontario's economic development patterns.

E. MINVILLE (ED.): Collected studies 'Notre Milieu' – *Notre Milieu, L'Agriculture, Montréal économique, La Forêt, Pêche et chasse* – Montreal, Ecole des Hautes Etudes Commerciales and Editions Fides, 1943-6.
Extensive works of description applying to the latter part of the thirties. Their importance has by now become historical.

CHAPTER

4

ECONOMIC FLUCTUATIONS

The economic growth described in the two preceding chapters is comforting. Looked at from above and from a distance, the material progress of capitalistic economies is impressive, and justifiably so. Yet if we look closer, we soon discover that advances and recessions are about equal in number. It is typical of economic growth to lack continuity, indeed one might even talk of a rule, since the expansion and contraction phases follow one another in a more or less regular fashion. This alternation of phases has been going on since the industrial revolution. Although we do not know whether what happened in the past is a sufficient indication of what will happen in the future, nevertheless cycles have occurred and undoubtedly they still do occur at the present time.

A. The Lessons of the Past

Because everything is dependent on everything else in social life, very few phenomena escape such a more or less cyclical pattern. Whether we take salaries, prices, national income, employment, or production, we observe from one quarter to another or from one year to another rising trends followed by falling trends, all trends being more or less pronounced according to particular circumstances. This fact can be verified from several hundreds of statistical series. We can therefore represent economic activity by a figure like the following:

Index of economic activity,

or Y

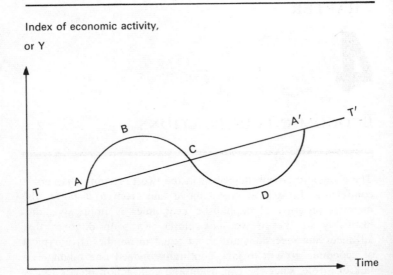

The horizontal axis is time – months or years, for example. On the vertical axis is the index by which economic activity is measured: the value of industrial production (Y). The slope of the line TT' reflects a long-term trend to expansion: in spite of recessions and taking all things into account, production is increasing. But this line TT' is not an observation, it is a calculation. What we observe is the line ABCDA' upon which we can distinguish four phases which define a complete cycle. AB is the expansion phase, BC the recession phase, CD the depression phase, and DA' the recovery phase. Point B is a peak; Point D is a trough. These two turning-points serve to identify the cycles; the distance that separates them measures the amplitude (and thus the importance) of the fluctuations on the vertical axis and the duration of the cycle on the horizontal axis. The series used for such graphs are usually corrected for seasonal variations.

We distinguish the specific cycle which expresses the evolution of a particular statistical series (wholesale prices, for example) from the reference cycle which applies to the whole of the economy. Although studies of business cycles have been little developed in Canada, the principal peaks and troughs in general economic activity since 1919 are reasonably well known. (See Table 4:1.)

TABLE 4 : 1

Reference Dates and Duration of the Cycles, Canada 1919-61

Dates				Duration in months		
Peaks		Troughs		Expansion	Contraction	Complete cycle
		April	1919			
June	1920	September	1921	14	15	29
June	1923	August	1924	21	14	35
April	1929	March	1933	56	47	103
July	1937	October	1938	52	15	67
		February	1946			
October	1948	September	1949	32	11	43
May	1953	June	1954	44	13	57
April	1957	March	1958	34	11	45
November	1959	February	1961	22	16	38

SOURCES: 1919-54: E. J. Chambers, 'Canadian Business Cycles since 1919', *Canadian Journal of Economics and Political Science*, May 1958, p. 180. 1957-58: Department of Trade and Commerce, *Dating the 1957 Peak and the 1958 Trough of the Canadian Reference Cycle.* Ottawa, mimeo. 1959-61: Dominion Bureau of Statistics, *National Accounts, Income and Expenditure*, 1962, p. 8.

In the period 1919-1938 we record four cycles of very unequal length. The peaks of prosperity are June of 1920, June of 1923, April of 1929, and July of 1937. The troughs are April of 1919, September of 1921, August of 1924, March of 1933, and October of 1938. Three short cycles and one average cycle (see p. 83) show as follows: two and a half years, three years, eight and a half years, five and a half years.

Between the end of the war and the beginning of 1961, the table shows four short cycles varying from three years to almost

TABLE 4 : 2

Percentages of Decrease in Certain Indices of Economic Activity During Periods of Downturn
(exceptions as noted)

	Mar. 1920-July 1921	May 1929-Mar. 1933	July 1937-July 1938	Apr. 1953-June 1954	Apr. 1957-Mar. 1958	Nov. 1959-Feb. 1961
Industrial production	21.0	53	8.2	4.3	3.5	3.4*
Wholesale prices	32.2	31	10.2	1.5	0.2	+0.8
Exports	45.2	66	32.5‡	7.1	+1.2†	19.6
Construction	40.7	90	52.0‡	51.0§	5.0	41.1
Gross national product	(14.0)#	(42)	(2.0)	2.7	+0.5	0.6

*In 1957-58 and 1959-61, the indexes used were:
  industrial production: monthly index of volume adjusted for seasonal variation
  wholesale prices: monthly general index
  exports: monthly index of physical volume
  construction: monthly value of building permits
  gross national product: in 1959-61, quarterly figures seasonally adjusted at annual rates in constant dollars in 1957-58, the constant dollars indexes
    were not readily available. Current dollars were used.
†A plus sign denotes an increase. These figures are exceptions in the table.
‡April 1937 to February 1938.
§April 1953 to January 1954.
#The rates in brackets compare years as of December 31 instead of peaks and troughs.

SOURCES: From 1920-21 to 1953-54, the figures are taken from I. Brecher and S. S. Reisman, *Canadian-American Economic Relations*, Part I, Royal Commission on Canada's Economic Prospects, pp. 11-90. For 1957-58 and 1959-61, the figures are taken from Dominion Bureau of Statistics, *Canadian Statistical Review*. The reference dates are not exactly the same as those of Chambers reproduced in Table 4 : 1.

six years, with peaks in October of 1948, May of 1953, April of 1957, and November of 1959.

Like the length of the periods of contraction (or recession) and expansion, the size of the fluctuations is highly variable. *The amplitude measures the severity or the rigour of the contractions as well as the intensity of the expansion phases.* To see this, we need only calculate the percentages in variation of values between peaks and troughs and inversely. If employment, for example, decreased by 10 per cent in one contraction period and by 25 per cent in another, we can say that the second was more severe than the first. By making such calculations on certain statistical series, we can compare the severity of the contractions in Canada since 1920. Table 4:2 gives results of this comparison as far as February 1961.

It becomes evident from this table that the depression of 1920-21, although of short duration, was very pronounced. The most severe and the longest was the depression of 1929-33. That of 1937-38 lasted for a year and was less severe than that of 1920-21. The post-war downturns have been light in comparison to those of the pre-war period. This final observation confirms certain other studies which have established that in several countries fluctuations have been a great deal less pronounced since 1946.

Table 4:3 describes economic activity 1946-1964 in a more general way without referring to the precise turning-points of the business cycle. Less rigorous as to method than Table 4:2, Table 4:3 and the graph are also perhaps more suggestive.

The evolution of the G.N.P. can be divided into six periods since 1946. From 1946 to 1949 the growth was very slow. In fact, real income per person remained stationary.[1] This was a period of reconversion of the economy as a consequence of the

---

1. Since the population increases at a rate of about 2 per cent per year, the G.N.P. must increase by more than 2 per cent for per-capita income to show an advance.

war; the pressure on prices was very strong, notably in 1947 and 1948, and unemployment was quite low. From 1950 to 1953 the economy was going through a period of evident prosperity during which the growth of the G.N.P. was very rapid. The year

**Rate of Growth of the Gross National Product;
Rate of Unemployment 1946-64**

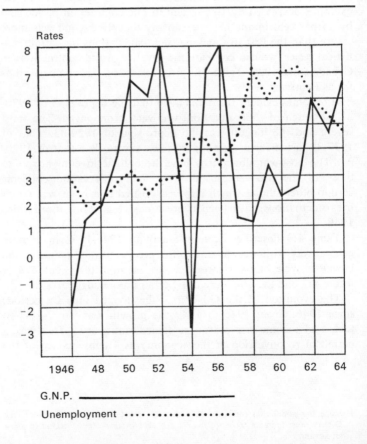

TABLE 4 : 3

Indexes of Economic Activity

	Changes in the G.N.P. in constant dollars (1949) %	Rates of unemployment %	Price increases %
1946	−2.0	3.0	2.1
1947	1.2	1.9	9.7
1948	1.9	2.0	12.8
1949	3.8	2.7	4.0
1950	6.9	3.2	3.1
1951	6.1	2.4	10.6
1952	8.0	2.9	5.0
1953	3.8	3.0	0.4
1954	−2.9	4.6	2.0
1955	7.1	4.4	0.0
1956	8.0	3.4	3.8
1957	1.3	4.6	3.0
1958	1.1	7.1	1.8
1959	3.4	6.0	2.6
1960	2.2	7.0	1.6
1961	2.6	7.2	0.6
1962	6.0	6.0	1.6
1963	4.6	5.5	1.8
1964	6.5	4.7	2.3

NOTE: The 1964 price index is the G.N.P. implicit prices series.

SOURCES: *National Accounts, Income and Expenditure, The Labour Force*, and the *Canadian Statistical Review*. Ottawa, Queen's Printer.

1951 was a year of inflation, but in 1952 the rise in prices was held in check in spite of quickly expanding production. A peak was reached in May 1953 (Table 4:1), so that the annual average growth of the G.N.P. was smaller than in 1952; prices were stable. A rather serious recession marked 1954: this was the third phase.[1] The fourth consisted of a blaze of prosperity in 1955, 1956, and the beginning of 1957. Prices were held in check, but unemployment did not have time to disappear: there was little decrease from the recession of 1954. Then came five long years of stagnation (during which a peak was reached in November 1959, but a peak of lean years), a period when income per capita completely stopped rising. Prices rose in a quite unnatural way[2] and unemployment was excessive, at a rate of 6 to 7 per cent of the labour force. The awaited recovery finally came in 1962 and was maintained in 1963 and 1964. Unemployment went down in 1964 to 4.7 per cent.

The graph reproduces the figures of the table. One notes the wide fluctuations in economic activity, and on the other hand the persistence of unemployment, or rather the rising trend in unemployment until 1961.

Economic fluctuations are an almost universal phenomenon in industrialized countries because they are fundamentally due to the competitive system of these countries. Because of its geographical position and the direction of its foreign trade, Canada is particularly sensitive to fluctuations in the American economy. From the studies that have been made on this subject,[3] it is well established that the turning-points in the Canadian business cycle coincide in large part with those of the American cycle but that the amplitude of the fluctuations is smaller in Canada.

The method of reference dates for the identification of cycles

1. The imprecision of the method is illustrated here: if the peak is May 1953, and the trough June 1954 (Table 4:1), the second part of 1954 is a period of expansion and not of recession.

2. This pattern of rising prices combined with high unemployment was a result of a policy of monetary restraint and the consequent overvaluation of the Canadian dollar during most of this period.

3. I. Brecher and S. S. Reisman, *Canadian-American Economic Relations*; E. J. Chambers, '*Canadian Business Cycles*'; W. A. Beckett, *Indicators of Cyclical Recessions and Revivals in Canada*, published in N.B.E.R., Business Cycle Indicators, Vol. 1, edited by G. Moore, New York, 1961. On the Canadian cycles there should also be cited V. W. Malach, *International Cycles and Canada's Balance of Payments, 1921-33*, Toronto, 1954.

is based exclusively on the behaviour of the statistical series. If reference is made instead to categories that have been developed as explanations of cycles, we will generally distinguish the *short cycles* of a duration of about three years, which depend on variations in business inventories; the *average cycles* (called the Juglar cycles, after the man who discovered them in 1857) of a duration of about eight years, which are deemed to depend on variations in investment;[1] the *long cycles* (Simon Kuznets and Moses Abramovitz) running between fifteen and twenty years, which relate to population changes and construction; and the *long waves* (the Kondratieff cycles, reported for the first time in the twenties) of a duration of about fifty years, which are said to be explained by major innovations.

In Table 4:1 we have observed the inventory cycle which is

TABLE 4 : 4

Business Cycles: Volume of Production of Durable Goods, United States 1865-1938

	Trough to trough	*Number of years*	*Peak to peak*	*Number of years*
1st	1865-1876	11	1872-1882	10
2nd	1876-1885	9	1882-1892	10
3rd	1885-1896	11	1892-1907	15
4th	1896-1908	12	1907-1920	13
5th	1908-1921	13	1920-1929	9
6th	1921-1932	11	1929-1937	8
7th	1932-1938	6		

SOURCES: A. Burns and C. Mitchell, *Measuring Business Cycles*, National Bureau of Economic Research, New York, 1946, quoted by A. Hansen. *Business Cycles and National Income*, Norton, 1951, p. 24.

1. Since the sources of these first two cycles are hardly distinguishable, they may be considered as one category only. In any case, these are the ordinary business cycles.

the cycle revealed by the method we have used. We have encountered the average cycle on one occasion (see p. 77). Table 4:4, using United States statistics, provides further illustration of this kind of cycle.

The troughs given here represent years of severe depressions which have nothing in common with the post-war recessions appearing in Table 4:1. To be more precise, the decline in production from peak to trough has at no time been less than 25 per cent. Between 1929 and 1932 the decrease in production amounted to 69 per cent.

The 'long waves' have often been illustrated by wholesale prices in England and the United States:

> 1st cycle:
>> 55 to 60 years.
>> rise 1790-1815-1820
>> drop 1820-1845-1850
>
> 2nd cycle:
>> 45 to 50 years.
>> rise 1845-1850-1873
>> drop 1873-1895
>
> 3rd cycle:
>> 45 years.
>> rise 1895-1920
>> drop 1920-1940

Common sense will tell us that a depression occurring in the course of a long movement of expansion will be shorter and less pronounced than one that takes place during a long movement of decline. The severity of the depressions of 1882-1885 and 1929-1933 may partly be explained by this fact.

B. Short-term Forecasting

The study of economic fluctuations is directed principally towards short-term forecasting, towards the 'forecast of the present' as a French economist has expressed it. A close examination of the recent past, of what happened in previous booms or recessions, is indeed one of the systematic techniques used for predictions. But short-term forecasting has by now become in itself a field of specialization where sophisticated training and a good deal of experience are required for success.

In Canada, very little forecasting is reported to the public. Certain private organizations do publish regular analyses on the current economic situation and on trends and outlook, but the government, as a matter of policy, publishes nothing. In this it follows the example of the United Kingdom, though most other countries publish their forecasts. Until the spring of 1965 it was even impossible to know exactly the methods used in Canada by the government, since for some unaccountable reason they were guarded as if from the devil.[1]

1. SOME FORECASTING TECHNIQUES

The Business Cycle Indicators.

Short-term economic forecasting dates from the work of W. M. Persons at Harvard University during the First World War. *These writings led to the construction of a 'barometer' consisting of the famous curves A, B, and C which were to predict the turning-points in the business cycle.* Here curve A represented three series of leading indices (speculation indices); curve B, five series of coincident indices (business indices); and curve C, two series of lagging indices (from the money market). This barometer correctly predicted the short crisis of 1920 and the recovery of 1922. But it met with a resounding failure in 1929.

Although later rehabilitated, the Harvard barometer has given way to other techniques. Among these, what are called the diffusion indices of sensitive indicators deserve a brief description. *From the Harvard barometer the idea is retained of separating certain statistical series that lead, coincide, or lag behind, in reference to the turning-points. A diffusion index is calculated by counting up, each month, how many of these series are rising and dividing the number obtained by the total number of series con-*

1. The current Canadian techniques are exposed for the first time in a 1965 publication of the Organization for Economic Co-operation and Development. See the Suggested Readings.

sidered. When the percentage is below 50 a recession is indicated, and when it is above 50 an expansion is indicated. This is an essentially mechanical approach like that of the barometer and has the serious disadvantage of not giving any warning when it is about to fail. To this method belongs the notion of reference cycles and specific cycles referred to in the first section of this chapter. Following the publication in 1950 by the National Bureau of Economic Research in the United States of an important study on statistical indicators, the same indicators were applied to the Canadian economy and it was found that they move in the same way in the Canadian business cycle as they do in the American. These indicators are grouped as follows to form four diffusion indices:

(a) *The leading indices*
  1. industrial common stocks prices;
  2. residential construction permits;
  3. commercial construction permits;
  4. weekly hours of work (manufacturing);
  5. corporation profits (quarterly);
  6. wholesale prices of capital goods;
  7. new orders for equipment goods;
(b) *The coincident indices*
  8. industrial employment;
  9. number of unemployed;
  10. industrial production;
  11. gross national product (non-farm, quarterly);
  12. cheques cashed;
  13. railway transportation;
  14. wholesale prices;
(c) *The lagging indices*
  15. average hourly earnings (manufacturing);
  16. retail trade;
  17. inventories (manufacturing);
  18. rate of interest on day-to-day loans;
  19. consumer credit.
(d) *Total of the above indices*

A private organization in Toronto, General Research Associates, uses these original American indices, with Canadian imports and exports added, as the basic Canadian indicators in a systematic forecasting framework. Some of the indicators are published monthly, some quarterly, by the *Canadian Statistical Review*. The Canadian government does not use the technique directly to establish its forecasts, but it does make use of it, along with the whole forecasting apparatus, to assess, evaluate, and correct forecasts obtained otherwise.

Surveys.

A second forecasting technique, more widespread in Germany and France than in Canada, consists of periodic surveys on the intentions or perspectives of entrepreneurs and consumers. It is best illustrated in Canada by the survey of the Department of Trade and Commerce on investment plans, called *Private and Public Investment in Canada, Outlook*. This survey, which began to be published in 1946, covers residential and non-residential construction, and machinery and equipment. All sectors and industries are included except agriculture and fisheries, for which other sources of estimation are used. Residential construction plans are obtained from the local offices of the Central Mortgage and Housing Corporation.

The first inquiry regarding investment plans for a particular calendar year is conducted in October of the previous year on a preliminary basis through personal interviews with the managements of about one hundred large firms. The main survey is made in December and covers 20,000 establishments. Finally in June revisions of the December estimates are supplied by about 4,500 firms. Only the last two surveys are published.

The Department of Labour compiles a biannual report on the employment situation, with forecasts for the following six months on the labour force, employment, and unemployment, based on quarterly surveys of the manufacturing industry. Although they are not published, it is known that the forecasts are in the form of diffusion indices showing the percentage of entrepreneurs who expect a rise in employment in the next months. It is, of course, the change in this percentage that is important; the expected level of employment is not expressed in figures. The department also conducts regular and numerous interviews with people in industry on the general economic situation and perspectives. The reports of these interviews help to assess the quantitative material.

Experts in the field will say that to be worth anything surveys of intentions must be done regularly and interpreted carefully on the basis of past experience. It is only after a good many years of close and constant examination of expectations against subsequent actual results that the surveys take on a real significance and become reliable indicators for predictions and policy.

Market Analysis.

Market analysis is an integral part of any forecasting apparatus. It may be used to predict the level of activity in certain industries, sectors, or commodities where alternative forecasting techniques are not reliable enough, or it may be introduced to break down the aggregates and check for consistency. Suppose that investment plans show a large projected increase in capacity in given industries; capital output or other ratios will give output estimates which must be consistent with the general level of demand and with the distribution of the demand among the main categories of commodities. Market analysis is useful in this disaggregation process.

Market analysis is widely used in Canada to predict exports (about 100 categories), imports, and non-commercial transactions relative to the balance of payments.

Econometric Models.

The Department of Trade and Commerce makes use of a general econometric model for the purpose of making annual or quarterly forecasts of general economic activity. Because, as already stated, the government keeps such matters very much to itself, it is not possible to describe this model here, but we shall give a brief explanation of the method used.

An econometric model is essentially a quantitative system

describing the interrelations between economic variables. Contrary to the preceding business cycle indicators, which are selected without any logical sequence, the mathematical model attempts to predict the event working from certain known facts (the exogenous variables) and then from the relations that exist between these known facts and the facts one is seeking to predict (the endogenous variables). Thus the propensity to consume is a relation between consumption and income. If the income and the relation are known, the consumption may be found by a simple calculation. Similarly, if imports are a stable and known function of the level of income the income figure allows us to deduce the import figure. The characteristic liaison between two variables often involves a time-lag. Today's consumption may depend on yesterday's income rather than on current income; investment is often described as being a function of the consumption of a previous period. Such time-lags are very useful in forecasting when they are known and stable, the knowledge of one day leading directly to the knowledge of the next. Generally, econometric models are set up in rigorous mathematical form and make thorough use of the interdependent relations that are to be found in great number in economic activity. In the Netherlands and in the United States, the econometric technique is widely used as a forecasting instrument.

The present Canadian econometric model uses about sixty equations. The exogenous variables, whose values must be predicted or assumed by other methods, are exports, public expenditure, and residential construction. The dependent variables are of course the G.N.P., the main categories of income and expenditure, the general level of employment, unemployment, and prices.

2. THE GENERAL FRAMEWORK: THE 'NATIONAL BUDGETS'

Since the economic activities of the country are recorded in the national accounts, this framework is the obvious one within which to organize forecasting. Put simply, the end result of a comprehensive forecasting program is a whole set of national accounts calculated in advance. By analogy with the projected annual government revenue and expenditure, such 'prospective' national accounts could be called a *national budget*. As defined, a national budget is a classifying device or a framework rather than a forecasting technique. An econometric model may be translated easily into an economic budget if the model is sufficiently general, but in most countries the other techniques of obtaining information and data are used as well.

Even as a simple device, however, a national budget adds something specific in so far as any set of accounts ensures consistency between partial estimates. Moreover, the forecasts are presented in the budget in a form that is already familiar to users of the national accounts.

All governments that do any forecasting at all do it in the general framework of the national accounts. Canada is no exception. Indeed, since the national accounts became complete in their modern form, a good deal of attention has been given in this country to their use for the purpose of forecasting.[1]

The techniques used are now fairly standard practice. The differences from country to country are mainly in emphasis. In the Netherlands, the mathematical methods are given a larger part in over-all forecasting than in other countries, but even where the iterative and pragmatic approach predominates the models are there in the background.

In Canada, the main steps in arriving at the economic budget are as follows:

As stated earlier, the surveys of investment plans supply figures for projected expenditure on non-residential construction, residences, machinery, and equipment. Projected government expenditure is taken from the budgetary estimates. Exports of goods and services are estimated by direct study of the conditions prevailing in foreign markets, and imports on the basis of a preliminary forecast of the level of the G.N.P. To get the total expenditure, consumers' expenditure and business inventories must be added. Consumers' expenditure is (in part) a fairly

1. Stewart Bates, 'Government Forecasting in Canada', *Canadian Journal of Economics and Political Science*, August 1946, pp. 361-78.

stable function of income in the short run, so that again the figures may be derived from the estimated changes in income. Inventories by contrast are one of the most difficult items to predict. An estimate is made on the basis of changes in non-farm production, the ratio of inventory to sales, changes in consumer demand for durables, and the phase of the business cycle. This estimate is less reliable than the others.

On the income side of the national accounts, labour income is comparatively stable; corporation profit is the unstable component. Labour income is estimated partly from the surveys referred to previously, partly from known changes of productivity and unit labour costs, from the estimated pressure on the labour market, and so forth. Corporation profits on the other hand are projected essentially on the basis of previous cyclical behaviour. Most of the other components of the national income are derived from relatively stable ratios involving items already estimated.

From the first chapter the reader will have learned that it is possible to derive or estimate missing figures by going from the expenditure to the income side of the national accounts and conversely. The econometric model fills the remaining gaps and serves as a general control device. In the end, the projected change in the G.N.P. is established and all possible inconsistencies are forcibly removed (when logic fails, the calculators do it).

In case this too brief account of forecasting should leave the impression of a more or less mechanical operation, it must be strongly emphasized that judgment and rigorous economic theorizing are absolutely indispensable. One final example will suffice. Suppose that the total demand forecasts exceed the total supply forecasts. The analyst has to decide not how the accounts will balance but how the economy will. And there are many possibilities. Will the adjustment take place through rising prices, through increased output, or through increased imports, to cite only a few? Each one of the equilibrating mechanisms calls for a particular set of revisions to the estimates and probably for a different end result on the over-all forecast.

Since 1946 the governments of Canada and the United States have been required by law to pursue a policy of full employment without inflation and thus ensure the economic stability of their countries. They acquit themselves daily of this heavy responsibility, but the only regular means by which they report to the people are, in Canada, the annual budget speech, and in the United States, the Economic Report of the President.

The main objects of these two documents are to review the economic situation and to announce the economic policy that the government intends to follow during the coming year. Ideally, this policy should be based on studies of current economic conditions and on explicit forecasts, and these should be made public. The current situation is adequately examined in the White Paper[1] which accompanies the Canadian budget speech, but no predictions concerning the near future are included.

The budgetary documents are made up of two parts: the first is a review of economic conditions in the year just ended and the second is an analysis of the government accounts. These documents are not intended to support specifically any changes in government policy that the Minister of Finance may propose in his speech. By contrast, in the United States, where comprehensive forecasts likewise are not included in the Economic Report of the President, a detailed analysis is provided of the effects expected from the economic policy being proposed. This analysis is contained in the Report of the Council of Economic Advisors.[2]

The Canadian budget speech does contain, however, the expected rate of growth of the gross national product. For the year 1965 the expected rate was 7.0 per cent. Incidentally, the actual rate proved to be 10.5 per cent. The only purpose of the inclusion of this rate is to justify the estimates of government revenue. But how is it possible to have informed public discus-

1. A White Paper is a document that is tabled before the House of Commons and published as a supplement to the reports of the debates.

2. Economic Report of the President transmitted to the Congress together with the Annual Report of the Council of Economic Advisors, Washington, D.C.

sion on proposed policies if nobody outside government circles knows what the economic situation of the country is likely to be in the near future? No wonder that little in the budget speech gets public attention except proposed changes in taxes that directly affect the individual.[1]

SUGGESTED READINGS

ORGANIZATION FOR ECONOMIC CO-OPERATION AND DEVELOPMENT: *Techniques of Economic Forecasting*, Paris, 1965.
A description of methods used by governments in short-term economic forecasting in Canada, the U.S.A., France, the United Kingdom, the Netherlands, and Sweden. Probably the best introduction to the field.

T. N. BREWIS, H. E. ENGLISH, A. SCOTT, AND P. JEWETT: 'Economic Forecasting', chapter 9 of *Canadian Economic Policy*, revised edition, Toronto, Macmillan, 1965, pp. 214-31.
Examines the Canadian forecasting techniques and their usefulness.

E. J. CHAMBERS: 'Canadian Business Cycles since 1919', *Canadian Journal of Economics and Political Science*, May 1958, pp. 166-89.
An article that tries to identify the Canadian reference cycle dates and their relationship with U.S. reference dates.

T. M. BROWN: 'A Forecast Determination of National Product, Employment and Price Level in Canada, from an Econometric Model', in *Models of Income Determination*, Studies in Income and Wealth, Vol. 28, National Bureau of Economic Research, Princeton University Press, 1964, pp. 59-86.
The paper presents an econometric model developed for the

---

1. The Department of Economics at the University of Montreal publishes a monthly review, *Canadian Economic Outlook,* based on examination of several hundred statistical series which are kept constantly up to date. Several other non-governmental organizations, including the National Industrial Conference Board and several brokerage houses, publish regular analyses of Canadian economic activity.

Canadian economy and suggests how it could be used to determine income and employment and to predict the future behaviour of the economy.

W. A. BECKETT: 'Indicators of Cyclical Recessions and Revivals in Canada', in *Business Cycle Indicators*, Vol. 1, ed. G. Moore, New York, National Bureau of Economic Research, 1961, pp. 294-322.
Some of the techniques of business cycle measurement and analysis developed by the National Bureau of Economic Research are tested in a Canadian setting.

J. MERAUD: 'Analyses des tendances récentes, indices précurseurs et tests conjoncturels', *Cahiers de l'Institut de sciences économiques appliquées*, Supplement No. 116, August 1961.

D. G. HARTLE: 'Predictions Derived from the Employment Forecast Survey', *Canadian Journal of Economics and Political Science*, August 1958, pp. 373-90.
The article summarizes the results of an analysis of the predictions derived from data obtained by the Employment Forecast Survey from 1946 until 1957. These predictions were little known outside government circles. See also the complete study: *The Employment Forecast Survey*, University of Toronto Press, 1962.

A. E. SAFARIAN: *The Canadian Economy in the Great Depression*, University of Toronto Press, 1959.
A factual and analytical presentation of the Canadian experience with economic fluctuations in the thirties.

I. BRECHER AND S. S. REISMAN: *Canada–United States Economic Relations*, Royal Commission on Canada's Economic Prospects, Ottawa, Queen's Printer, 1957.
In part I, the authors discuss the transmission of business cycles from the U.S. to Canada.

D. B. SUITS: 'Forecasting and Analysis with an Econometric Model', *American Economic Review*, March 1962, pp. 104-32.

An actual econometric model of the U.S. economy is presented as well as its use as a forecasting instrument. An excellent exercise in applied economic theory.

J. JOHNSTON: *Econometric Methods*, New York, McGraw-Hill, 1963.
Provides a self-contained development and explanation of econometric methods. For students who have already done some work in statistics.

G. HABERLER: *Prosperity and Depression: A Theoretical Analysis of Cyclical Movements*, Geneva, League of Nations, 1941.
A basic text on business cycles.

CHAPTER

5

THE DISTRIBUTION OF INCOME

A. Determinants of Income

The distribution of income among people is essentially a problem of price. Although labour is not a merchandise, we have to apply the concepts of supply and demand to it if we are to have an understanding of the phenomenon of income distribution and of the problems underlying economic inequality. *Thus wages and salaries are explained by the supply of and the demand for the worker's services. 'Supply' here is a substitute for the more general rule of scarcity.* The scarcer a product, the greater its price. The same applies to labour. All things being equal (individual qualifications especially), the worker who is the rarest of his kind relative to the demand will earn the most money. Babe Ruth and Maurice Richard were exceptional in their professions: they could thus command high returns. The doctor and the engineer are scarcer in relation to public demand than is the labourer, and therefore earn more. *On the demand side is the concept of marginal productivity, that is, the additional contribution to the value of the service produced that can be imputed to each additional worker.* He who contributes more to the increase in the value of the product receives a higher remuneration, all else being equal. If one service or product is more highly regarded by the consumer than another service or product, its value will be correspondingly higher and so will the income of the man who has offered it on the market. Productivity (or the demand for labour) depends primarily not on the personal merits of the worker, but rather on the demand for the product or for the service of the worker. Whatever the skill with which an artisan fashions an object, the object will be without economic value and the artisan without money if nobody wants it. To increase his income each worker must either increase his productivity, if he can do so in the consumer's terms, or else make himself scarcer. Since it is often easier to influence supply than demand, certain groups, trades, and professions sometimes seek to restrict their number in order to increase their incomes. It is easy to set more difficult examinations for candidates, to forbid foreigners to enter the profession, and so on. *Productivity and scarcity, then, are the two fundamental factors that explain the remuneration for work, and consequently the distribution of income and goods among workers.*

Most differences in income can be attributed to differences in productivity. For example, a forty-year-old worker generally earns more than a twenty-year-old worker. This is because experience increases his output. Similarly, education commands a price because it also increases output. The differences in wages between men and women are attributable in part to differences in productivity (because of age and types of occupations). So it is with differences in wages between industries and between occupations.

B. Inequality of Income: An Ethical and Economic Problem

A good many people refuse to accept that the distribution of income should be dependent upon scarcity and productivity. Opponents of the capitalistic system have always attacked its inequality of distribution, declaring that 'to each according to his needs' should replace the capitalistic dictum 'to each according to his work'. If the inequality of income merely posed a problem in social ethics it would be easier to correct; the problem, however, is economic as well as social, and it has not been solved by anyone, communist or capitalist. What happens is that a greater equality in distribution may decrease savings and investment and consequently the rate of growth of the economy. Let us take

$50,000 to be divided between two individuals A and B. In the first case each has $25,000 at his disposal and consumes $10,000. The total consumption is $20,000 and the savings are $30,000. In the second case A receives $5,000 and B $45,000. A's consumption can be only $5,000 while B's can remain at $10,000. Total consumption is $15,000 and savings are $35,000. *A conflict thus arises between social goals and economic goals.* It is only during a period of depression that a more equalitarian distribution will not risk compromising other objectives. At that time savings are excessive, and they can therefore be reduced without inconvenience.

These general observations will permit a more balanced evaluation of the following data on income distribution.

C. Wealth and Poverty in the World

Let us first examine the distribution of income throughout the world. We all know that it is at this level that incomes are the most unequally divided. In 1949 the United States, with only 7 per cent of the world's population, commanded 42 per cent of its income. At the other extreme, the twenty-five poorest countries, in which the average annual income was below $100, accounted for 54 per cent of world population but only 9 per cent of world income. The situation has not changed appreciably since that time.

In Table 5:1 statistics are given showing the national income per capita of several countries. The reader should pay particular attention not to the absolute figures but rather to the comparison between them. Even for comparative purposes these figures are so rough and the bases for calculation so tenuous that we should add a 'more or less' to our conclusions. It becomes evident from the table that the United States has an average income of about thirty-five times that of China or India, about three times that of the U.S.S.R., and about twice that of the United Kingdom, Germany, or France. Among the richest countries Canada, Switzerland, and Sweden ranked after the United States in 1961. The reader will notice that there have been some significant changes over the years.

TABLE 5 : 1

National Income Per Capita of Selected Countries in U.S. Dollars

	1953	1957	1961
United States	1,908	2,108	2,800
Canada	*1,318*	*1,472*	*2,000*
Switzerland	995	1,244	1,800
Sweden	910	1,171	1,800
West Germany	482	711	1,500
United Kingdom	930	955	1,500
Denmark	740	869	1,500
France	600	720	1,450
U.S.S.R.	441	500	900
Italy	307	404	800
Republic of Ireland	416	451	700
Argentina	366	402	500
Japan	197	252	450
Mexico	207	233	300
China	60	64	75
India	60	64	75

SOURCE: P. A. Samuelson, *Economics*, 6th edition, New York, McGraw-Hill, 1961, p. 111.

Instead of the national income per capita, the United Nations now publishes statistics on the rate of growth of the domestic product of several countries. These statistics are more trustworthy but less revealing. They do not express the income level already reached, but only the rate of change over a certain period.

The differences in income between the various countries are primarily differences in the degree of economic development. Certain countries are still at the pre-industrial stage whereas others have long since achieved industrialization. The differences between these two types of countries are enormous: one might say that they are differences in kind. In comparison, the differ-

TABLE 5 : 2

**Average Annual Rates of Growth of
Real Gross Domestic Product Per Capita**

	Period	*Rate*
United States	1953-61	1.1
Canada	*1953-61*	*1.0*
Sweden	1953-61	3.4
United Kingdom	1953-61	2.2
France	1953-61	3.7
West Germany	1953-61	5.7
U.S.S.R.	1951-59	8.5
Italy	1953-61	5.4
Argentina	1953-61	0.4
Japan	1954-61	8.8
India	1953-60	1.4
China	1953-58	9.5

SOURCE: United Nations, *Yearbook of National Accounts Statistics*, 1963, pp. 318-19. The figures for the U.S.S.R. and China are taken from the 1961 issue and apply to the 'material domestic product'.

ences between the industrialized countries themselves are insignificant.

D. The Rich and the Poor in Canada

Just as income is unequally distributed between countries, so it is between the various regions of the same country. The distribution of personal income in Canada is given in Table 5:3 by provinces. Ontario and British Columbia have the highest incomes, and the prairie provinces come next. Quebec is situated at the centre of the distribution. The Atlantic provinces are poorest.

When we speak of analysing the distribution of income, we do not mean primarily the geographical distribution but rather the distribution among citizens according to the income class to which they belong.

In this sense it may be said that Canada is among the countries in which there is least inequality in the distribution of income.

TABLE 5 : 3

Geographical Distribution of Per-Capita Personal Income

	1956		1963	
	$	As a percentage of the national average	$	As a percentage of the national average
Newfoundland	749	55.0	1,029	59.3
Prince Edward Island	788	57.9	1,075	61.9
Nova Scotia	971	71.3	1,283	73.9
New Brunswick	895	65.7	1,151	66.4
Quebec	1,149	84.4	1,504	86.7
Ontario	1,594	117.1	2,019	116.4
Manitoba	1,325	97.3	1,664	95.9
Saskatchewan	1,392	102.2	1,890	108.9
Alberta	1,456	106.9	1,747	100.7
British Columbia	1,667	122.5	1,957	112.8
Yukon and Northwest Territories	1,387	101.9	1,333	76.8
Canada	1,361	100	1,734	100

SOURCE: Dominion Bureau of Statistics, *National Accounts*.

Many readers, rightly, will consider it unsatisfactory from a social point of view to be able to say no more than this. Table 5:4 shows that the median income per non-farm household[1] in 1961 was $4,262, which means that 50 per cent of the households earned less and 50 per cent earned more than this figure. The poorer half of the non-farm population earned approximately 24 per cent of the personal income. It can also be seen that a third of the households earned less than $3,000, or 10.5 per cent of the total income. In a country as rich as Canada it will no doubt come as a surprise to many, especially when they consider the general level of prices, that a third of all those not living on farms earn less than $3,000 a year. In the population as

1. The term household here includes both complete families and individuals living alone or living with unrelated persons.

a whole the situation is worse than this, because if farm households were included in the calculations, the division of income
would undoubtedly appear even more unequal.

The inequality of incomes is more clearly illustrated if we plot
the figures along what is called a Lorenz curve.

**Distribution of non-farm Income: Lorenz Curve
Canada, 1961**

Percentage of total income

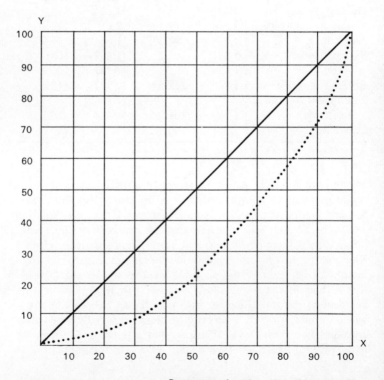

Percentage of total number of households

TABLE 5 : 4

Non-Farm Income Distribution, Canada 1961

Income group $ per year	Families and unattached individuals			Total income (million $)	Income	
	1 Number (thousands)	2 Percentage of total	3 Cumulated percentage	4 Total income (million $)	5 Percentage of total	6 Cumulated percentage
Under 1,000	475	9.9	9.9	249	1.1	1.1
1,000 – 1,999	501	10.4	20.3	741	3.2	4.3
2,000 – 2,999	575	12.0	32.3	1,442	6.2	10.5
3,000 – 3,999	662	13.8	46.1	2,340	10.2	20.7
4,000 – 4,999	706	14.7	60.8	3,176	13.7	34.4
5,000 – 7,999	1,307	27.3	88.1	8,045	34.8	69.2
8,000 – 9,999	313	6.5	94.6	2,801	12.1	81.3
10,000–14,999	188	3.9	98.5	2,313	10.0	91.3
15,000 and over	73	1.5	100.0	2,006	8.7	100.0
	4,800	100		23,113	100	

Average income $4,815
Median income $4,262

SOURCE: Dominion Bureau of Statistics, *Distribution of Non-Farm Incomes in Canada by Size*, 1961.

On the X axis we place the distribution of households (column 3 of Table 5:4) according to income classes, and on the Y axis the distribution of incomes (column 6 of Table 5:4). The diagonal of the chart gives us an absolutely equalized distribution of income, in which 20 per cent of the households would earn 20 per cent of the income, 70 per cent of the households would earn 70 per cent of the income, and so on. The actual distribution of income is represented by the line to the right of the diagonal. The wider the divergence between the two curves, the more unequal are the incomes.

According to certain data that it would take too long to describe here, incomes are distributed more equally in Canada than in the United States, particularly in the highest income classes.

Since 1951 the distribution in Canada has not changed much. The changes that can be observed, however, are in the direction of greater equality, as Table 5:5 shows.

TABLE 5 : 5

**Income Distribution of Non-Farm Families
and Unattached Individuals, Canada 1951 and 1961**

Percentage of households starting with the lowest income groups	*Percentage of income (cumulated)*	
	1951	*1961*
20	4.0	4.2
40	13.6	16.2
60	31.7	34.6
80	54.3	59.9
100	100	100

SOURCE: Dominion Bureau of Statistics, *Distribution of Non-Farm Family Income in Canada by Size*, 1951 and 1961.

E.   The Government Reducing the Inequality in Income

Suppose we wish to modify the distribution of incomes. What can be done? Theoretically, we could choose to act upon the factors that control distribution (productivity and scarcity). But to pursue our objective in this manner would require superhuman patience, and besides it must be admitted that we could not be certain of the result because the method would be a very indirect one. The government has at its disposal, on the other hand, several methods that are much more efficient. The first of these is taxation. In Canada it is the personal income tax particularly that affects distribution. By changing the structure of this tax the government can modify the inequality of incomes at will. It first does this by setting the tax to be paid on a percentage-of-income basis, so that at 10 per cent, for example, an income of $1,000 is taxed $100, and an income of $5,000 is taxed $500. The government does more than this. It establishes progressive taxes: that is, the higher the income the higher the rate. An income of $1,000 is taxed at 10 per cent, let us say, and one of $5,000 at 20 per cent. In the first case the tax is $100, in the second $1,000. All industrialized and 'capitalist' countries reduce the inequality of incomes in this way through taxation that takes more from the rich than from the poor.

Columns 1 and 2 of Table 5:6 are analogous to columns 2 and 5 of Table 5:4, but the data on which they are based are not comparable. It is the comparison between columns 2 and 3 that particularly illustrates how taxation decreases the inequality of incomes. Those who have earned incomes of $15,000 and over in 1962 received 8 per cent of the total income but paid 21.4 per cent of the total tax; that is, their share in the total tax was almost three times their share of the total income. But if we calculate the tax paid by those who earned less than $3,000, we see that for incomes equal to 19.9 per cent of the total income the tax levied amounted to only 8.1 per cent of the total taxes. Column 4 may also be compared to column 2. Here we find the distribution of disposable income: that is, the income remaining after the tax has been paid. Inequality has been reduced to a certain extent.

The government may employ several other methods for making income distribution either more or less equal. Inflation and higher yields on government bonds will, as a general rule,

TABLE 5 : 6

Effect of Income Tax on Income Distribution, Canada 1962

Income classes $ per year	1 Percentage of returns to total returns	2 Total class income as a percentage of total income assessed	3 Tax payable as a percentage of total tax payable	4 Disposable income as a percentage of total disposable income
Under 1,000	11.1	1.3	0.1	1.5
1,000 – 1,999	16.5	6.5	1.7	7.0
2,000 – 2,999	18.5	12.2	6.3	12.8
3,000 – 3,999	17.3	16.1	10.9	16.6
4,000 – 4,999	14.2	17.1	13.8	17.3
5,000 – 7,999	16.7	27.1	28.4	27.0
8,000 – 9,999	2.4	5.8	7.8	5.6
10,000–14,999	1.8	5.9	9.6	5.5
15,000 and over	1.5	8.0	21.4	6.7

SOURCE: Calculations made from *Taxation Statistics*, 1964, Department of National Revenue.

increase the inequality of income. On the other hand the structure of government expenditure, in particular transfer payments for purposes such as social security, favours the less fortunate.

F. Certain Explanatory Factors Relating to Differences in Income

We cannot take into account all the factors that explain the differences in income between citizens. Here, however, are some statistical data concerning the influence exerted by certain of these factors.

1. AGE

Table 5:7 indicates the relation between age and income.

TABLE 5 : 7

Family Income According to the Age of the Head of the Family, Canada 1961

Age	Median income $
24 and under	3,895
25-34	4,797
35-44	5,313
45-54	5,400
55-64	4,826
65 and over	2,809
All families	4,866

SOURCE: Dominion Bureau of Statistics, *Distribution of Non-Farm Incomes in Canada by Size*, 1961.

2. EDUCATION

Table 5:8 distributes income by educational levels. The spread of the distribution is from 1 to 2 between an elementary and a university education. These figures under-estimate the influence of education because important sub-categories in each class are not taken into account. For example, the earnings figure for those with university education is a median that includes the earnings of people who spent a year at university and the earnings of graduates. The earning differential is very large between these two sub-categories so that the figure goes down for the category as a whole. Nevertheless the importance of education stands out clearly.

3. OCCUPATIONS AND INDUSTRIES

Among the other factors that affect the distribution of income or the structure of salaries and wages, occupations and industries are most often cited. But these are derived factors in the sense that it is not the occupation as such that causes a rate of salary to be high or low, but rather some particular circumstances affecting the occupation. For example, a doctor may earn more

TABLE 5 : 8

Median Earnings of Men According to Schooling and Age, Canada 1961

Schooling and age	Total wage-earners reporting earnings (thousands)	Median earnings $
Elementary		
15-24	214.6	1,737
25-44	722.0	3,316
45 and over	586.4	3,256
Secondary		
15-24	421.5	2,287
25-44	921.6	4,401
45 and over	419.8	4,435
University		
15-24	57.7	1,565
25-44	191.5	6,105
45 and over	86.7	6,664

SOURCE: Census of Canada 1961, Series 71.

in one country than in another because he is scarcer or perhaps because health insurance is paid directly out of the consolidated revenue of the government. If one occupation can command a higher wage, it is often because the required level of qualification is higher. The explanation then lies in the level of qualification that happens to be demanded rather than in the occupation itself.

This is equally true of differences in wages between industries. In order to explain these we must look further than at the industries *per se*: we must inquire about the amount of capital invested per employee, the qualifications needed, the size of the establishments, and so forth.

On the whole it would seem that a good part of the differences in incomes are attributable, on the supply side, to the levels of competence and skill achieved through education and experience, and, on the demand side, to the amounts of capital invested per employee and to the general economic efficiency of individual firms. Additional comments on labour earnings are presented in the next chapter.

SUGGESTED READINGS

A. R. OXENFELDT: *Economics for the Citizen*, New York, Rinehart, 1953.

An introduction to income distribution in a market economy is presented in non-technical terms, especially in chapters 7, 8, and 9.

AMERICAN ECONOMIC ASSOCIATION: *Readings in the Theory of Income Distribution*, Philadelphia, Blakiston, 1951.

A compendium of important articles dealing with several aspects of distribution.

H. D. WOODS AND S. OSTRY: *Labour Policy and Labour Economics in Canada*, Toronto, Macmillan, 1962.

Wages in Canada according to occupations, industries, and regions are discussed in chapters XIV to XVII.

T. W. SCHULTZ: *The Economic Value of Education*, New York, Columbia University Press, 1963.

Part III especially discusses the consequence of a higher level of education on income.

G. S. BECKER: 'Investment in Human Capital: A Theoretical Analysis', *Journal of Political Economy* (Supplement), October 1962.

Education, as an explanation of income differentials, is discussed among other topics. See also the article by B. A. Weisbrod in the same supplement.

CHAPTER

6

THE LABOUR MARKET

The institutional aspects of the labour market are of particular importance in explaining wages and the allocation of labour resources. The trade union movement in particular has transformed the conditions under which labour appears and behaves on the market, and has introduced a number of rigidities concerning wages and other conditions of work, so that the study of trade unions has become indispensable to an understanding of that particular but very important market.

The object of this chapter is to describe briefly the evolution of employment and wages in Canada, and then to give some rather fragmentary information about the trade union movement.

A. The Labour Force

The first points to consider about the labour force are the number of workers and the rate at which this number is increasing. Table 6:1 breaks down the total population figure in order to make clear the concept of the labour force (line 4 of the table). In Canada in 1964 there were 6.9 million people in the civilian labour force out of a total population of 19.2 millions. This figure is derived as follows: *from the total population is first subtracted all who are 13 years of age and under, to obtain the active population.*[1] Next the number of people in the armed

1. This expression is not commonly used in English. It may be defined as the population of working age.

forces is subtracted, in order to obtain the *active civilian population*. The concept of the labour force is arrived at by subtracting from this active civilian population all students (14 years of age and over), housewives, old people, and all those who do not work for gain. *The labour force may be defined, then, as that portion of the total population fit for employment and willing to work for gain.* Finally a distinction must be made between the employed and the unemployed members of the labour force. The unemployed are those without a job but seeking work. *The figure for the total labour force corresponds, in theoretical language, to the quantity of labour that is offered at a given moment at the going wage rate.*

TABLE 6 : 1

Labour Force in Canada, 1964 Average

	In thousands
1. Total population	19,237
2. Active population (total population 14 years of age and over)	12,864
3. Active civilian population	12,745
4. Total civilian labour force	6,920
5. Civilian labour force employed	6,595
agriculture	624
non-agriculture	5,972
6. Civilian labour force unemployed	325

SOURCE: Dominion Bureau of Statistics, *The Labour Force.*

It can readily be deduced from Table 6:1 that the number of workers will vary from year to year under the influence of changes both in the total population and in what is called the participation rates. Let us first look at the population factor.

1. CHANGES IN THE SIZE OF THE TOTAL POPULATION

Chapter 2 has already given some information on the rate of

growth of the population, showing, for example, that the average annual rate of growth was 2.9 per cent between 1951 and 1956 and 2.68 per cent between 1956 and 1961, representing an increase of 4.2 million, or 30 per cent, in the decade 1951-61.

Increase in population is caused by natural growth (the surplus of births over deaths) and by net immigration (the surplus of immigration over emigration).

TABLE 6 : 2

Population Increases, Canada 1931-64, in thousands

	Total population	Total increase	Natural increase	Net immigration
1931	10,376.8			
1941	11,506.6	1,129.8	1,221.8	−91.9
1951	14,009.4	2,502.8*	1,972.4	168.4
1956	16,080.8	2,071.4	1,471.7	599.6
1961	18,238.2	2,157.4	1,722.0†	436.4†
1964	19,271.0	1,032.8	962.0†	70.8†

*Newfoundland adds 361,000 inhabitants not counted in the last two columns.
†Estimates.

SOURCES: *Canada Year Book*, 1961 and 1962, and Bank of Canada, *Statistical Summary*. Total Population is on June 1.

Table 6:2 indicates the relative importance of natural increase and of immigration in the increase in population since 1931. It is clear that before the war the population movements showed a net emigration, since the figure for net immigration, 1931-41, is negative. Immigration was heaviest from 1951 to 1956, no doubt because of Canada's prosperity throughout this period. Net immigration in those years contributed almost 30 per cent of the total increase. In 1957 the number of immigrants reached a maximum of 282,164; the trend was reversed in the period 1958 to 1961: 124,851, 106,928, 104,111, 71,689. In 1962 it was 75,000, and in 1963, 93,000. From 1956 to 1961, net immigration contributed 20 per cent to the population increase. Between

1961 and 1964, its contribution fell quite sharply to 7 per cent. Population movements are very sensitive to employment opportunities in Canada; this applies not only to immigrants, whose number is more or less regulated by policy, but also to emigrants (mainly to the United States), whose number is not controlled by Canada.

2. PARTICIPATION RATES

These constitute the second factor influencing the number of workers. *The participation rate is the ratio of the labour force to the active population, and may be expressed as a percentage.* Other definitions of the participation rates are used, but this one is sufficient for our purposes here. Labour force participation rates vary in a significant manner over a period of time as well as in different localities.

TABLE 6 : 3

Participation Rates of the Active Population in the Labour Force

	Men	*Women*	*Total*
1955	82	23.9	52.9
1958	81.7	26.3	53.9
1960	80.9	28.0	54.3
1962	79.3	29.1	54.1
1964	78.4	30.5	54.3

SOURCE: Dominion Bureau of Statistics, *The Labour Force* and the Supplement of September 1960.

The participation rate increased by 1.4 per cent from 1955 to 1964 for the total labour force. (This percentage increase represents 97,000 more workers in 1964 than if the participation rate had remained the same as in 1955.) This total results from opposite trends in the employment of men and women.

The participation rate of males has been decreasing because they have been staying longer at school and, at the other end, retiring earlier; that of females has been increasing markedly because married women work more and more outside the home.

More precise statistics would also show that participation rates vary according to age. A knowledge of the age structure of the population – that is, the proportions of the various age groups in its make-up – and whether it is changing rapidly or slowly, is therefore important for understanding the past evolution or predicting the future evolution of a country's labour force. Finally, participation rates, particularly those of women, vary under the influence of general economic conditions.

As a result of the operation of these two factors – changes in the total population and changes in the participation rates – the Canadian labour force increased by about 145,000 persons per annum between 1955 and 1964.

TABLE 6 : 4

Increase in the Labour Force, Canada 1955-64, in thousands

	Total labour force	Increase	Percentage of increase
1955	5,610		
1956	5,782	172	3.0
1957	6,003	221	3.8
1958	6,127	124	2.0
1959	6,228	101	1.6
1960	6,403	175	2.8
1961	6,518	115	1.8
1962	6,608	90	1.3
1963	6,737	129	1.9
1964	6,920	183	2.7
Average annual increase		145	2.3

B. Employment and Unemployment

When we come to examine how the economy has absorbed these

new workers, we have to take note of the fact that during the period 1955-1964 the number of unemployed was considerable. It follows that the economy did not in fact create sufficient new jobs. See Table 6:5.

TABLE 6 : 5

Increase in the Labour Force, New Employments, and Variation in the Number of Unemployed (in thousands)

	Increase in the labour force	New jobs	Variation in the number of unemployed
1956	172	221	−49
1957	221	140	+81
1958	124	−30	+154
1959	101	161	−60
1960	175	99	+76
1961	115	94	+21
1962	90	168	−78
1963	129	147	−18
1964	183	231	−48
Total for the period	1,310	1,231	+79
Annual average	145.5	137	+8.5

SOURCE: Calculations made from Dominion Bureau of Statistics, *The Labour Force*.

For the whole period, an average of 145,500 additional persons presented themselves each year on the labour market, but the average number of new jobs created was only 137,000. There has been, then, a lack of 8,500 jobs per year, on the average. The total of unemployed workers at the beginning of the period was 246,000; therefore it was 325,000 (an increase of 79,000) at the end of 1964. One can make similar calculations from Table 6:5 for each year taken separately. Thus we see that in 1962 there were 168,000 new jobs created, while the labour force increased by only 90,000; the unemployed were then drawn upon to fill the jobs and their number was reduced by 78,000. This was a prosperous year. Similarly in 1964 there were 231,000 new positions created and additions to the labour force were 183,000. The number of the unemployed was therefore reduced by 48,000.

In addition we should note that an average of 22,000 jobs a year were eliminated from agriculture between 1955 and 1964, so that in fact the total absorption of the labour force exceeds by 22,000 (per annum) the number of jobs shown in the table. It could also be deduced from these figures that, had it not been for the emigration of agricultural workers to industry and services, the new jobs would have been sufficient, by and large, to absorb the additional workers. But this deduction, we must hasten to add, is purely arithmetical; it would be a mistake to impute unemployment to agricultural workers who change their occupations, simply because the figures happen to fit. On the other hand such a phenomenon is a valuable clue to the nature of unemployment. We shall see later that this case is one of those that correspond exactly to the concept of structural unemployment.

Table 4:3 gave unemployment figures as a percentage of the labour force. First, we notice that unemployment is sensitive to cyclical variations, since it was higher during the recessions of 1954 and 1958 than during years of prosperity such as 1951, 1956, or 1962. *In so far as it varies in accordance with general economic conditions unemployment (or under-employment) is called 'cyclical'.* This particular type of unemployment calls for an economic policy of expansion aimed at maintaining and encouraging expenditure – lower taxes, increased government expenditure, and lower interest rates. Cyclical unemployment is characterized by a generalized deficiency in over-all demand.

On the other hand unemployment is structural if it is caused by permanent changes in domestic or foreign consumer demand, by technological changes that reduce the labour coefficient in production, by the exhausting of natural resources in a region, by structural modifications in the management or in the ownership of corporations such as to bring about the disappearance of cer-

tain plants, or by a lack of balance between the available skills of the workers and the new skills required. Theoretically, unemployment of this type is quite insensitive to cyclical variations; it persists even during periods of general economic expansion. It is clearly localized, contrary to cyclical unemployment, which prevails in all parts of the country. It is limited to certain regions; and it is limited to certain readily identifiable industries. We have several pieces of evidence that Canadian unemployment is not merely cyclical in nature. One is that after three years of very rapid expansion from 1962, unemployment in 1965 was still as high as 5 per cent of the labour force. A second is the progressive transformation of agriculture into a more capital-intensive industry, which transformation, as we have seen, is accompanied by a persistent reduction in the number of jobs. A third is that in some areas of the Atlantic provinces high unemployment has persisted for several years.[1] Some economists have said that the technological changes that have taken place in the shipbuilding and lumbering industries, combined with the progressive replacement of coal by other sources of energy, largely explain this phenomenon. *Finally, the competition from imports, as, for example, in the textiles industry in Quebec, exerts increasing pressure for productivity advances, which mean, in a traditional industry, important reductions in the number of jobs available.*

The third important form of under-employment in Canada is seasonal unemployment. The seasonal variations in employment result partly from various customs and traditions such as the Christmas holidays, but particularly from climatic conditions which make it difficult to maintain production during the winter. In the Atlantic provinces and in the eastern part of Quebec, where a high proportion of the workers are engaged in seasonal industries, seasonal reduction in employment can easily lead to an unemployment rate of more than 10 per cent of the total

---

1. The regional component of unemployment is especially important in Canada. The following percentages are a breakdown of the national rate of 6.0 per cent in 1962: Newfoundland, 17.5; the Maritimes, 8.9; Quebec, 7.5; Ontario, 4.3; Prairies, 3.9; British Columbia, 6.7. Taken from *Unemployment in Canada*, Dominion Bureau of Statisics.

labour force. It has been estimated that even under conditions of (cyclical) full employment the unemployment rate in the middle of winter could rise to 4 per cent in Canada as a result of the seasonal factor alone. When the general conditions of employment deteriorate, there is a corresponding aggravation of seasonal – and, for that matter, structural – unemployment, since workers cannot find other occupations.

The labour force is distributed among occupations and among

TABLE 6 : 6

**Distribution of the Labour Force by Occupation Group,
Canada 1931-61**

	1931 %	1961 %	Changes %
All occupations	100	100	
White-collar	*24.4*	*38.6*	*14.2*
Proprietary and managerial	5.6	7.9	2.3
Professional	6.1	10.0	3.9
Clerical	6.6	12.9	6.3
Commercial and financial	6.1	7.8	1.7
Transportation and communication	*6.3*	*7.8*	*1.5*
Services	*9.3*	*10.8*	*1.5*
Personal	8.3	9.3	1.0
Protective and other	1.0	1.5	0.5
Blue-collar	*27.5*	*27.1*	*−0.4*
Manufacturing and mechanical	11.5	16.4	4.9
Construction	4.7	5.3	0.6
Labourers	11.3	5.4	−5.9
Agriculture	*28.8*	*10.2*	*−18.6*
Other primary	*3.8*	*2.9*	*−0.9*
Not stated	—	2.6	—

NOTE: Occupations on the basis of 1951 classification.

SOURCE: N. M. Meltz, *Occupational Trends in Canada*, 1931 to 1961. Department of Labour, Report No. 11, September 1963.

industries. Changes over time in occupations and industries call for adaptation on the part of the workers and foresight on the part of public authorities and of management in educational and training programs. Let us look at the major changes that have taken place since the early thirties.

Information on occupational changes between 1931 and 1961 is set out in Table 6:6. The striking changes affect the white-collar occupations and agricultural workers. The proportion of the first group increased by 14.2 per cent; the proportion of the second decreased by 18.6 per cent – from 28.8 per cent of the labour force in 1931 to 10.2 per cent in 1961. The increasing share of white-collar occupations in contemporary employment is a little less dramatic than the declining share of agriculture, but it is surely as important. All the sub-categories of white-collar people advanced, but the clerical occupations made most rapid progress; the increase is almost 100 per cent. The small relative decline in blue-collar occupations is the result of opposite trends in the sub-categories. Manufacturing, mechanical, and construction workers took an increased share of the total labour force, but labourers lost considerable ground, accounting for only 5.4 per cent of the labour force in 1961 compared with 11.3 per cent in 1931. Service occupations as well as transportation and communication show a modest relative increase of 1.5 per cent.

The major factor explaining occupational changes is technology. And technology works at two different levels: first, in changing techniques or methods of production within industries, and second, in introducing new products that make for a different industrial structure. Another important factor is the gradual increase in consumption standards along with higher incomes, by which the structure of demand is modified.

As can be inferred from such a process of change, it is difficult to keep changes in occupations and changes in industries separate, because some of the basic factors operate on the one kind through the other kind. It is all the more important, then, to examine as well the trends in the industrial distribution of the labour force. These trends may be seen in Table 6:7.

Because the headings in the occupational schedule of the Canadian census are misleading, it may be useful to note that an occupation defines a type of work performed and relates to the worker, whereas an industry defines a commodity or a group of commodities produced. A labourer may thus work in several different industries. In the primary sector, however, the occupation and the industry are, for all practical purposes, the same.

The marked decline in employment in agriculture is compensated for by increased employment in the service, trade, and manufacturing industries. The service industries are leading: they have increased their share of the labour force by 9.4 per cent and have become the most important sector as regards employment. As Table 6:7 shows, the services now require more labour than

TABLE 6 : 7

Distribution of the Labour Force by Industry Group, Canada 1931-61

	1931 %	1961 %	Changes %
All industries	*100*	*100*	
Agriculture	28.7	9.9	−18.8
Other primary	4.3	4.0	−0.3
Manufacturing	18.5	23.0	4.5
Public utilities	0.6	1.1	0.5
Construction	6.4	7.2	0.8
Transportation and communication	7.1	7.0	−0.1
Trade	9.9	14.4	4.5
Finance and insurance	2.4*	3.5	1.1
Services	17.9	27.3	9.4
Unspecified	4.3	2.4	−1.9

*Finance only.

SOURCES: 1931: N. M. Meltz, 'Factors Determining Occupational Trends in the Canadian Economy', Department of Labour, mimeo, 1961.
1961: Richard Béland, 'Tendances et structure de la main-d'oeuvre', Province de Québec, mimeo.

manufacturing does. Obviously the services will become in the future as important to employment as agriculture was in the past; and perhaps, one may add, with some of the same characteristics such as low productivity, low wages, and disguised unemployment.

C. Wages

The index of hourly earnings for all jobs in Canada (1949 = 100) went from 119 in 1951 to 188 in 1963, an increase of 58 per cent. The retail price index during the same period rose from 114 to 133.0 (1949 = 100), an increase of only 11.7 per cent. Since nominal wages increased more rapidly than retail prices, the purchasing power of these wages increased. In fact, real wages rose from 104.7 in 1951 to 144.7 in 1963, an increase of 38.2 per cent.

TABLE 6 : 8

Real Wages in Canada, 1951-63

	Index: 1949 = 100
1951	104.7
1956	125.9
1959	134.0
1960	137.1
1961	139.2
1962	142.2
1963	144.7

SOURCES: Department of Labour, *Wage Rates, Salaries and Hours of Labour*, and Dominion Bureau of Statistics, *Consumers' Price Index*.

Over a long period the trend of real wages follows the changes in labour productivity, although the two are not exactly parallel at all times. (A question that is being debated at the present time is whether salaries have had a tendency in the long run to increase somewhat more rapidly than productivity.) Increases in the productivity of labour result from several factors, of which the main ones are:

1. technological progress and the general growth of knowledge;
2. increase in the capital-labour ratio;
3. improvement in quality of the labour force (education, training);
4. higher coefficient of utilization of existing capacity;
5. within industries the substitution of more efficient for less efficient establishments;
6. growth in the relative importance of the more productive industries.

Among these factors, advances in knowledge and technology have probably contributed most to the rise in the standard of living.

If labour earnings increase more rapidly than productivity, workers obtain a larger share of the national income. But ordinarily such a tendency will result in higher prices, so that the real wage may remain the same.

The average earnings mentioned up to now give a very incomplete idea of the various aspects of labour income. Let us therefore add some information on the wage structure according to occupations, industries, and regions.

Agricultural workers are the lowest paid. The other groups, in order of increasing income, are: industrial workers, semi-skilled workers, skilled workers, and, at the top of the ladder, professional workers and business managers. Between 1941 and 1951, the wage spread had a tendency to contract within occupations, and this movement appears to have continued during the fifties. The principal factor tending to lessen the disparities in wages is the general spread of education in society, which increases the proportion of skilled to unskilled workers.

On the other hand, workers with similar skills in the same type of occupation in the same market may receive different wages according to the industry they happen to be in. This is illustrated in Table 6:9 for unskilled labour. The figures represent a kind of floor rate in the industry.

TABLE 6 : 9

Hourly Wage Rates of Labourers in Selected Industries, Canada 1963

	$
Breweries	2.34
Primary iron and steel	2.13
Iron castings	1.76
Machine tools	1.69
Paints, varnishes, and lacquers	1.69
Industrial machinery	1.68
Sheet-metal products	1.66
Sawmills	1.62
Soft drinks	1.61
Brass and copper products	1.61
Machine-shop products	1.53
Planing mills	1.34
Wooden furniture	1.19

SOURCE: Department of Labour, *Wage Rates, Salaries and Hours of Labour*, 1963.

The high-wage industries are mainly characterized by large establishments, high capital-labour ratios, and a labour force primarily masculine and more specialized than the average. The low-wage industries have opposite characteristics. As Table 6:9 shows, the differentials in the basic wage rate between industries may reach 100 per cent. There has been practically no reduction of these disparities in recent years.

Finally, regional disparities in wages are also common, but on the average they are less pronounced than industrial disparities. Table 6:10 gives some information on this point. The pattern is well known: wages are high in Ontario and the West and low in Quebec and the Atlantic provinces. Given the level of aggregation (the whole manufacturing industry), however, and the different industry mix as between provinces, these differences in wages are much less significant than is generally expected. Other evidence confirms that a 20 per cent difference in wage rates between Nova Scotia and Ontario is the relevant order of magnitude. Regional disparities have not been reduced to any great extent for several years.

TABLE 6 : 10

Average Hourly Wages in Manufacturing in Eight Provinces, Canada 1964

	$
British Columbia	2.58
Alberta	2.13
Saskatchewan	2.17
Manitoba	1.88
Ontario	2.17
Quebec	1.86
New Brunswick	1.88
Nova Scotia	1.83

SOURCE: Dominion Bureau of Statistics, *Man-hours and Hourly Earnings*, December 1964.

D. The Trade Unions

The development of trade unionism has led to major modifications in the organization of the labour market since the nineteenth century.

1. IMPORTANCE OF TRADE UNIONS

What is the importance of the trade union movement in Canada? One method of measurement is to take the number of union workers compared to the total number of workers. *This is what is called the trade union penetration rate.*

Trade unions had their greatest development during the period 1941-1951: the proportion of union members among the total

TABLE 6 : 11

**Union Membership, 1931-64, and Total Paid Workers
in the Non-Agricultural Sector, Canada,
annual averages**

	Union membership (*thousands*)	Total non-agricultural paid workers (*thousands*)	Percentage union members
1931	311	2,006	15.5
1941	462	2,538	18.2
1951	1,029	3,623	28.4
1954	1,268	3,840	33.0
1961	1,447	4,798	30.1
1963	1,449	5,133	28.2
1964	1,493	5,360	27.8

SOURCES: Department of Labour, *Labour Organizations in Canada*, Table 1, and *Canadian Statistical Review*. The figures on the labour force are taken from the latter and are not the same as those given by the Department of Labour.

non-agricultural paid workers rose from 18.2 to 28.4 per cent. The percentage continued to increase until 1954 and has become more or less stabilized since that time at a slightly lower level. The trade unions included within their ranks a little more than one-quarter of the total wage-earners in 1964.

The distribution of union members by industry reveals some interesting characteristics, but the information is so approximate (it is based on the reports of union locals) that the Department of Labour ceased to publish it in 1959. Table 6:12, however, gives reliable private estimates for 1961.

This table is a little difficult to read. For each of the three areas covered, the first column refers to a percentage distribution of total union members. It tells us where the union members are in the economy of the area; the second column is the penetration rate, that is, the number of union members as a percentage of the total labour force.

TABLE 6 : 12

Union Membership: Percentage Distribution by Industry, 1961

	Quebec		Ontario		Canada	
	Distribution by industry %	Percentage of union members to labour force	Distribution by industry %	Percentage of union members to labour force	Distribution by industry %	Percentage of union members to labour force
Primary	*6.0*	*33*	*6.0*	*59*	*8.6*	*56*
Forestry	2.2	21	2.3	100	4.0	65
Fisheries	—	00	—	00	0.3	43
Mining	3.8	53	3.7	48	4.3	51
Secondary	*60.2*	*37*	*61.1*	*44*	*50.8*	*42*
Manufacturing	50.8	38	48.5	42	39.9	41
Construction	9.4	31	12.6	56	11.0	43
Tertiary	*33.5*	*15*	*32.2*	*15*	*39.8*	*18*
Transport and communications	18.1	56	14.6	61	20.2	57
Public utilities	1.0	18	3.2	60	2.5	50
Trade	2.6	5	3.0	5	3.4	6
Services	11.8	10	11.4	10	13.7	12
Total	*99.7*	*24*	*99.3*	*27*	*99.2*	*26.8*
Total membership	353,347		550,040		1,399,391	

NOTE: The figures are not strictly comparable to those of Table 6 : 11.

source: Calculations supplied by Professor L. M. Tremblay of the University of Montreal. The documents used were the 1961 Census of Canada and unpublished data on union membership prepared by the Department of Labour.

Reading the first columns, we learn that the trade union movement has spread into all sectors of activity and that the main
concentration of union activity is in the manufacturing industries,
which employed some 40 to 50 per cent of the union members in
1961. The second columns show the degree of unionization in
each sector and, by inference, the potential development for the
future. Unionization in transport and communications, public
utilities, and mining, in Canada as a whole, had reached 50 per
cent or more in 1961; in manufacturing it had reached 40 per
cent. Where the trade unions have not yet occupied the field in
force is obviously in the trades and services sectors, where the
unionization in 1961 was of the order of 10 per cent. It is easy to
see that future advances by the trade unions will take place in
these sectors. Indeed, although the 1961 figures were the latest
available at the time of writing, there are good indications that
the trade unions were making inroads in trade and services
between 1961 and 1965. The degree of unionization differs little
between Quebec and Ontario. Quebec manufacturing is less
unionized by the small margin of only 4 per cent. The difference
is large in forestry but it is due to legal problems.

2. TRADE UNION ORGANIZATION

The organization of the trade union movement is relatively complex. At the base of the pyramid several different types of unions
group together workers of various categories. These locals may
in turn be associated on a geographical basis (city councils, for
example) or on an industry basis (the Federation of Textile
Workers). At the top level there are two separate national
organizations in Canada.

The following are the main types of unions:

(a) *The craft union* is composed of workers belonging to the
same craft or trade. Each member must be capable of carrying out all the operations demanded in his trade. All must
have undergone the same apprenticeship. This type of
union generally includes only a small part of the total numbers of workers in a modern industrial enterprise.

(b) *The multiple craft union* includes workers whose trades are related. The members are not qualified to carry out the operations of all the crafts concerned. Several unions of this sort result from mergers among craft unions.

(c) *The extended craft union* aims at including in its ranks workers within the same trade but with varying degrees of competence. Integration takes place on a vertical scale and takes in skilled, semi-skilled, and non-skilled workers. One example is the International Union of Machinists and Machinists' Helpers.

(d) *The semi-industrial trade union* groups together all workers, whether skilled or not, who contribute directly to the production of an establishment. Workers belonging to the auxiliary services are excluded.

(e) *The industrial trade union* is made up of all the workers, without distinction, employed by a single establishment or a firm.

These unions may form associations based upon all imaginable forms of jurisdiction – trades, plants, industries, regions, provinces, countries, or the North American continent. Since unions recruit their members in a great variety of ways, jurisdictions may easily overlap and lead to conflicts.

Today we have two central labour bodies in Canada – the Canadian Labour Congress (C.L.C.) with more than 1.3 million members and the Confederation of National Trade Unions (C.N.T.U.) with about 130,000.

At the beginning of the century the central labour body of the United States, the American Federation of Labour (A.F. of L.) stepped up its organizing activities in Canada. It thereby played an important role in the organization of the central labour congress of that period, the Dominion Trade and Labour Congress (D.T.L.C.), founded in 1883, which became the Trade and Labour Congress of Canada (T.L.C.C.) in 1892. Tensions arose which led to the breaking away of twenty-three unions previously affiliated with it. These unions then formed a federation which, in 1908, was called the Canadian Federation of Labour. Its principal aim was to safeguard and promote the national autonomy of the movement. However, the subsequent breaking away of the Quebec unions greatly reduced this federation. In the western provinces other labour unions not affiliated with the T.L.C.C. were formed at various times, notably the One Big Union (O.B.U.) in 1919, but it proved impossible to establish a stable Canadian body of any size. In 1927, however, the All Canadian Congress of Labour was formed, and this Congress, in 1940, joined with the Canadian unions expelled from the T.L.C.C., under pressure from the A.F. of L.–C.I.O. (Congress of Industrial Organizations), to create the Canadian Congress of Labour (C.C.L.). In 1956, after seventeen years of separation, the C.C.L. joined forces with the T.L.C.C. and so created the Canadian Labour Congress (C.L.C.). Again the American example was followed, since a merger of the A.F. of L. and the C.I.O. had taken place in 1955. In Canada the merger was carried out at the federative level only, with the industrial unions preserving their former freedom of action.

The great majority of members of the present C.L.C. are also members of American trade or industrial unions (hence 'international unions'). Again we are faced with the usual Canadian problem of American influence. What is the real extent of this influence?

The autonomy of the C.L.C. in regard to American organizations is recognized not only in practice but also in a formal agreement between the C.L.C. and the A.F. of L.–C.I.O. The C.L.C. has complete freedom of action and full jurisdiction in Canada. But between the Canadian locals and the American unions the problems that arise are somewhat more complex. The dues are fixed by the whole union, in which the Canadian locals are in a minority; the funds are deposited in Canadian banks, however, and there appears to have been no systematic transfer of union funds across the border.[1] The representation of Canadian unions on the boards of the large unions is often

---

1. The first Annual Report of the Corporations and Labour Unions Returns Act Administration indicates that payments by residents to international unions

proportionately higher than the number of Canadian members. The decision to strike is left to the local; the requirement that the union's approval be obtained before the strike fund may be drawn on is rarely more than nominal. Finally, the policies concerning negotiation of collective agreements are for the most part established in Canada. It may be concluded that the formal liaison between the Canadian and American unions does not impose a very serious limitation on Canadian freedom of action. It is obvious that American influence does make itself felt at various levels, but, generally speaking, it does so without arousing too much opposition, at least in the open.

A factor contributing to the autonomy of Canadian trade unions has been the existence since 1921 of the Canadian and Catholic Confederation of Labour (C.C.C.L.), which in 1960 became the Confederation of National Trade Unions (C.N.T.U.). Catholic trade unions, which had been formed in Quebec at the beginning of the century, created this organization by joining together in 1921. During the 1920s the development of Catholic trade unionism was not spectacular. In 1932 the C.C.C.L. was made up of seventy-five unions, eight central councils, and four industrial federations. The number of members was about 26,000. Since the last war, however, the Confederation has shown a rapid development. Thanks to new management and a more modern outlook, it began to follow more aggressive lines of policy which it still pursues and which have led to its playing a decisive role in important strikes such as that at Asbestos in 1949. At the beginning of the 1950s its membership had reached 100,000. In the sixties, the C.N.T.U. has made swift advances on new fronts, among such as teachers, engineers, nurses, and civil servants, and has succeded in inducing important existing groups to affiliate with it.

---

amounted to 22 millions in 1962 and direct outlays by the unions for residents, to 12.6 millions. Even if there were overhead costs and other indirect expenditures by the unions for their Canadian membership, it is very unlikely that the net benefits belong to Canadians. Again, in spite of declarations to the contrary, the Americans do obtain funds and resources from Canadians.

SUGGESTED READINGS

A. E. KOVACS (ED.): *Readings in Canadian Labour Economics,* Toronto, McGraw-Hill, 1961.
Articles dealing with the history of the labour movement in Canada and with researches in the area of collective bargaining and labour legislation in Canada.

H. D. WOODS AND S. OSTRY: *Labour Policy and Labour Economics in Canada,* Toronto, Macmillan, 1962.
The most comprehensive analysis of labour policy, wages, and labour supply and organization in Canada.

CANADA: *Manpower and Employment,* Proceedings of the Special Committee of the Senate, Ottawa, Queen's Printer, 1960-61.
An important report on the trends in manpower requirements and utilization in Canada; analysis of the growth and characteristics of the labour force.

H. A. LOGAN: *Trade Unions in Canada,* Toronto, Macmillan, 1948.
A classic history of labour organization in Canada.

P. HARVEY: 'Plein-emploi national et plein-emploi régional au Canada depuis la guerre', *L'Actualité économique,* April-June 1956, pp. 5-26; also 'Conjoncture et structures: les perspectives spatiales du plein-emploi au Canada', *ibid.,* October-December 1956, pp. 383-405.

Employment, Unemployment and Manpower, Fifteenth Annual Conference, Industrial Relations Centre, McGill University, Montreal, McGill University Press, 1964.
See especially the communications of J. P. Francis, P. P. Proulx, and John H. G. Crispo, on the Canadian labour market, unemployment, and training requirements.

CHAPTER

7

INDUSTRIAL ORGANIZATION

Goods and services are produced by business firms. *Firms (or enterprises) may be defined as decision-making units and are distinguished from establishments or factories where the goods or services are actually produced.* A firm may include several establishments. Thus a Steinberg store is an establishment; the Steinberg corporation is a firm made up of all the establishments under the control of its board of directors. *We must also distinguish between a firm and an industry. All the establishments manufacturing an identical product, or giving an identical service, together make up an industry.* We speak of the clothing industry to designate the total clothing-producing activity in the country. A business firm may easily belong to several industries at once, since a large firm carries on a great variety of activities: we need only think, for example, of the cafeterias and the trucks operated by a large brewing company. The activities of even a single establishment might be classified in several industries.

A. Types of Enterprises

The several kinds of enterprises must first be separated into two broad categories. On the one hand we have state enterprises, called in Canada Crown corporations, and on the other hand, private enterprises. Among Canadian Crown corporations are departmental corporations (branches and services), agency corporations, and proprietary corporations. We shall explain these terms later. Among private enterprises distinction is made between individual business firms, partnerships, corporations, and co-operatives. Table 7:1 shows the relative importance of the various kinds of private enterprise in the manufacturing industry.

TABLE 7 : 1

Types of Ownership in Manufacturing Industries, Canada 1961, by percentages of establishments, employees, and value of shipments

	Establishments %	Number of employees %	Selling value of factory shipments %
Individual ownership	34.4	3.7	1.7
Partnerships	9.4	1.9	1.0
Corporations	53.8	93.6	95.8
Co-operatives	2.4	0.8	1.5

SOURCE: Dominion Bureau of Statistics, *Type of Ownership and Size of Establishments Engaged in Manufacturing in Canada, 1961.*

This traditional method of classification is not of particular interest to us, not only because the form of ownership is not important in itself for economic analysis, but also because production and employment are now concentrated to such an extent in the corporations that the other business firms are of negligible importance. As the table shows, more than 95 per cent of manufacturing production comes from the corporations. Since corporations on the whole are much larger than the other types, it is not surprising to find that they make up only 53.8 per cent of all establishments, by number, or that individual ownership, for example, still accounts for 34.4 per cent of the total.

A comparison of columns 2 and 3 is useful in indicating the relative levels of the productivity of labour in the various enterprises. Individual companies require 3.7 per cent of the labour force in order to manufacture 1.7 per cent, by value, of the products sold. Partnerships, too, require a higher percentage of labour than they contribute to production, but the opposite applies both to corporations and co-operatives.

The predominance of corporations has become constantly more marked in the period since the end of the war. In 1946, individual companies accounted for 47.3 per cent of all establishments, partnerships for 16 per cent, co-operatives for 3.3 per cent, and corporations for only 33.4 per cent. It must be emphasized that these are statistics of the manufacturing industries. *They do not apply to trade and services, in which, no doubt, individual enterprises still maintain a leading position[1] in certain fields*. Manufacturing technology has made great advances, but its application is so expensive that the capital required is generally beyond the resources of individuals. In fact, the major disadvantage of the individual enterprise is its limited financial resources. The *partnership*, in which two or more persons divide the responsibility and the profits, faces several difficulties, in that the capital is not freely transferable, and authority is divided as a rule. The unlimited responsibility of each partner should logically require the complete equality of all the partners, in regard to both their personal wealth and their shares in the company; such conditions are difficult to find, and even where they are, the partnerships do not easily last very long. Estimates are that 'only one partnership in three survives the first two years'.[2]

The joint-stock company or corporation is the innovation par excellence of the capitalist system. It is not an association of persons but an association of capital subscriptions. The stockholders (or shareholders) are very numerous and are recruited, so to speak, on the floor of the stock exchange. Such an enter-

---

1. In 1951 individual ownership contributed 3.3 per cent of sales in manufacturing but 11 per cent in the wholesale trade, 38.3 per cent in the retail trade, and 37.5 per cent in services. R. Bellan, *Principles of Economics and the Canadian Economy*, McGraw-Hill, 2nd edition, 1963, p. 29.

2. J. E. Smyth and D. A. Soberman, *The Law and Business Administration in Canada*, Toronto, Prentice-Hall, 1964, p. 461. The legal aspects of partnerships are complex and a subject-matter to themselves. They are not given here.

prise, if it has the confidence of the public, can mobilize considerable resources. It is, moreover, immortal, since shares may be freely exchanged. The corporation belongs to the owners of the common stock; they have the right to vote at meetings and the dividends on their shares depend on the profits. The corporation may issue preferred shares which do not grant the right to vote but which do carry the right to be paid dividends (usually at a fixed rate) before the common stock. Finally, the corporation (in this it cannot be distinguished from other forms of enterprise) may issue bonds and debentures. These are borrowings which bear a fixed rate of interest and do not give the right to vote. If the company is dissolved, bonds and debentures must be repaid before shareholders receive anything. The return on these three types of securities is directly proportional to the risk incurred. The return on the common stock can rise as high as the fortunes of the company take it, say, on an average between 6 and 15 per cent, while the return on preferred shares is usually about 5 or 6 per cent and on bonds and debentures about 4 or 5 per cent.

In the above types of enterprises the producer and the consumer of the product are never the same person. *In the co-operative, on the other hand, these roles are merged.* In a consumers' co-operative the entrepreneur or producer is the man who consumes the product. In a producers' co-operative the entrepreneur is the man who sells his products or his services.

The *government corporations* that we shall mention here are those under the jurisdiction of the federal government. They are generally called 'Crown corporations'. The *departmental corporations*, ten in number, are 'responsible for administrative, supervisory or regulatory services of a governmental nature'.[1] They are: the Unemployment Insurance Commission, the Dominion Coal Board, the Atomic Energy Control Board, the National Research Council, the Agricultural Stabilization Board, the Canadian Maritime Commission, the Director of Soldier Settle-

---

1. C. A. Ashley and R. G. H. Smails, *Canadian Crown Corporations,* Toronto, Macmillan, 1965, p. 99.

ment, the Fisheries Prices Support Board, the National Gallery of Canada, and the Director, the Veterans' Land Act. These organizations, having no independent sources of revenue, draw on the federal budget for their funds. The *agency corporations* are 'responsible for the management of trading or service operations on a quasi-commercial basis, or for the management of procurement, construction, or disposal activities'.[1] This usually means that their activities show a deficit which is made up from public funds. They are ten in number: Atomic Energy of Canada Limited, Canadian Arsenals Limited, Canadian Commercial Corporation, Canadian Patents and Development Limited, Crown Assets Disposal Corporation, Defence Construction Limited, National Battlefields Commission, National Capital Commission, National Harbours Board, and Northern Canada Power Commission.

Finally the *proprietary corporations* are industrial, commercial, or financial enterprises which are ordinarily required to conduct their operations without parliamentary appropriations.[2] In fact some of them, at times, do come to Parliament for funds. Thirteen in number, they are: the Canadian Broadcasting Corporation, the Canadian National Railways, the Canadian Overseas Telecommunication Corporation, Central Mortgage and Housing Corporation, Cornwall International Bridge Company Limited, Eldorado Aviation Limited, Eldorado Mining and Refining Limited, Export Credits Insurance Corporation, Farm Credit Corporation, Northern Transportation Company Limited, Polymer Corporation Limited, The St. Lawrence Seaway Authority, and Air Canada.

Other Crown corporations have been incorporated under special Acts and are not included in the preceding lists. They are: the Bank of Canada, the Canada Council, the Canadian Wheat Board, the Eastern Rockies Forest Conservation Board, the Halifax Relief Commission, the Industrial Development Bank,

1. *Ibid.*, p. 111.

2. *Ibid.*, p. 126.

the National Productivity Council, and the Northern Ontario Pipe Line Crown Corporation.

B. Size of Establishments

The phenomena of size and concentration must attract the attention of the economist far more than the differences in forms of ownership. Let us first consider the question of size. Rightly or wrongly, in explaining productivity great importance is generally attached to the size of establishments. Indeed, this is expressed succinctly in the stock phrase *economies of scale.* The costs of operation are supposed to be higher below a certain volume of production than they are above it. At the other end of the cost curve, it is possible for an establishment to become too large; then there are *diseconomies of scale. There is therefore an optimum size that it is in the interest of the entrepreneurs to discover and at which they should operate.* Business establishments have generally become larger and larger over the years. This phenomenon is attributable to technological change, to the enlargement of markets (increases in population and income), to increases in savings and capital, to the increased efficiency of methods of administration, to the security offered by the diversification of activities, and to the advantages of specialization.

Other reasons why individual businesses have become big may be less honourable. Competition may have been reduced or suppressed in the process in order that the market could be controlled and prices raised. When a large firm is established through a merger of leading competitors, there may be objective advantages achieved in the public interest – in terms of increased productivity, for example – but competition is reduced thereby. The end result is a mixed blessing. In any case, no one must believe that a large-scale operation is *ipso facto* proof of efficiency, dynamism, and social progress.

The two measures of size most often used currently are the value of production and the number of employees. The first measure is relative rather than absolute. In fact, what Table 7:2 provides us with is a measure of inequality in the size of the establishments.

TABLE 7 : 2

Size of Manufacturing Establishments, Canada 1949 and 1961

Production in thousands of dollars	1949		1961	
	Percentage of the number of establishments	Percentage of the total value of production	Percentage of the number of establishments	Percentage of the total value of production
0–25	45.0	1.1	27.1	0.4
25–50	13.6	1.4	14.0	0.7
50–100	12.5	2.5	13.7	1.3
100–200	10.0	4.1	12.9	2.5
200–500	9.0	8.0	13.8	5.9
500–1,000	4.1	8.3	7.3	6.9
1,000–5,000	4.1	25.3	8.7	24.8
5,000 and over	1.1	49.0	2.5	57.5
Total	99.4	99.7	100	100

SOURCE: Dominion Bureau of Statistics, *Type of Ownership and Size of Establishment Engaged in Manufacturing in Canada, 1961*.

If we add the figures for 1961 in respect of establishments producing goods to the value of $1 million and over, we see that in that year they amounted to 11.2 per cent of all establishments, but that this 11.2 per cent of the establishments together turned out 82.3 per cent of Canada's manufacturing production. To put it in another way, to eliminate about 90 per cent of the manufacturing establishments (some 30,000) would only reduce production by about 18 per cent.[1]

Looking at the figures for the small establishments, we find that in 1961, 67.7 per cent of all establishments (the total of the first four lines) produced only 4.9 per cent of the total manufacturing production. A similar calculation of inequality may be made for 1949, but the differences between the years are negligible. This means that the small business concerns increased in size as much as the big firms between 1949 and 1961. The value of output per establishment was $349,000 in 1949, and $645,000 in 1959.[2] Prices having increased by 49 per cent, the value of the 1959 production is $433,000 in 1949 prices, which means that a real increase of 24 per cent in the average size of establishments took place over the ten-year period.

When size is measured by the number of employees instead of by the volume of production, the measure of size differs from the preceding to the extent that productivity itself differs in accordance with the size of the establishments. This is because a number-of-employees index does not take account of productivity increases. We know that the number of employees per establishment was 32.7 in 1949, and 36.0 in 1959. The increase was only 10 per cent. We can therefore deduce that the difference between the 24 per cent increase of the preceding paragraph and this 10 per cent is due to the increase in productivity between 1949 and 1959.

---

1. This is one way of illustrating statistics; since business establishments are highly interdependent in matters of production, no political party, obviously, should carry out this suggestion.

2. 1959 figures are used here for the purpose of the following calculations.

We have pointed out that the inequality of establishments is a measure of relative size. There are obviously several measures of absolute size. A given corporation annually sells a million dollars' worth of products, a certain establishment has 100 employees – these are absolute measures. A piece of information of this kind is of no help in explaining economic phenomena, but it is quite helpful in satisfying one's curiosity.

Table 7:3 lists several of the largest enterprises in Canada, with the value of their assets in 1963. The list is not complete within the range adopted because the author was not able to find the necessary information.

TABLE 7 : 3

Seventeen of the Largest Firms in Canada, 1963

	Total assets million $
Royal Bank of Canada	5,713
Canadian Imperial Bank of Commerce	5,248
Canadian National Railways	4,519 (1962)
Bank of Montreal	4,275
Canadian Pacific Railway	2,917
Sun Life Assurance Company	2,691
Bank of Nova Scotia	2,674
Toronto-Dominion Bank	2,461
Bell Telephone Company	2,347
Hydro-Québec	2,050
Aluminum Company of Canada	1,469
Manufacturers Life Insurance Company	1,258
Brazilian Traction	1,068
London Life Insurance Company	1,011
Imperial Oil	1,002
Great-West Life Assurance Company	963
Banque Canadienne Nationale	905

SOURCE: 'Survey of Industrials', *The Financial Post, 1964.*

Probably the largest business enterprise in the country is the Royal Bank of Canada, which had assets of more than five and a half billion dollars in 1963. By way of comparison, total expenditure for the province of Quebec was one billion, and that of the federal government was seven and a half billions in 1963. In second place is another bank. Of the seventeen enterprises, fifteen have assets exceeding one billion dollars. It is striking to notice that there are only three manufacturing enterprises in this list: the remainder are banks, insurance companies, and public services.

This observation leads us to examine more closely the measure of size provided by the value of assets. If we had taken the value of output produced during the years the list would have been very different. *This is because the relation between assets and output is different in different industries. This relation is called the capital-output ratio.* For Canadian National Railways the ratio is 4 (for $4 billion of assets there was $1 billion of revenue in 1961). But for insurance companies the capital-output ratio is 5.7. For banks it is 18. On the other hand, for the manufacturing industry in 1960 the ratio was 0.8. The higher the capital-output ratio the greater the over-estimation of the size of the enterprise when value of assets is used as a measure rather than annual receipts. This is particularly clear with banks and, at the other extreme, with manufacturing enterprises. In order to produce an annual revenue of $1.00 the manufacturing industry requires a capital of approximately $1.00. The banking business needs a capital of $18.00 in order to produce the same amount of $1.00.

Capital-output ratio is very important in economic analysis.[1]

---

1. Assets and sales are oversimplifications of capital and output. To get at the theoretical concepts, several adjustments to the business accounts are required to take care of valuation difficulties. Output, in any case, is value added, not total sales.

C. Concentration in Industry

If the size of business enterprises is of great interest because of its influence on the cost of production and more generally on efficiency, concentration is equally important because of the influence that it exerts on the kind and the intensity of competition. Concentration is a measure of the importance of individual enterprises or establishments in an industry. *Concentration is higher in an industry when the number of establishments (or enterprises) is smaller.* To take the extreme case, concentration is at its maximum when there is only one supplier of a product.

Concentration may be measured in several ways. These two indexes are among the most currently used:

1. The number of establishments required to produce a given percentage of the industry's total output. Let us say that in order to obtain 80 per cent of the production of industry A, it is sufficient to take two of the largest establishments, whereas in industry B it takes 50: industry A is more concentrated than industry B.

2. The second measure is the inverse of the first. This is the percentage of the industry's production held by a given number of establishments. The three largest establishments of industry C, for example, account for 95 per cent of total production, and in industry D the three largest produce 60 per cent: industry C is more concentrated than industry D.

Table 7:4 gives some figures on concentration in Canadian manufacturing industries in 1961.

Concentration is a more complex phenomenon than it seems at first sight. To find the multiple factors that influence the degree of concentration in an industry it is necessary to understand the arithmetical relationships between the variables incorporated in the measurement. Four factors are brought to play: the number of establishments (denoted by N), the size of the establishments (E), the size of the industry (I), and the inequality in size of the establishments (D).[1] Concentration is designated by C.[2]

We can write:

$$E = \frac{I}{N} \qquad (1)$$

The size of the establishments is equal to the size of the industry divided by the number of establishments. This is a definition. On the other hand, and also by definition:

$$N = \frac{C}{D} \qquad (2)$$

The number of establishments in an industry is higher if C is large (if the concentration is low) for a given value of D; N is higher if D is small (if the inequality is great) for a given value

---

TABLE 7 : 4

Concentration in the Forty Leading Manufacturing Industries, Canada 1961 — number of establishments required to include 80 per cent of the employees of the industry (not including head-office employees)

	Number of establishments
1. Motor vehicles	2.8
2. Rubber tires and tubes	4.1
3. Iron and steel mills	5.6
4. Tobacco products	7.1
5. Smelting and refining	10.5

---

1. Inequality is the percentage of establishments required to obtain a given percentage of the total employment in the industry. If this percentage is small inequality is high and vice versa. By contrast, concentration is the *number* of establishments required to obtain a given percentage of the total employment in the industry. When this number is small, concentration is high and vice versa.

2. The following relationships are taken from G. Rosenbluth, *Concentration in Canadian Manufacturing Industries,* Princeton University Press, 1957.

6.	Railroad rolling stock	10.9
7.	Aircraft and parts	12.6
8.	Flour	15.4
9.	Cotton yarn and cloth	16.9
10.	Synthetic textiles	18.5
11.	Major electric appliances	18.7
12.	Communications equipment	20.7
13.	Electric industrial equipment	20.9
14.	Petroleum refining	21.0
15.	Breweries	21.7
16.	Industrial chemicals	24.5
17.	Motor vehicle parts	25.5
18.	Structural metal fabrication	29.3
19.	Slaughtering and meat packing	42.1
20.	Wire and wire products	45.6
21.	Pulp and paper	60.4
22.	Miscellaneous paper converters	62.5
23.	Miscellaneous metal fabrications	78.4
24.	Miscellaneous foods	81.9
25.	Fruit and vegetable preparations	93.9
26.	Shoe factories	96.9
27.	Printing and publishing	101.1
28.	Miscellaneous machinery	117.8
29.	Metal, stamp and press, etc.	131.1
30.	Men's clothing	148.6
31.	Pasteurizing plants	218.1
32.	Soft drinks	241.1
33.	Women's clothing	317.4
34.	Household furniture	346.7
35.	Butter and cheese	401.1
36.	Sash and door planing	403.4
37.	Feeds	415.7
38.	Printing and bookbinding	513.5
39.	Bakeries	776.4
40.	Sawmills	810.2

SOURCE: Calculations made from Dominion Bureau of Statistics, *Type of Ownership and Size of Establishment Engaged in Manufacturing in Canada, 1961.*

of C. If we suppose C = 4, N will be equal to 5 if D = .80. But if D were equal to .5 (the inequality would be greater) N would be equal to 8 for the same value of C.

The transformation of expression (2) gives

$$C = N\,D \qquad (3)$$

which by (1) becomes

$$C = \frac{I \times D}{E} \qquad (4)$$

C is higher and concentration is lower when the industry is important, when inequality in the size of the establishments is low (D is high), and, finally, when the establishments are small (E).

If one asks what the factors are that govern concentration in industry the answer is: all the factors that act directly upon I, D, and E. One example will suffice. We said previously that technology has had the effect of increasing the optimum size of business establishments.[1] According to our equation (4), C will decrease under this influence so that indirectly the evolution in technology can be held partly responsible for the tendency to an increase in concentration. Other factors act in the opposite direction. In the case of a rise in income, for example, there will be an increase in I if imports are held constant.

The level of concentration in the market has a considerable effect on competition. It is doubtful whether the intensity of competition is inversely proportional to the level of concentration, as is often supposed. It is beyond doubt, however, that the nature of competition is changed as concentration is increased. To simplify the argument, let us suppose on the one hand a situation with 500 competitors, and on the other a situation with only five, these in a country the size of Canada being clear examples of a low and a high level of concentration. Compared to a market structure of 500 competitors, a market structure of only five presents a completely different picture in respect of

1. Page 138.

competition. In this case one's competitors' reactions to any move are of prime importance, whereas in the low-level case they may be considered as almost negligible. It follows that the dangers of collusion are infinitely greater. Resort to monopolistic practices in every imaginable form is probable: price control, market sharing, advertising based on product differentiation (often artificially created) rather than competitive pricing, control of local markets and sites, competition for marginal and accessory advantages connected with the product in an artificial way (buy X soap and get a piece of stainless steel cutlery for 29c), resale price maintenance practices, price agreements, mergers of firms following dubious competitive drives, and so forth.

Yet it is equally probable that a highly concentrated industry will have new products that are a great deal cheaper than the old, newer and more economical methods, and increased productivity thanks to research and better equipment; in short, a dynamism that is, on the whole, to the consumer's advantage.

SUGGESTED READINGS

E. S. MASON (ED.): *The Corporation in Modern Society*, Cambridge, Harvard University Press, 1959.
A collection of papers pertaining to important aspects of the modern corporation.

G. ROSENBLUTH: 'Concentration and Monopoly in the Canadian Economy', in *Social Purpose for Canada*, ed. M. Oliver, University of Toronto Press, 1961, pp. 198-248.

G. ROSENBLUTH: *Concentration in Canadian Manufacturing Industries*, Princeton University Press, 1957.
The classic book on the subject.

R. B. HEFLEBOWER AND G. W. STOCKING (EDS.): *Readings in Industrial Organization and Public Policy*, Homewood, Ill., R. D. Irwin Inc., 1958.

C. A. ASHLEY AND R. G. H. SMAILS: *Canadian Crown Corporations*, Toronto, Macmillan, 1965.

J. E. SMYTH AND D. A. SOBERMAN: *The Law and Business Administration in Canada,* Toronto, Prentice-Hall, 1964.
Part 5, pp. 448-520, describes the legal aspects of partnerships and corporations.

CHAPTER

8

THE ANTI-COMBINES LEGISLATION

A. Historical

The first anti-combines legislation in Canada was introduced in 1888. At that time pressures exerted on Parliament by small businessmen led to the setting up of a Combines Investigation Commission. Confirming the allegations and fears of the small tradesmen, the investigators brought to light a series of agreements between various big producers. Restrictive measures were apparently very widespread, ranging from sugar to coffins to barbed wire.

Following this investigation, in 1889 Parliament passed an Act for the Prevention and Suppression of Combinations Formed in Restraint of Trade. Although incorporated into the Criminal Code in 1892 as Section 520, the Act proved totally inoperative until 1900. Indeed, the legislators had taken the precaution of specifying that to break this law an individual would have to commit an illegal act within the meaning of the 'common law'. The Act, therefore, established no new criminal offence.

In 1900 the Act was amended to eliminate the loophole clause. Undue restriction of competition became in itself a criminal offence. Substantially this remains the situation to the present time.

In 1909 a wave of mergers swept through the Canadian economy shortly after a similar movement in the United States: fifty-eight business firms and $361 million in capital were involved.

Faced with an aroused public opinion, Parliament in 1910 passed 'an Act to provide for the Investigation of Combines, Monopolies, Trusts and Mergers'.

The intention was to provide legislation that would be complementary to the Criminal Code. In essence the law of 1910 adds to the former provisions machinery for the application of the Act: thenceforth, at the request of six citizens, a judge could order an inquiry by an *ad hoc* commission of three members. The report of this commission was to be published. If there was in fact an infraction of the law, and if the guilty party should persist in his attitude, legal action would be taken.

Two Acts were passed in 1919 to replace that of 1910, which had proved ineffective, in particular because of the transitory nature of the investigating commissions. The Board of Commerce Act provided for the setting up of a permanent organization responsible for enforcing the legislative provisions against combines. The Combines and Fair Prices Act added to the provisions of 1910 a prohibition against undue stockpiling of the necessities of life and one against realizing exaggerated profits through unreasonable prices. These Acts also gave the federal government the power to issue 'orders to cease and desist' in these civil matters, a fact that caused the Privy Council to declare both Acts unconstitutional in 1921. Thenceforth the federal government would restrict its actions in this field to the provisions of the Criminal Code, abiding by the terms of the Act of 1910.

In 1923 Canadian combines legislation was finally consolidated. The most important sections of the Combines Investigation Act, which came into effect in that year, are still in effect.

The legislation of 1910 was strengthened in the 1923 Act by the appointment of a permanent officer, called first a Registrar and in 1937 a Commissioner, to be responsible for enforcing the provisions of the Act and the Criminal Code. The Commissioner could institute an inquiry either at the request of six citizens or on his own initiative; he was to gather and evaluate the evidence and submit his report to the Minister concerned (the Minister of

Labour until 1946 and the Minister of Justice since that time). In 1937 publication of this report was made mandatory. During the Depression, as a result of the influence of the policies of Roosevelt in the United States, attempts were made to allow certain price agreements in commerce and industry. An Act to this effect, the Dominion Trade and Industry Commission Act, was passed in 1936, but it was rejected by the Supreme Court as *ultra vires*. The most recent amendments to the Act of 1923 were made in 1952 and 1960.

B. The Present Act

Let us examine the nature and structure of the Combines Investigation Act as it now stands, taking the 1952 and 1960 amendments into account.

1. PROCEDURES

Until 1960 Canada's anti-trust legislation consisted of sections 409 to 412 (after changes in the numbers) of the Criminal Code and the Combines Investigation Act. In 1960, among other important amendments, the two legislative texts were consolidated into one by inserting the provisions from the Criminal Code into the Combines Investigation Act.

(a) Administrative Responsibility.

Since the recommendations of the MacQuarrie report were adopted in November 1952,[1] the Combines Branch of the Department of Justice has been divided into two distinct agencies. One, under the Director of Investigation and Research, is responsible for making inquiries into restrictive practices and for obtaining documentary evidence.[2] The other, the Restrictive Trade Practices Commission, is responsible for appraising the evidence submitted to it by the Director, for hearing witnesses or persons referred to or implicated by any allegation contained

1. S. C. 1960, ch. 45, art. 5 and 6.

2. R. S. C. 1952, ch. 314, art. 5

in the document submitted by the Director, and, finally, for submitting the report to the Minister of Justice.[1] An objection had been raised that the Department of Justice, under the former arrangement, was at once judge and party to the dispute. This argument is highly debatable since the body actually doing the judging was never the Department of Justice but the courts. In any case, the amendment of 1952 adds a supplementary tribunal to that of the regular courts.

(b) Investigation Procedures.

The Director of Investigation and Research begins his inquiries either of his own accord (at the request of the Department of Justice) or at the request of six Canadian citizens.

Generally, as a first step, he uses information already available. After this he may decide to carry out a formal detailed investigation to establish proof of a violation of the Act. For this purpose the officials of the Department of Justice may search premises and seize any documents. The Director or his appointed representatives may summon witnesses and, if necessary, require sworn statements. He prepares the statement of evidence and submits it to the Restrictive Trade Practices Commission and to the parties under investigation.

(c) The Commission Report.

On receiving this statement from the Director, the Restrictive Trade Practices Commission sets a date for hearing the case, at which time the Director presents argument in support of his statement. For their part, the persons against whom allegations have been made in the Director's report have the right to be heard before the Commission. Having heard all the evidence, the Commission prepares and submits its own report to the Federal Minister of Justice.

Every report of the Commission must be published within thirty days of its receipt by the Minister unless the Commission recommends to the contrary.

1. S. C. 1960, ch. 45, art. 16.

(d) Jurisdiction and Special Proceedings.

The superior provincial courts try cases involving combines, mergers, and monopolies. Since 1960, however, the Exchequer Court has had jurisdiction in common with the superior courts. It is now the judicial body before which cases of monopolistic arrangements that have important economic implications are heard and tried. Thus, in cases of this kind it replaces the provincial courts, which formerly had sole jurisdiction in such matters. The Act also provides for restraining orders granted by the Courts when an infraction is about to be committed.

2. PROHIBITED PRACTICES

(a) Agreements.

The Act prohibits suppliers from making agreements to fix prices, to limit production or distribution, or to restrict others from entering their trade or industry. The form of the agreements is of little importance: *their illegality resides in the harm done to the public interest by the limitation on competition that they entail*. Notwithstanding the illegality *per se* of such agreements, the 1960 amendment to the Act explicitly permits corporations to participate in arrangements relating to exchange of statistics, definition of product standards, exchange of credit information, co-operation in matters of research and development, and restriction of advertising. But the legislation adds that such practices must not unduly lessen competition or they will be considered offences.

(b) Monopoly and Merger.

The legislation prohibits mergers and the establishment of monopolies that are of such a nature as to injure the public interest. It defines a merger as the acquisition by one or several persons of any control over or interest in the whole or a part of a competitor's business, or of control of markets or sources of supply, that has the effect of lessening competition to the detriment of or against the interest of the public.

As for the term *monopoly*, it pertains to enterprises that control a large part or the whole of a particular trade or industry and are likely to operate against the public interest.

(c) Commercial Practices.

Under this head we can group together four commercial practices that are prohibited: (i) *Loss-leaders*. The Act prohibits the supplier from 'selling goods at prices unreasonably low having or designed to have the effect of substantially lessening competition or eliminating a competitor'. (ii) *Discrimination*. A supplier may not offer one customer a preferred price that is not available to another who is willing to buy in 'like quality and quantity'. Moreover, when a merchant or a supplier makes advertising or promotional allowances he must grant them to all his competing trade customers in proportion to their purchases. Finally, a supplier must not vary his selling prices in different areas of the country with the purpose of 'substantially lessening competition or eliminating a competitor' in any such areas. (iii) *Misleading price*. The Act prohibits the supplier from making, in his sales promotion, a materially misleading representation concerning the real price of a product or the price at which the product is ordinarily sold. (iv) *Resale price maintenance*. A dealer or manufacturer is prohibited from setting a specific or a minimum price for the resale of his products, from setting a maximum discount or a minimum mark-up whether such mark-up or discount is expressed as a percentage or otherwise.

3. PENALTIES

The penalties provided under the Act are:

1. publication of reports;
2. imposition of fines or prison sentences;
3. reduction or removal of customs duties;
4. revocation of patents and expunging of trade-mark registrations;
5. an order to cease and desist (introduced in 1952);
6. forced dissolution in the case of merger or monopoly.

The publication of reports alerts public opinion and exposes the incriminated companies to considerable loss of prestige. The president of the United Kingdom Board of Trade once expressed his confident opinion 'that publicity itself will operate in the majority of cases to cause a monopoly or association which is acting against the public interest, to change its habits.'[1] In the minds of Canadian parliamentarians publicity has also been of the greatest importance; this was especially true of Mackenzie King, who introduced the Acts of 1910 and 1923.

The maximum prison sentence is two years. Since 1952 the legislation has not set maximum fines; the amounts are left to the court's discretion. Before 1952 the maximum fines were $10,000 and $25,000 for persons and corporations respectively. These were much too low. But it should be noted that from 1952 until the time of writing no fine exceeding $25,000 has been imposed. Imprisonment as a penalty has remained a dead letter.

Resort to tariff reductions, rescinding of patents, and expunging of trade marks has been very rare. Dissolution has never yet been ordered by the courts. Finally, the author is aware of two cases (1953 and 1959) in which the court issued an order 'to cease and desist'.

C. A Short Appreciation

1. THE ESSENTIAL NATURE OF THE ACT

A criminal offence exists, according to Canadian law, whenever competition has been reduced to a substantial degree. The competitive system appears essential to Canadian legislators in order to bring about both efficiency and justice for the Canadian people. Commercial practices have thus been evaluated from the point of view of maintaining competition rather than by direct reference to a public interest clearly defined beforehand.

The argument of the reasonable nature of the prices that are fixed by cartels has been put forward many times by defendants, but judges have all decreed that such a consideration was not

---

1. Quoted by F. A. McGregor in E. H. Chamberlin (ed.), *Monopoly, Competition and Their Regulation*, London, Macmillan, 1959, p. 372.

within the competence of the court. A judgment as to the 'reasonable' nature of prices must come under the jurisdiction, not of the judicial courts, but of a government regulatory agency that is in a position to have a thorough knowledge of the evolution of the whole of the economy. The other economic arguments, such as the stabilization of industry, the low level of profit, or the non-restrictive nature of agreements, as well as the greater efficiency of the firms involved in monopolistic practices, have been similarly rejected by the Canadian courts.

We can readily admit that the attitudes of the courts are defensible from the economic point of view. As Professor Machlup[1] has pointed out, the combine in no way settles the problems of excess productive capacity and instability in production and prices. Indeed, he stresses the fact that in the first we are often confronted with an expanding industry in which there are probably some producers who are more efficient than others: thus monopolistic practices would only protect the high-cost producers. In the case of instability, which primarily concerns raw materials and agricultural products, it is not the competition that causes the instability, and consequently monopolistic agreements will have little effect on it. As for serving as palliatives or as remedies for instability, monopolistic agreements are much less effective for such purposes than other types of intervention.

It is also by reference to the maintenance of a competitive system that we must judge the other practices prohibited by the Act. Hence price discrimination among several sellers or several buyers, when it has no economic justification such as differences in the volume of purchases, is illegal. Indeed, it is contrary to the very essence of competition that a dollar should have a different purchasing power depending on the individual buyer or seller. Moreover, discriminatory pricing policies are always aimed, in the final analysis, at assuring a monopolistic or monopsonistic[2]

1. F. Machlup, *The Political Economy of Monopoly*, Baltimore, Johns Hopkins University Press, 1952, p. 56 ff.

2. Monopsony: a buyer's monopoly

position in a given market. A similar reasoning is behind the prohibition against prescribing resale prices to the retailer. The competitive system can function only if each economic agent, whatever his position in the market, is free to make his own decisions.

Anti-trust legislation in the United States draws its inspiration from the same source as Canadian legislation. Both accept as a criterion of criminal offence the fact *per se* of restricting competition. In general the American laws provide for severer penalties than the Canadian. In Great Britain, on the contrary, no commercial practice is forbidden as such. The British Commission on Restrictive Trade Practices judges on the basis of economic criteria (reasonable prices and profits, efficiency, nonrestriction of production, etc.). The administration of such legislation is not made easier as a result, but it does have the advantage of being incorporated within the framework of an over-all economic policy.

2. ITS EFFECTIVENESS

For several reasons the effectiveness of Canadian anti-combines legislation is rather limited. The main reason is that the federal government is able to base its legislation only on the Criminal Code, since civil law comes under the jurisdiction of the provinces. Those who violate the Criminal Code naturally must belong to the category of criminals. It can easily be understood that the courts are hesitant to condemn as a criminal the president of a large company who has fixed a price with his competitor during a game of golf or who has decided to buy out a rival company that has been giving him trouble. In one sense these practices are much too widespread for all the suspected criminals to be effectively prosecuted at once. It can also be understood that in order to obtain convictions on criminal grounds irrefutable proof is demanded. The very nature of the offences makes such proof extremely difficult to establish; agreements, for example, are verbal in most cases. It has been said that the only ones who ever get caught are either simpletons or publicity seekers. In short, many observers are of the opinion that criminal prosecutions in this domain are both unsuitable and ineffective. Nevertheless prosecutions in the civil courts are at the present time impossible at the federal level.

On the other hand, penalties are quite moderate in Canada. As already stated, fines have never exceeded $25,000 for corporations. The most costly conviction was that of the paper companies in 1960 when the court imposed fines totalling $240,000 on seventeen companies that had acted in combination to purchase pulpwood.

Partly because of the lack of financial resources available to the Department of Justice, partly because of the difficulties of applying the Act, the record of government activity in seeking out infractions of the law and in instituting legal proceedings does not make for a very thick file.

Between 1952 and 1962, forty-eight reports were submitted to the Department of Justice, an average of 4.8 per year.[1] From 1923 to 1940 the annual average was 1.5. Most of the investigations have dealt with trade agreements, but there has been a tendency to greater diversification over the last few years. In respect of mergers there has been little success: three cases have been terminated – those in the match, beer, and sugar industries – and only in the first case was there a conviction.

Twenty-one reports were submitted to the Minister of Justice between July 24, 1957, and the end of March 1962. Four led to convictions, one to acquittal, seven to abandonment of the proceedings (six through lack of proof, because the Commission did not recommend prosecution, and one because the situation had been corrected voluntarily), and nine were pending at one stage or another of the proceedings.[2] This five-year balance sheet is evidently quite unsatisfactory. One cannot help thinking that either Canadians are a very virtuous people or our investigations

1. *Report of the Director of Investigation and Research, Combines Investigation Act, 1962*, p. 34.

2. *Ibid.*, Appendix II.

are wrongly directed. Professors Rosenbluth and Thornburn[1] are of the latter opinion. They have shown that the proceedings that have been instituted have never touched upon more than a very small percentage of the Canadian markets open to the domination of cartels or monopolies. They have deduced from this a rule according to which it is presumed that the Canadian government is occupied more with minor violations of the law than with the serious violations that would implicate the country's most important corporations and industries.[2]

SUGGESTED READINGS

L. A. SKEOCH: 'The Combines Investigations Act', *Canadian Journal of Economics and Political Science*, February 1956.
An excellent introduction to Canadian legislation on the subject. Must not be read as a description of the actual situation in every detail.

H. E. ENGLISH: 'Competition and Policy to Control Restrictive Practices' and 'Other Policies Affecting Competition', in Brewis *et al.*, *Canadian Economic Policy*, revised edition, Toronto, Macmillan, 1965, chapters 2 and 3.
Analysis of the extent to which the Canadian government aids or obstructs the process of resource allocation through private markets.

G. ROSENBLUTH AND H. G. THORNBURN: 'Canadian Anti-Combines Administration, 1952-1960', *Canadian Journal of Economics and Political Science*, November 1961, pp. 498-508. Same title, University of Toronto Press, 1963.

1. G. Rosenbluth and H. G. Thornburn, 'Canadian Anti-Combines Administration, 1952-1960', *Canadian Journal of Economics and Political Science*, November 1961, pp. 498-508. See also the book under the same title published in 1963 by the University of Toronto Press.

2. The major part of this chapter is taken from a much more detailed text that Professor Gerald Marion had prepared for the 1962 session of the Canadian Institute of Public Affairs (ICAP) which in turn was based upon *La Politique canadienne sur les monopoles*, Montreal, Editions Bellarmin, 1957.

V. BLADEN: 'Monopoly and Competition in Canada', in *Monopoly and Competition and Their Regulation*, ed. E. H. Chamberlin, London, Macmillan, 1959, pp. 3-20.
In the same book see also the article by F. A. McGregor, 'Preventing Monopoly: Canadian Techniques'.

AMERICAN ECONOMIC ASSOCIATION: *Readings in the Social Control of Industry*, New York, Blakiston, 1949.
A survey of articles concerned with public policy toward industrial organization and control.

S. STYKOLT: 'Combines Policy: An Economist's Evaluation *Canadian Journal of Economics and Political Science*, February 1956.

R. CAVES: *American Industry: Structure, Conduct, Performance*, New York, Prentice-Hall, 1964.

Part two

MONEY AND FINANCE

CHAPTER

9

THE MONEY MARKET

A. Nature of the Market

The money market consists of transactions in short-term securities. Details of these securities will be given later. The expression 'financial market' or 'capital market' is ordinarily reserved for transactions in long-term securities.

Prior to 1953, the money market in Canada consisted only of a relatively limited and fixed volume of short-term government bonds, and there was practically no trading except within the banking system, a fact that considerably restricted the Central Bank's freedom of action. From 1953 on, several institutional changes led to the development of a short-term market which became more active after the middle of 1954. The most important changes were as follows:

(a) The institution of weekly sales of 91-day treasury bills in 1953. These treasury bills were sold at auction for the first time on March 1, 1934, and from 1937 on, sales were held each fortnight.[1,2]

(b) The periodical sale of new issues of short-term government bonds.

---

1. The government also made use of deposit certificates between 1942 and 1954, whereby the banks made loans to the government for short periods but without submission of tenders.

2. The treasury bills do not bear a nominal rate of interest. They are sold at a discount and redeemed on maturity at par. The effective rate of interest or

(c) The institution of purchase and resale agreements between the Bank of Canada and a certain number of Canadian investment dealers.[1] The agreements allow these dealers to become 'authorized dealers' in treasury bills and Canadian government bonds. There were fifteen authorized dealers at the end of 1963. The agreements allow investment firms other than the chartered banks or the government to have access to the Bank of Canada for carrying on operations that are very similar to rediscounting. Each dealer is granted a line of credit renewable each month, but it is not in his interest to avail himself of this privilege except as a last resort.

(d) The institution in 1954 of day-to-day loans of a minimum value of $100,000 granted by the chartered banks to the authorized dealers on a guarantee of short-term securities. The interest on these loans is generally slightly lower than the return on treasury bills, but fluctuates considerably according to circumstances. It has already varied from a low of ⅜ of 1% to a high of 6%.

(e) The 1954 agreement between the Bank of Canada and the authorized dealers, under which dealers can borrow securities (bills or bonds) of a certain term from the bank, on the guarantee of securities of a different term, so that they can fill the order of a particular client.

(f) The introduction of the arbitrage mechanism, a sort of tele-

---

yield is the difference between the purchase price and par value, given the period of time involved. On a 91-day treasury bill, the yield is given by the formula $P_n = P_o \left[1 + \dfrac{i \times 91}{365} \right]$ where P_n is the par value, P_o the purchase price, and i the actual yield. It may be found easily that a one-hundred-dollar treasury bill will yield around 4% for 91 days if the price paid is $99; it will be 3.25% if the price paid is $99.194.

1. By virtue of these purchase and resale agreements the Bank of Canada consents to buy from the authorized dealers either 91-day treasury bills or other short-term government bonds on condition that it will resell them to the authorized dealers in less than 30 days at a price stipulated in advance and such that the return on this discount operation is the same as the bank rate. For the dealers this rate is very high, but this method of borrowing money is also very useful.

phonic market linking the Montreal and Toronto dealers, which allows the two centres to maintain a uniform price for securities of the same term.

All of these measures, combined with other favourable circumstances, have caused a great increase in the number of buyers and sellers of treasury bills in Canada. Whereas in 1954 (December 31) the treasury bills outstanding amounted to $180 million, in 1964 they reached over $2 billion. A very important market in short-term securities now exists.

Those party to the money market pursue different goals according to whether they are on the side of the government, which issues bonds to finance its activities, or on the side of the buyers, the banks, and the dealers, who do not wish the liquid assets at their disposal to remain inactive.

This market was organized with a view to making efficient use on a so-called day-to-day basis, or for other short periods, of any cash balances that otherwise would have remained idle. This creation of a stronger market achieved a second aim of procuring for the Bank of Canada more efficient control over the monetary system than was possible when the market was weak and could be disrupted by any intervention. Another aim was for the Canadian government to secure additional financing through the sale of short-term government securities. The system of deposit certificates has therefore been replaced. One can get some idea of the large volume of liquid assets that are offered or demanded on the short-term market by examining the amounts outstanding at the end of 1964:

    day-to-day loans: $215 million;

    91-day treasury bills: $2.1 billion;

    federal bonds of a term of under two years: $3 billion;[1]

---

1. Strictly speaking, federal bonds of a term of under 3 years should be included here.

> short-term bonds, including treasury bills issued by certain provinces and cities, the total of which has not been calculated.

Still another aim was to broaden the market for private short-term securities, although these are still of little importance in the money market. Sales finance companies are almost the only companies to issue private short-term securities, called 'Finance Company Notes', regularly exchanged on the market. In recent years these have amounted to about $700 million outstanding. The bank acceptances introduced in June 1962, which are based on private short-term securities, also show interesting possibilities. These amounted to $150 million outstanding at the end of 1965. The balance of the private short-term securities account for $300 million.[1] These, then, are the types of securities exchanged on the short-term market in Canada.

It may be that only a few hundred people understand how the short-term market functions, and yet the money market plays a very important role in the economic life of the country. The principal agents engaged in this market are the federal government's Department of Finance, the eight chartered banks, the two savings banks of the Province of Quebec, and some 270 jobbers in securities.

Just as in any market where there is competition between buyers and sellers, the money market contributes to the efficient distribution of the financial resources of the country, and makes it possible to keep liquid assets active even when very short periods of time are involved.

The most important auction sale in the country takes place at noon on the Thursday of each week at the Bank of Canada. Officials of the Department of Finance, assisted by certain employees of the Bank of Canada, open the underwriters' letters of tender for the purchase of the treasury bills offered by the government of Canada (an average of $135 million per week

---

1. Corporate paper, with original terms of one year or less, issued by firms other than the sales finance companies. *Report of the Royal Commission on Banking and Finance*, Appendix volume, 1964, p. 257.

in 1965). This auction sale is carried out in the purest banking tradition without anyone having to raise his voice – this is perhaps the reason why it passes unnoticed by most citizens – yet a very large part of Canada's liquid assets are at stake, since the securities traded amount to more than $5 billion outstanding.

These weekly auctions require a series of quick decisions. The treasurers of the large corporations must put in their orders to the commercial banks or to the investment dealers; the investment dealers must fix their tenders on the basis of their clients' orders and the sales they expect to make; the agents of the chartered banks must review the state of their liquid assets and attempt to take the market's pulse; and the administrators of the Bank of Canada must form their own estimate of the country's money supply and decide on the value of the treasury bills they are going to buy and the price they will offer. Treasury bills are purchased in denominations of $1,000, $5,000, $25,000, $100,000, and $1 million. The average individual rarely takes the trouble to invest his idle funds because he usually holds rather insignificant amounts, but the situation is different for the chartered banks, the investment dealers, and the large corporations, whose liquid assets are often very large. When large sums remain idle or inactive, they not only provide no return for their owners, they also make the financial structure of the country much more rigid. Taking the case of a large corporation that has at its disposal a temporary but considerable amount of idle money – because it will have to pay dividends within a few weeks' time, for example – it can still put these liquid assets to use in the interval by buying short-term securities which are easily negotiable, or convertible into cash at very short notice. Conversely, a corporation needing money for a short period of time can sell off the short-term securities that it holds in order to obtain it. In brief, the short-term market reduces the operating costs of corporations and at the same time increases the mobility of short-term capital. In addition to providing the government with a relatively inexpensive method of financing, the money market procures a considerable degree of control for the Bank of Canada because of the frequent movements of funds and the increased sensitivity of the system to changes in the money supply. For their part, the commercial banks can adjust their reserves from day to day by lending or by borrowing on the market, or by the purchase or sale of these same short-term securities. Thus available liquid assets are utilized more efficiently.

B. The Department of Finance

The government finds in the short-term market an efficient and inexpensive method of financing its activities: it tries to ensure that part of the national debt is made up of short-term bonds, in order both to reduce interest charges and to answer current needs in balancing its cash holdings and expenditures. The cost to the government is·determined on a competitive basis, the price of the bonds being fixed by the market. The average return to the bond buyers represents the average cost of borrowing to the government.

This method of financing, which has long been in force in certain countries (it was begun in England in 1877), was introduced into Canada in 1934 by the Department of Finance.

It is the Department of Finance which presides over the auction sale that takes place each Thursday noon. It is the Department which receives the tenders submitted by the Bank of Canada, the chartered banks, and the investment dealers. It is the Department, acting through its representatives, which opens the sealed tenders. The highest acceptable tender is completely filled at the offered price; the second-highest tender is also filled at the offered price; and so it continues until the week's issue has been completely sold. Generally the total of the tenders exceeds the value of the bills offered, so that the lowest tenders are not filled. The average yield on the issue is calculated and published by the Bank of Canada. At the request of the Department of Finance the Bank also publishes the price limits (the high and low bids). The same client (bank or dealer) will often submit several tenders at different prices since he evidently does not know how many will be accepted beforehand. Those whose tenders are accepted must collect their certificates or their bonds by 3 p.m. of the day following.

To guard against the possibility of the buyers failing to submit enough tenders to absorb the whole weekly issue, the Bank of Canada generally submits a reserve bid in an amount equal to the total week's issue. It should be noted that the Bank is not obliged to make this tender;[1] it does so with the object both of preventing any agreements aimed at increasing the interest rate or at boycotting an issue, and of permitting the government to obtain all the money it requires. The amount of the weekly issues is decided on the basis of the cash held by the government, of its expected receipts and expenditures, and of the due dates of the outstanding bonds.

The preceding remarks give a far from comprehensive account of the multiple roles assumed by the Department of Finance in the money market. It also exerts an influence on monetary regulation through the decisions it makes regarding the national debt, and is responsible for the policy and the administration of several special accounts (the Exchange Fund Account, the Securities Investment Account, the Purchase Fund,[2] etc.) with the Bank of Canada as its executive agent. In this respect two important government decisions may be cited: the decision of December 1961, to intervene in the foreign exchange market by selling Canadian dollars to lower the exchange rate; the decision in the summer of 1958 to make a massive exchange of 6.4 billion dollars' worth of short- and medium-term bonds for longer term bonds. (The latter episode was an extraordinary venture which caused interest rates to rise at a time of unemployment and recession although it was never demonstrated that the operation was absolutely necessary.) Finally, the Department influences the reserves of the chartered banks by its distribution of its current deposits between the Bank of Canada and the chartered banks.

---

1. At the time of the sale of the 20th of August 1959, a period of intense speculation, the reserve bid of the Bank of Canada could not be found, according to Professor Scott Gordon. See *The Economists Versus the Bank of Canada*, Ryerson Press, Toronto, 1960, p. 30.

2. The Purchase Fund dates from 1961, and serves to mitigate undesirable fluctuations in bond prices.

C. The Bank of Canada

1. OBJECTIVES

The preamble to the law incorporating the Bank of Canada reads as follows: 'Whereas it is desirable to establish a central bank in Canada to regulate credit and currency in the best interests of the economic life of the nation, to control and protect the external value of the national monetary unit and to mitigate by its influence fluctuations in the general level of production, trade, prices and employment, so far as may be possible within the scope of monetary action and generally to promote the economic and financial welfare of the Dominion . . .'[1]

From this text we can deduce that the objectives of the Bank are twofold: first, to avoid the depreciation of the national currency in world markets; and second, to pursue within the country a policy of economic stability that will avoid depression or inflation to the extent that monetary policy can serve these ends.

2. ORGANIZATION AND STRUCTURE

The Bank of Canada is a central bank responsible for the application of monetary policy in the general interest of the country. In conformity with the recommendation of the Royal Commission on Banking and Currency (1933), the government founded the Bank of Canada on July 3, 1934, as a private institution. After shares had been offered for public subscription in the amount of $5 million, the Bank became the property of 12,000 shareholders. It began its operations on March 11, 1935.

After the election of the Liberal government in 1935, the Bank was partially nationalized in 1936. The government increased the Bank's capital by $5.1 million, thus assuring itself of majority control. It appointed half the directors and gave them each two votes. By 1938 nationalization was completed: the government bought back all the shares held by the public and reduced the Bank's capital to $5 million. In addition to the Governor and the Deputy Governor, the twelve directors were

1. Quoted from the Annual Report of the Bank of Canada, 1960.

henceforth appointed by the government. The Governor is appointed for a period of seven years and cannot be deprived of his office without parliamentary intervention; he has the right to veto any decisions of the Board of Directors.

The principal problem created by the organization of the Bank of Canada concerns the relations between the Bank and the government. From the very beginning of the Bank's operations this proved to be a highly controversial question, as we have noted above, and it remains so today.

In the main, the problem is the degree of independence or autonomy that the Bank should enjoy in regard to the government. At the outset there was a fear of political intervention, and that is why the Bank was established as a private enterprise. Later it was feared that private interests would dominate. Mackenzie King frequently stated that the Bank should be *the government bank* because the government alone was representative of the general interest and the sovereignty of the people. Once the Bank had been nationalized, however, it was deemed necessary to preserve the institution from political interference: hence the guarantees given to the Governor of the Bank.

A related problem arose as to the Bank's responsibility for monetary policy. Was it the monetary policy of the Central Bank or the monetary policy of the government that was to be followed? In theory, no conflict could arise, but in practice, what would be the situation if the Governor disagreed with the Minister of Finance on the policy to be followed, since the Minister could not rescind the Governor's appointment? In 1941 the Minister of Finance (Ilsley) declared[1] that the monetary policy carried out by the Bank must be the government's monetary policy, and that in case of disagreement it would be necessary for the Governor of the Bank to resign. Statements made by Governor Towers in 1954 and by Governor Coyne in 1956 showed that they concurred with this view; and when Louis Rasminsky was appointed Governor in July 1961, he declared:

---

1. Not without correcting a previous statement.

'In case of disagreement between the Governor and the Bank, the Government has the right and the duty to give instructions to the Bank on the policy to be followed.'[1] Nevertheless, from 1958 to 1961 the relations between James Coyne, then Governor of the Bank, and the government were highly strained. A number of economists even publicly demanded the Governor's resignation. It finally became necessary to present an act of dismissal before Parliament to get the Governor to agree to offer his resignation.

Events of this kind have led several observers to think that the independence of the Bank's Governor is excessive and should be reduced. After having considered the proposals put before it, the Royal Commission on Banking and Finance maintained the ultimate responsibility of government in monetary policy fully, while stressing the need for the Bank to retain its independence in carrying it out. The Commission took the view that a continuing directive from the government to the Bank would be impractical and would destroy the Bank's independence. Instead it favoured a clause in the Bank of Canada Act giving the Cabinet power, through an Order in Council, to issue a directive to the Bank that would automatically lapse after 30 days. That directive would be as specific as possible and be made public along with a statement from the Governor. In essence, then, the Commission felt that government should have the power to prevail when there was a fundamental issue between the Minister of Finance and the Governor of the Bank. But at the same time it expressed the view that extraordinary precautions should be taken to ensure that the device could not be used in the normal course of events.[2]

3. POWERS AND FUNCTIONS

Conflicts between the government and the Bank of Canada are rare because in Canada the Central Bank is more closely connected to the government than in many other countries. In

1. Annual Report of the Bank of Canada, 1962.

2. *Report of the Royal Commission on Banking and Finance*, 1964, pp. 539-45.

Canada the Central Bank fulfils three functions that are properly governmental in nature: it is the fiscal agent of the government; it has managed the public debt since 1938; and it administers the Exchange Fund Account, the Securities Investment Account, and the Purchase Fund. If only to carry out its supporting role, the Bank must be in constant communication with the Department of Finance. It should be noted that with its close ties to the government, the Bank even runs the risk of putting the special interests of the government before the interests of the nation as a whole. A rise in the interest rates, for example, might be beneficial to the country, but represent a rise in the public debt charges to the government. *A priori*, then, it is the Bank's excessive submission to the views of the government that should be feared, rather than its opposition to them.

The confusion of roles has certain advantages in bringing about greater cohesion between the government and the Central Bank in carrying out monetary policy. The danger is that monetary policy may be subordinated to management of the public debt.[1]

The principal functions of the Central Bank are *to adapt the money supply* (currency held outside banks, and chartered banks, deposits) *to the needs of the economy, and to insure that interest rates move in the desired direction.* This is monetary management. To this end the Central Bank has held a monopoly on the issue of bank notes since 1944, and in 1950 it bought up all the other bank notes still in circulation. It is required by law to maintain gold reserves equal to at least 25% of its note and deposit liabilities, but the application of this rule was suspended in 1940 and has never been put back in force. *Since 1940, then, Canada's currency has not been backed by gold*, and as far as the redemption of its bank notes with gold (convertibility) is concerned, the Bank has not been required to do this since 1934. The Bank receives deposits from the government, from the Canadian chartered banks, and from central foreign banks with-

1. E. P. Neufeld, *Bank of Canada Operations and Policy*. University of Toronto Press, 1958, chapter I, notably page 19.

out paying interest; it can purchase without restriction United States government bonds, United Kingdom bonds with a maturity of less than six months, and, since 1954, all securities issued by Canadian governments (before 1954, operations in long-term securities were subject to restrictions); it can also lend money to Canadian chartered banks and governments, on security, for periods of less than six months.[1,2]

The nature of the operations of the Bank of Canada appears clearly in the balance sheet on the opposite page.

A quick examination of the Bank of Canada's assets shows that the Bank does not hold any gold as a guarantee for the notes it issues; it buys long- and short-term securities (the volume of long-term securities is notably higher), but it does not buy any provincial or municipal government securities, although allowed to do so by law. While certain of the Canadian government securities may be held as a result of purchase and resale agreements with investment dealers, on the date of this particular balance sheet the Bank was not holding any, nor had it made any advances to chartered banks. Finally, there is the Bank's investment in its subsidiary, the Industrial Development Bank.

On the liabilities side are the bank notes issued by the Bank, with which it pays (in part) for the assets that it procures, the deposits of the Canadian government and the chartered banks, and the Bank's foreign currency liabilities.

4. INSTRUMENTS OF MONETARY MANAGEMENT

Monetary policy is applied through changes in the money supply and the interest rates.

1. Article 18K of the Bank of Canada Act allows the Bank to buy commercial securities of a term of less than 90 days without the endorsement of a chartered bank. The purchase of stocks or private debentures is neither explicitly permitted nor forbidden.

2. The two Quebec savings banks (La Banque de la Cité et du District de Montréal and La Banque d'Economie de Québec) also have access to the Bank of Canada. They are operating under a separate Savings Bank Act. Their powers and functions are somewhat different from those of the chartered banks. See chapter 8 of the *Report of the Royal Commission on Banking and Finance*, pp. 147-54.

TABLE 9 : 1

Balance Sheet of the Bank of Canada
as of December 31, 1964, millions of dollars

Assets			Liabilities		
1. Foreign currencies		111.0	1. Notes in circulation		2,380.6
2. Total Government of Canada direct and guaranteed securities		3,064.3	Held by chartered banks	355.1	
Treasury bills	478.7		Others	2,025.5	
Short-term securities			2. Canadian dollar deposits		986.6
(two years and under)	349.2		Government of Canada	68.9	
Other maturities	2,236.4		Chartered banks	882.1	
3. Bankers' acceptances		—	Other	35.6	
4. Investment in the Industrial Development Bank		212.5	3. Foreign currency liabilities		44.9
5. All other accounts		254.1	4. Capital stock, reserves, and other accounts		229.8
Total Assets		3,641.9	Total Liabilities		3,641.9

SOURCE: *Bank of Canada, Statistical Summary.*

The money supply (or the stock of money) is the sum of the means of payment available to the public. The statistical measurements of it are elastic, because they depend on the definition of 'means of payment' and of 'public'.

For general purposes, 'means of payment' is limited to coin, bank notes, and deposits in the chartered banks. Consequently all securities (stocks and bonds) are excluded, even if these securities are highly liquid. Also excluded are deposits in the *caisses populaires*–credit unions, and in the trust and mortgage loan companies, because these deposits have been made with bank notes that have already been counted.[1] In Canada, the meaning assigned to 'public' in statistical measurement is equally arbitrary. The federal government is excluded from the definition, but the other governments are included, as well as all non-financial and financial institutions and corporations. It should also be noted that currency outside the banks represents only 13% of the money supply as it is defined here (Table 9:2).

In order to influence the money supply and the economy's level of liquidity, the Bank of Canada can increase or reduce the reserves of banks and other financial institutions, it can affect the level and variations of interest rates, and it can adopt various procedures that are designated in Canada as 'moral suasion'. The observations we have made concerning the extension of the money market are sufficient to illustrate the methods of persuasion available to the Bank of Canada. The discussion here will therefore be limited to the first two instruments of control.

The open-market operations by which the Bank influences

1. Some day the definition of 'money supply' will have to be revised. The bank notes held by the public should all be identical. At present those which are put into the *caisses populaires*–credit unions, or the trust and mortgage loan companies, are reserve bank notes worth $\frac{1}{r}$ times the others, where r is the cash ratio of those institutions, because they allow deposits to be created in the same way as those of the chartered banks. To be logical, all those bank notes held by institutions accepting deposits should be excluded from the bank notes held by the public, and the deposits of these institutions should be added to the money supply.

TABLE 9 : 2

Money Supply as of December 31, 1964, millions of dollars

Currency outside banks — notes	1,958	
Currency outside banks — coin	225	
Demand deposits in chartered banks	4,510	
Money supply excluding savings and other notice deposits in chartered banks		6,693
Personal savings and other notice deposits in chartered banks		10,340
Total money supply		17,033

SOURCE: *Bank of Canada, Statistical Summary, Supplement* 1965.

cash reserves are not peculiar to Canada, but, unlike some foreign central banks, the Bank of Canada does not limit its purchases to short-term government bonds. The possibilities of Central Bank intervention in the Canadian market are much greater than they were a few years ago for several reasons – because the short-term market has expanded considerably since 1954, because the public debt provides a large volume of government securities, and because the major part of these securities are now purchased by Canadian residents from domestic savings (non-residents reduced their holdings of federal government securities from 32.5% of the total in 1938 to 3.8% in 1956 and 5.2% in 1965).

In 1954 an amendment to the Act was passed which granted the Bank of Canada the power to alter the cash ratio of the chartered banks. *This ratio is the percentage of deposit liabilities that the chartered banks must maintain in the form of bank notes or deposits in the Bank of Canada.* From 1935 to 1954 the statutory minimum cash ratio was 5%. Since 1954, the Bank Act has stipulated a cash ratio of 8% of Canadian dollar deposits; but instead of requiring that it be maintained for each day of the month, as formerly, it is now required only as the average over the month. For this purpose a calculation is made of the average holdings of the notes and Canadian dollar deposits in the chartered banks for the four consecutive Wednesdays of the month, and of the average holdings of the deposits in the Bank of Canada for the working days of the month.

The Bank of Canada has never altered the statutory cash ratio of 8%. In fact, such an alteration must be considered as an instrument of last resort, for it is highly desirable to maintain a stable ratio. The Bank of Canada would probably change the ratio only if open-market operations should prove powerless to counteract unfavourable changes in the reserves.

In May 1956, at the request of the Bank of Canada, the chartered banks agreed *to maintain an additional or secondary reserve of liquid assets in the form of treasury bills and day-to-day loans.* The total of cash and secondary reserves must represent at least 15% of their deposit liabilities. This additional restraint has strengthened the Central Bank's control to a certain extent, and helps to maintain the price of treasury bills and lower the interest rate in the short-term market.

The Bank of Canada makes advances of money to chartered banks and to governments. It can do so on a promissory note but it can also rediscount (or discount a second time) securities that have first been discounted by the chartered banks for the benefit of their customers. *The discount rate or the Bank Rate is the interest rate that the Central Bank sets for its advances or its rediscount operations.* In several cases, as we have already seen, the Bank can require investment dealers to buy back the securities they have sold under purchase and resale agreements. In this way the Bank assures itself of being a 'lender of last resort'. It forces the investment dealers, so to speak, to hang on to their securities.[1]

The rediscount rate was not used by the Bank of Canada as

1. Strictly speaking, these agreements are investments for the Bank of Canada.

an instrument of monetary management for very long. From 1935 to 1955 it was only changed twice: in 1944, when it was lowered from 2½% to 1½%; then in 1950, when it was raised to 2%. The period from February 1, 1955, to November 1, 1956, was the only one in which the rate was changed by the Bank as a policy. It was changed six times during this period, and just when its effectiveness could have been ascertained, it was decided to make it a 'floating' bank rate, fixed at ¼ of 1% above the average tender rate on treasury bills of the preceding week. The object was to encourage and strengthen the short-term bond market and to ensure that the Bank would remain a lender of last resort. It must be recognized, however, that such a measure was not necessary since to obtain this objective, the Bank is only required to maintain *in fact* its rate above the market rate. Fixing the rate in advance has thus introduced an element of useless rigidity and has, moreover, deprived the rediscount rate of the important functions it once had of influencing the expectations of savers and investors, and of clearly announcing the monetary policy that the Bank intended to adopt in the near future.

TABLE 9 : 3

Bank Rate, June 1962 to December 1965

June 24, 1962	6%
November 13, 1962	4%
May 6, 1963	3½%
August 3, 1963	4%
November 24, 1966	4¼%
December 6, 1965	4¾%

SOURCE: *Bank of Canada, Statistical Summary, Supplement* 1965.

In June 1962, the Bank introduced a dual rate. For general purposes it was suddenly raised to 6%; but for transactions with the investment dealers under the purchase and resale agreements, it remained at ¼ of 1% above the tender rate on treasury bills. This is an excellent compromise, since the measure allows the market to be maintained (a 6% rate applied to the investment dealers would probably have caused them to drop out) without sacrificing the requirements of monetary policy. The 'official' Bank rate has been changed from time to time as Table 9:3 indicates.

It is not possible to discuss the interest rate structure in relation to the term of the loans here, but since this is an important subject, Table 9:4 gives figures on some representative securities.

TABLE 9 : 4

Interest Rate Structure in Canada,
Average Annual Yield of Certain Securities, 1956-1962

	Day-to-day loans	Treasury bills (3-month bills)	Federal security maturity: June 15/67-68	Federal security maturity: Oct. 1/79
1956	2.56	2.85	3.50	3.56
1957	3.45	3.76	4.34	4.09
1958	1.70	2.25	3.67	3.98
1959	4.21	4.81	4.89	4.87
1960	2.94	3.20	4.79	5.04
1961	2.55	2.81	4.56	5.01
1962	3.84	4.05	4.51	5.07
1963	3.28	3.56	4.32	5.01
1964	3.60	3.75	4.44	5.12

NOTE: From 1956 to 1962, the average annual yield was based on monthly averages; for 1963 and 1964, the average end-of-month yield was used.

SOURCES: *Bank of Canada Statistical Summary* and *Supplements*.

D. The Chartered Banks

When a Canadian citizen thinks of banks, he generally has the chartered banks in mind. This name comes to them from the federal charters that grant them legal existence. Unlike the Bank of Canada, the chartered banks are private companies, of which the oldest and most important is the Bank of Montreal, dating from 1817. Although they are not numerous, being only eight in number,[1] the number of branches, 5,784 in 1964, is higher in proportion to population than in any other country. The establishment of multiple branches is a feature characteristic of the Canadian banking system, in contrast to the large number of separate banks in the United States. It is claimed that the structure of the Canadian banking system accounts for the excellent reputation that these banks have always enjoyed, the remarkable security they have assured their depositors in periods of financial crisis, and the services they have rendered throughout the whole country in spite of distances and the low population density. No doubt administrative controls and monetary policy itself are also easier to apply for this reason; however, price competition

TABLE 9 : 5

Number of Banks and Branches in Canada

	Number of banks	Total Number of branches
1902	34	747
1930	10 (1931)	4,083
1940	10	3,311
1950	10	3,679
1962	8	5,332
1964	8	5,784*

*207 of which are abroad.
SOURCES: *Canada Year Book*, 1963-4, and Canadian Bankers' Association.

between banks to attract depositors and borrowers has never been very keen. Co-operation rather than competition seems the rule; the lack of open friction among the members of the Cana-

1. Three of which hold 70% of all bank deposits.

dian Bankers' Association, since its establishment in 1891, has been an eloquent witness to this fact.

The same simplicity and order characterizes the legislation governing the chartered banks. A single general Bank Act controls the commercial banking business, and this Act, carefully edited with the collaboration of all concerned at the time of Confederation, was adopted in 1871 and has been revised at regular ten-year intervals since then.

The chartered banks are deposit and credit banks. *Their essential function is to supply short-term credit for industrial or commercial purposes*. The discounting of commercial bills of a three-month term is a typical banking operation. Lending on the collateral security of primary products held in inventory (such as wheat or lumber) for the period they are being shipped to the customer is also a long tradition in Canada (dating from 1859).[1] Since 1944 especially, banks have sought to multiply their services. To commercial loans proper, banks have added consumer loans, with or without chattel mortgages, insured mortgage loans of a longer term,[2] and farm loans and loans to fishermen on the partial guarantee of the federal government. The Export Finance Corporation of Canada Limited, which finances exports on a one- to five-year basis, was founded by the eight chartered banks together. In 1963 two banks (with three trust companies) set up a subsidiary in Montreal to extend medium- and long-term industrial credit. Although the banks are moving into these new fields of activity only with caution, they are tending to become all-purpose banks.

A maximum interest rate on bank loans has been fixed by law since 1777. From 1871 to 1944, the Bank Act fixed it at 7%; then it was reduced to 6% in 1944. This ceiling on the interest

1. Section 88 of the Bank Act.

2. The banks have suspended their investments in insured mortgages since 1959, because the rising cost of money (see Table 9:4) coupled with the 6% limit on bank loans and the cost of administering mortgage loans made such investments unprofitable.

rate has become the centre of a major controversy ever since the Royal Commission on Banking and Finance recommended that it be removed. According to the Commission, the 6% ceiling is inequitable as the banks are prevented from attracting business which can be attracted by other institutions. More importantly the ceiling works against the borrowers it purports to protect, because the other lenders charge higher rates than they would if they were not artificially protected from the banks' competition. In any case the banks already get more than 6% on a variety of operations and this is done with the full knowledge of all concerned.[1] Canadian banks have been paying interest on savings accounts since 1832, and allow their customers to draw cheques on them. They also render numerous accessory services such as accepting payment for the bills of certain utilities (electricity, telephone, etc.).

The assets of the chartered banks at the end of 1964 amounted to $18.6 billion. Of this total, loans made up about 60%, investments 32% or so, and cash holdings in the form of bank notes and deposits in the Bank of Canada 8%. The banks' investments are short-, medium-, or even long-term. They include not only federal government bonds but also provincial and municipal government bonds, as well as private securities.

The balance sheet which has been drawn up in Table 9:6 gives a statement of the principal activities of the chartered banks in Canada. The critical entries on this balance sheet from the point of view of monetary management are obviously the cash holdings, or liquid reserves (see Bank of Canada notes and deposits), since these holdings determine the upper limits of the credit that may be granted by the banks. The cash ratio has remained slightly higher than 8% since 1954, and cannot go below

1. *Report of the Royal Commission on Banking and Finance*, pp. 364-9. The removal of the 6% ceiling would also allow the banks to enter the field of conventional mortgages – another important recommendation of the Commission.

TABLE 9 : 6

Balance Sheet of Chartered Banks
as of December 31, 1964, millions of dollars

Assets		Liabilities	
Bank of Canada notes	383	Deposits	
Bank of Canada deposits	857	Government of Canada	696
Day-to-day loans	253	Provincial governments	202
Treasury bills	1,257	Personal savings and other notice deposits	10,440
Other Government of Canada securities	2,462	Other banks (mostly foreign)	183
Provincial and municipal government		Demand deposits	5,176
securities	679	Acceptances, guarantees and letters of credit	722
Corporate securities	487	Shareholders' equity	1,175
Call and short loans to stockbrokers and		All other liabilities	66
investment dealers	150		
Insured residential mortgages	851		
Loans in Canadian currency	9,260		
Customers' liabilities under acceptances,			
guarantees, and letters of credit	722		
Canadian dollar items in transit (net)	902		
All other assets*	398		
Total Assets	18,661	Total Liabilities	18,661

*These include bank premises, shares of and loans to controlled corporations, coin in Canada, Canadian dollar deposits with other banks, etc.

SOURCE: *Bank of Canada, Statistical Summary.*

8%, as we have previously noted. When the demand for loans is very pressing and the banks are short of cash reserves, they may borrow from the Bank of Canada and obtain advances the same day. More often they seek to sell off some of the securities they hold – the calling of day-to-day loans is one example of this. (In this case the bank can obtain a clearing cheque from the Bank of Canada the next day.) If it sells treasury bills in the market or to the Bank of Canada, it obtains its funds two days later. On government bonds maturing in less than five years funds are paid the third day after the sale, and on longer-term bonds the fourth day.

On the balance sheet of the chartered banks we find an entry 'Loans in Canadian currency' that calls for some additional figures. Table 9:7 divides these loans into several categories.

TABLE 9 : 7

Chartered Banks' Loans as of December 31, 1964, millions of dollars

1. Loans to provincial and municipal governments		393
2. Loans to grain dealers		148
3. Loans to finance the purchase of Canada Savings Bonds		198
4. Loans to instalment finance companies		299
5. Business loans		4,929
$5 million or more	787	
$1 to $5 million	1,103	
less than $1 million	3,040	
6. Personal loans		2,324
Against marketable securities	459	
Home improvement loans	72	
All other	1,793	
7. Loans to farmers		708
8. Loans to institutions		262
Total		9,261

NOTE: The last four classes of loans are called 'general loans'.
SOURCE: *Bank of Canada, Statistical Summary.*

Of the 9.2 billion dollars' worth of loans outstanding at the end of 1964 a little over half are general business loans and 2.3 billion dollars' worth are personal loans.

E. The Investment Dealers

Investment dealers are assuming increasing importance in the money market. We have already mentioned that fifteen investment houses have been granted lines of credit from the Bank of Canada to facilitate trading in short-term securities. These are no doubt the most active firms, but there are a great number of others who also engage in this trading activity. These are mainly the broker members of the Investment Dealers' Association, 185 in number, the members of the Bond Traders' Association of Toronto and Montreal, and the independent brokers. The first of these associations has reported that more than 400 brokers are engaged in the bond business in Canada, but this figure includes all bond brokers, not just those who deal in short-term securities.

These dealers, in addition to the numerous other functions they may perform, all act as agents in the purchase and sale of securities. The most important of these bond houses also buy and sell in their own name and generally hold a very large portfolio of securities. In firms of this type the broker's profit comes from the return on his inventory and from the difference between the purchase price and the sale price of these securities. From this gross profit must be subtracted the marketing costs, which are often very high, and the interest charges on loans contracted in order to acquire the securities.

For a long time banks were the only sources of credit for the investment dealers in Canada; but for some years now several other financial institutions have associated themselves with the banks in extending credit, so that investment dealers are now beginning to bear a close resemblance to 'discount houses' in England.

Of the 185 members of the Investment Dealers' Association in 1961, sixteen carried an inventory of securities worth about $5 million and more each, and seventeen others carried an inventory of $1 to $5 million. These investment houses alone sold 10 billion dollars' worth of short-term securities in 1961, which represents more than 90% of total dealers' sales.[1]

As the activities of the investment dealers extend beyond the bounds of the money market proper, this group will be dealt with more extensively in the following chapter.[2]

A statistical Table indicating the banking system's place in the market for federal government securities follows:

TABLE 9 : 8

Distribution of the Holdings of Government of Canada Direct and Guaranteed Securities by Type as of December 31, 1964, millions of dollars

	Bank of Canada	Chartered banks	Federal government accounts	General public	Total
Treasury bills	482	1,265	61	332	2,140
Maturity under two years	349	1,126	270	1,255	3,000
Maturity two years and over	2,284	1,336	438	5,944	10,002
Canada Savings Bonds	—	—	—	5,612	5,612
Total	3,115	3,727	769	13,143	20,754

SOURCE: Calculations made from *Bank of Canada, Statistical Summary*.

The outstanding securities of the federal government amounted to over $20.7 billion at the end of 1964. Sixty-three per cent of this sum was held by the 'public', that is, by the financial institutions, by other corporations, and by individuals. The proportion was much lower on the short-term security market. The

1. Memorandum of the Investment Dealers' Association to the Royal Commission on Banking and Finance 1962.

2. Chapter 10, section 2.

'public' held 15% of the treasury bills and 42% of the bonds of a maturity of two years and under. If the Canada Savings Bonds, which are not bought by the banks,[1] are excluded from these calculations, it is found that the Bank of Canada had 20.6% and the chartered banks 24.6% of all other federal government bonds. The banks' total share, exclusive of Canada Savings Bonds, thus came to 45%. In view of the large public holdings of marketable securities – 7.5 billion dollars' worth in 1964 – it can be concluded that transactions in federal bonds are truly conducted in the public market place: this is both right and necessary.

SUGGESTED READINGS

BANK OF CANADA: Briefs submitted to the Royal Commission on Banking and Finance, May 1962. An excellent summary of the Bank of Canada's operations.

BANK OF CANADA: *Report of the Governor of the Bank of Canada*, Ottawa, Queen's Printer, annual.
An annual survey of Canada's economic conditions and a discussion of the monetary policies adopted during the preceding year.

H. S. GORDON: *The Economists Versus the Bank of Canada*, Toronto, Ryerson Press, 1960.
A pamphlet on the status and recent policies of the Bank of Canada.

T. N. BREWIS, H. E. ENGLISH, A. SCOTT, AND P. JEWETT: 'Monetary Policy', chapter 9 of *Canadian Economic Policy*, Toronto, Macmillan, 1961.
A discussion of monetary policy in a Canadian setting.

---

1. Canada Savings Bonds are reserved for individuals and estates. Unlike other bonds, they are redeemable at par at any time.

E. P. NEUFELD: *Bank of Canada Operations and Policy*, Toronto University of Toronto Press, 1958.
A basic text on the operations of the Bank of Canada.

CANADA: *Report of the Royal Commission on Banking and Finance*, Ottawa, Queen's Printer, 1964. Final report and recommendations of the Commission.

R. C. MCIVOR: *Canadian Monetary, Banking and Fiscal Development*, Toronto, Macmillan, 1958, p. 263.
A useful historical narrative from the early days of New France up to 1956.

BANK OF CANADA: *Statistical Summary*. A monthly publication containing statistical material related to Money and Finance. An annual Supplement is also published covering the same fields.

CHAPTER

10

THE CAPITAL MARKET

There are two kinds of capital: *real* or *material capital, which consists of goods,* and *financial capital, which consists of claims upon others.* The ownership of a real asset is a claim on a thing; the ownership of a financial asset is a claim on a person or corporation. Real assets may be buildings, tools, or equipment; financial assets are bonds, equities, mortgages, and debentures.[1] *By the capital market is meant the total transactions affecting financial capital (or financial claims).*

Currency in circulation is one form of financial claims. (Bank-notes and savings deposits are merely particular kinds of claims.) The stock of money and the institutions creating it may therefore be included in the capital market and, indeed, they are included in the financial transactions accounts that we described in the first chapter and that we shall re-examine later. However, for purposes of the present description, everything dealing with currency and short-term securities has been placed in the preceding chapter under the heading 'The Money Market'. In this chapter we shall restrict ourselves to the examination of transactions in medium- and long-term securities.

---

1. A bond is a title (or a certificate) certifying that the bond-holder has loaned a certain sum of money under certain conditions (interest rate and maturity). An equity is a title of ownership; a mortgage is a claim on a building or a piece of land. The word debenture is generally reserved for bonds issued by private companies without a mortgage clause.

The aim of the first section is to place the financial institutions and the operations they perform in a strict accounting framework. The subsequent sections, B to J, will describe the principal financial institutions. The final section, K, will give a general outline of the capital market.

A. The Place of Financial Institutions in the National Accounts

1. A NATIONAL BALANCE SHEET

The existing capital is a stock or an asset outstanding. It is recorded in a balance sheet. As in the case of a private company a balance sheet can be drawn up for the whole nation. This would be a statement of the national wealth (or assets) in all its forms. Reduced to its essential headings, a national balance sheet would appear as follows:

Assets	*Liabilities*
1. Fixed (or real) assets	1. Net worth (accumulated savings)
2. Claims (financial assets)	2. Debt

The fixed assets consist of the material capital of the country; the claims form the financial capital. There is a correspondence between fixed assets and accumulated savings and between claims and debts.

2. A FINANCIAL TRANSACTIONS ACCOUNT

From the accounting of stocks we turn readily to the accounting of flows, i.e., the accounting of the transactions that have taken place during a certain period of time. To do this we record the changes that have taken place in the items of the balance sheet. Again we find a familiar nomenclature: an increase in real capital is an investment; an increase in claims is the amount of the net loans granted; an increase in net worth is savings; finally, an increase in debt is borrowing. The recording of savings and investments appears in the capital account, as we saw in Chapter 1; the recording of claims and debts appears in the financial transactions account. Here is an example of a financial transactions account.

Debit	Credit
1. Capital formation	1. Savings
2. Loans	2. Stock issues
3. Investments	3. Bond issues
4. Increase in cash holdings	4. Other borrowings

Numbers 2, 3, and 4 in each column are financial transactions proper, i.e., transactions in financial assets; number 1 is a transaction in real capital. It is in this way that the financial system can be connected with the economic activities included in the national product. From this perspective the financial system describes the ways and means by which the financing of economic activity is carried out.

Since we do not as yet have available a national balance sheet for Canada, we can examine neither the national wealth (material assets) nor the stock of financial assets. We do, however, have available certain integrated statistical data pertaining to the financial flows.[1] Table 10:1 shows the financial transactions for the year 1954, the most recent year for which such calculations have been made.

A table of financial transactions of this type is very difficult to interpret. The reader should now arm himself with patience. Let us first re-examine the conventions pertaining to *debit* and *credit* within the context of the financial transactions.

Debit refers to the utilization of funds, i.e., to all the forms in which receipts are retained or utilized. A positive debit is an increase in the assets of the sector under consideration. Thus an increase of bank deposits is a debit for the consumers (column

1. We are here talking about net financial flows. If we buy some securities for $50 and sell others for $30, then total purchases are $50 and net purchases are $20 ($50 - $30).

TABLE 10:1

National Transactions Accounts, millions of dollars, Canada 1954

	Consumers		Business non-financial		Business financial		Government		Rest of the world		Total	
	Dr.	Cr.	Dr.	Cr.	Dr.	Cr.	Dr.	Cr.	Dr.	Cr.	Dr.	Cr.
Saving minus Investment		809		−1,143		38		−131		427		0
1. Currency and deposits	921		180		10	793	−226	2	66	155	950	950
2. Instalment credit		37	62	−20	−45						17	17
3. Loans		98	1	111	148	−52	−17	30		−55	132	132
4. Claims on associated enterprises	85		363	671	36	217	127	2	392	113	1,003	1,003
5. Mortgages	436		8	932	477		11				932	932
6. Federal government bonds	−202		−4	388	306		−175	−573	−110		−185	−185
7. Other bonds and stocks	−12		197	678	538	76	102	338	320	53	1,145	1,145
8. Insurance and pensions	416					354		62			416	416
9. Foreign inheritances and migrants' funds	94	89							89	94	183	183
10. Other transactions and errors	9	715	700	−110	22	66	6	96		−30	737	737
Total	1,748	1,748	1,507	1,507	1,492	1,492	−174	−174	757	757	5,330	5,330

SOURCE: W. C. Hood, *Financing of Economic Activity in Canada*, op. cit., pp. 96 and 505.

2). Loans, the purchase of mortgages, the purchase of equities and bonds, and the payment of insurance premiums, are also debits.

Credit means the origin or source of the funds, i.e., the various ways in which transactors procure for themselves the means of payment. Saving is clearly a credit, but borrowing is also a credit, and so is the issuing of stocks and bonds. This is why the credit side of the financial transactions account corresponds to the liabilities of the balance sheet.

The sector nomenclature in the column headings should cause no difficulties, but certain items in the left-hand column require some explanation.

Saving minus investment is a sum carried over from the income and expenditure account, but the gross formation of real capital has been deducted from it. This amount is therefore the balance of the funds available for investment or for lending to other sectors, for repaying outstanding debts, or for leaving on deposit in the banks. In the case of the consumers this saving is positive ($809 million); for non-financial business it is negative. A negative saving obviously implies a borrowing or a need for borrowing. Governments also incurred a deficit ($131 million). Finally, we observe a positive balance of $427 million in the rest-of-the-world sector. Here we must take careful note: Canadians obtained funds from the rest-of-the-world sector representing the net balance of the international account. In other words, on current account, the balance showed a deficit and Canadians borrowed $427 million from non-residents. Hence it is through borrowing that we acquire additional financial resources, while we dispose of them through making loans. If we had a surplus balance, then by definition we would have been lending to the rest of the world. We would then have had less resources left for the other sectors and the sign affecting that figure would have been negative.

1. Currency and deposits: This item includes gold and foreign currency held by the Exchange Fund, currency and bank deposits, deposits in other institutions (*caisses populaires*, loan and trust companies, etc.). This item is a debit (or an asset) for the depositors and a credit (or a liability) for the institutions accepting the deposits. Consumers increased their holdings of currency and deposits by $921 million in 1954. Governments decreased theirs by $226 million. The financial institutions received the greater part of these deposits, $793 million.

2. *Instalment credit*: credit granted by retail dealers to their customers and by sales finance companies. Consumers made a net borrowing of $37 million, non-financial business made loans in the amount of $62 million and paid back debts of $20 million. Financial business decreased its loans by $45 million.

3. *Loans*: personal loans made by banks, *caisses populaires* and credit unions, and other institutions.

4. *Claims on associated enterprises*: financial transactions between associated institutions such as the financing of a subsidiary by the parent company, transactions between governments and Crown corporations, and claims of consumers on unincorporated enterprises. In fact, consumers increased their participation in individual businesses by the sum of $85 million, a sum that we find included in the increase of $671 million in credits for non-financial business.

5. *Mortgages*: loans guaranteed by a mortgage. Consumers loaned $436 million on mortgages; financial business, $477 million. The borrowers are the non-financial business sector ($932 million). Here we should recall the accounting convention by which transactions involving housing are classed in the business sector.

6, 7. *Stocks and bonds*: All securities are included regardless of term unless classified as claims on associated enterprises. On the debit side are the purchases or the sales (when the sign is negative) of securities, on the credit side the issues or the redemption (when the sign is negative) of securities. Thus consumers sold $202 million worth of federal government bonds. Governments paid off their bonds in the amount of $578 million, and various government agencies sold bonds in the amount of $175 million. Crown corporations, classed in non-financial business, issued bonds guaranteed by the federal government in the amount of $388 million. Finally, non-residents sold federal bonds in the amount of $110 million and bought $320 million worth of stocks and other bonds ($266 million of which were corporate securities).

Care must be taken not to confuse the issue of a bond by a corporation with the sale of a government bond held by the same corporation. The two operations procure funds for the company, but the first increases its liabilities whereas the second decreases the stock of bonds held. In the above accounts the issue of a bond is thus placed on the credit side and the sale of a government bond on the debit side bearing the minus sign.

8. Insurance and pensions: the policyholders' share of the life insurance and pension contracts. What is included in this item is the amount of consumer savings realized through the companies concerned. These savings are equal to the premiums paid less the payments received by the policyholders, plus the investment income of the companies minus their expenditures and profits.

9. Foreign inheritances and migrants' funds: Here are included primarily the funds of persons entering and leaving the country. In 1954 those who left the country took with them $94 million, and those entering brought in $89 million.

10. Other transactions and errors: transfers of existing assets, special deposit and trust accounts, accounts receivable and accounts payable, unclassified transactions, and the residual. The residual may be very large indeed. It amounted to 40 per cent of total consumer transactions in 1954. Students should therefore be reassured: there is still much work to be done in this field.

When we examine this table it becomes evident first of all, *that all sectors play a part in the capital market*. Financial institutions are intermediaries that facilitate the movement of funds from surplus sectors to deficit sectors, but by no means are they the exclusive transactors. As proof of this we note that in 1954 financial institutions effected only 28 per cent of the total financial transactions, $1,492 million out of $5,330 million. (There are several reasons why this figure under-estimates the importance of the financial institutions. We shall correct this later.) When an individual lends to another individual, for example on the guarantee of a mortgage, a financial institution does not enter the picture, but the transaction is none the less a financial one. In short, one must not equate financial institutions with the capital market.

In the second place, there appear in Table 10:1 the main categories of transactions that define the nature of the financial instruments that are exchanged in a capital market. The relative importance assumed by each category of transactions depends mainly on the economic conditions of the year under consideration. The same holds true for the surpluses and deficits of each sector. In 1951 the absolute total of surpluses and deficits in the eleven sectors of the Canadian national accounts represented 28 per cent of the G.N.P., and in 1954, a recession year, only 12 per cent. Although conditions exercise a considerable influence on these figures, we should nevertheless observe that in 1954 the increase in bank deposits contributed 18 per cent of the increase in total assets ($950 million out of $5,330 million), stocks and non-federal bonds 21 per cent, and claims on associated enterprises 18 per cent, which means that these three categories of transactions accounted for about 57 per cent of the total financial transactions. For each of the sectors taken individually, the financial transactions are restricted to a smaller number of categories. Consumers, for example, disposed of their funds by increasing their deposits (50 per cent), by lending on mortgages (25 per cent), and by purchasing life insurance policies and pension contracts (23 per cent). They parted with some of their federal government bonds (−11 per cent) in order to procure these assets, and also borrowed funds ($135 million). Consequently, for consumers the most important financial transactions in 1954 were bank deposits, insurance, and mortgages.

3. THE FINANCIAL INSTITUTIONS

What then are these financial institutions? All those that are tabulated in the Canadian national transactions accounts may be divided into ten groups:

1. banking
2. development corporations
3. *caisses populaires* and credit unions
4. government savings institutions[1]
5. life insurance companies
6. trust companies
7. mortgage loan companies
8. consumer loan companies
9. investment companies
10. other institutions.[1]

In order to complete the list of financial institutions two others should be added. The self-administered or trusteed pension funds are not included in the accounts because of lack of information. The stock exchanges, since they neither buy nor sell securities but merely provide a floor on which other parties may deal, also do not appear.

In the following sections we shall describe the nature and functioning of most of the financial institutions listed above. Number 1 has been treated in the previous chapter; numbers 4 and 10 will not be discussed here; but we shall deal with pension funds and with the stock exchanges.

B. The Stock Exchange

From the institutional point of view a stock exchange is a non-profit company formed by stockbrokers in order to facilitate

---

1. The government savings institutions are the Post Office Savings Bank, the Province of Ontario Savings Office, and the Alberta Treasury Branches. The total deposits in 1964 were $210 million. The other institutions include the fire and casualty companies, the fraternal benefit societies, certain government lending institutions such as the Agricultural Loans Commission, and government insurance institutions for such things as export credit.

trade in securities. The securities are the stocks and bonds of corporations and governments.[1] From the economic point of view a stock exchange is a market where securities are bought and sold. On the Montreal Stock Exchange, companies are not permitted to offer new issues of their shares; for this reason the Montreal Stock Exchange is said to be a secondary market. Companies listed on the Canadian Stock Exchange (also in Montreal) do have this privilege, and so both new shares and shares already held by the public are listed; the Canadian Stock Exchange is thus both a primary and a secondary market. The Toronto Stock Exchange is also both a primary and a secondary market.

After the shares of a given company have been listed on an exchange, each owner of shares is entitled to sell them, and they may be purchased through the intermediary of individuals or firms who, as members of the exchange, are authorized to engage in such trading.

1. HISTORICAL

The origin of stock exchanges goes back to the founding of the Amsterdam Exchange in 1602. In London, a hundred and fifty brokers joined together in 1762 in an association to encourage and regulate trading in securities. In 1773 these brokers moved into permanent quarters in the first stock exchange building in the world – the building that is still used for the same purpose today.

In Canada trading in securities dates from 1832 when the shares of the railway company that was to link St-Jean with Montreal were bought and sold. In 1863 eleven Montreal brokers formed a 'Board of Stock Brokers', but it was not until 1874 that the Montreal Stock Exchange was officially established, one hundred years after the London Exchange. When

1. Government and corporation bonds were formerly traded on Canadian stock exchanges. However, the practice has been discontinued altogether in Montreal and only a small number of bond transactions take place on the Toronto exchange, so that for all practical purposes we may say that only equities are traded on Canadian exchanges.

operations began, sixty-three securities were listed and about eight hundred shares a day were traded. By 1914 there were 182 listings and the daily trading volume was about 10,000 shares.

The Montreal Curb Market was founded in 1926. This second exchange was designed primarily to accommodate companies engaged in the exploration and exploitation of natural resources such as mines, natural gas, and oil. The shares traded are more speculative than those of the Montreal Stock Exchange, the conditions required for listing are less restrictive, the price of seats is lower, and so forth. In 1953 the name was changed to the Canadian Stock Exchange. In addition to the two Montreal exchanges there are exchanges in Toronto, Vancouver, Calgary, and Winnipeg. The Toronto Stock Exchange is by far the most active.

2. ORGANIZATION

The members of an exchange are individuals who have each bought a seat, i.e., the right to deal on the floor of the exchange. A member may be an individual trading on his own account or for other brokers or a partner or director of a brokerage firm. The Montreal exchange had seventy-seven members and the Canadian exchange ninety at the end of 1963. Since sixty-two members held seats on both exchanges, the combined membership was 105. The Toronto exchange had ninety-eight members, the Vancouver exchange forty-five, and the Winnipeg exchange thirty. The number of members is relatively small but it increased by 25 per cent between 1950 and 1963. The price of seats varies considerably from one year to another. In 1929 a seat on the Montreal exchange was worth $225,000, and a seat on the Canadian exchange $50,000. Prices were $35,000 and $9,000 respectively in 1964.[1]

The members of each exchange elect a board of directors annually. They share in the cost of the services of a president, vice-president, and secretary, who are all employed full time and

1. On the New York exchange a seat was sold for $250,000 in the summer of 1966.

are selected from non-members of the exchange.

The stock exchange as such has no financial interest in the securities that are exchanged on the floor, nor does it share in any way in the profits made by the buyers and sellers. Its essential aim is to encourage trading in securities while protecting the savings of the public. Its income is derived from the subscriptions paid by its members and by the companies whose shares are listed. Its activities are related to the acceptance of new members, the control of trading, the listing of company shares, and public information and general regulations.

There are relatively strict rules of admission to membership. As well as providing ample guarantees of honesty and solvency (with required amounts of capital), a candidate must be presented and sponsored by two members and must obtain the votes of a substantial proportion of the membership – two-thirds in Montreal, four-fifths in Toronto. Independent brokers are being replaced more and more by partners or directors of stockbroking firms.

Trading in securities is subject to very detailed regulations. The public interest is particularly involved with the listing requirements and the stipulations concerning credit margins and brokerage fees.

Equally strict, particularly on the Montreal exchange, are the requirements that a company must meet in order to have its shares listed. The Montreal Stock Exchange requires that it already have at least 300 shareholders, the Canadian Exchange 100; 20 to 25 per cent of the equities must be held by the public and must be available for trading in the market. While 'consistent earnings' is the general rule followed by the Toronto Stock Exchange for admitting industrial securities on the exchange, consideration is also given to the company's size and resources. Assets of $1 million and a working capital of $250,000 qualify a firm for listing if its earning potential is satisfactory. Each exchange (in theory at least) requires that the company provide complete information on its activities, on its financial situation, and on anything that is capable of influencing the price of its shares. Each reserves the right (and exercises this right from time to time) to suspend or withdraw from trading on the exchange the shares of any company if it considers that trading may injure the public interest in any way. These requirements, in a sense, are never adequate. There is still ample room for improvements, as the 1965 collapse of a large finance company illustrates. The 1964 *Report of the Royal Commission on Banking and Finance* suggested a number of measures to get more orderly trading of securities.

The stock exchange has its own language. While this language may seem mysterious to some of us, its mystery does not lie in its profundity but rather in the special terms used by its initiates. This is the mark of any well-organized profession, and stockbrokers, with their long tradition, are no exception.

Basically it is all very simple. In a large hall, which is called the 'floor', are the 'floor traders' or simply 'traders', who carry out the buying and selling orders of their clients. Two kinds of influence affect the price of a stock: the influence of definite objective facts relating to the stock's profit-earning potential, such as payment of a higher or lower dividend, or success or failure in obtaining an important contract; and the influence of fortuitous events or of subjective evaluations on the part of the buyers and sellers (as, for example, when ten large shareholders, with no prearranged plan, sell the stock on the same morning because they need money, or when an announcement is made that the President of the United States has come down with bronchitis). The stock exchange is the typical example of a perfectly competitive market in which price variations depend, not on the relatively stable costs of production, but on supply and demand which may change at any moment.

The forms assumed by transactions are numerous and complex. The techniques and conventions are too varied to be described here.[1] Let us examine only the roles of the investment dealers.

---

1. In this connection the vocabulary is important, and several expressions follow: Customers may give orders on listed stocks *at market price* or as *limit orders*,

There are several types of dealers. The *stockbroker* generally does not buy or sell for his own account but only for his customers. His income derives from his commissions. The dealer acting for his own account is the *jobber*, and his income results from the difference in the price at which he buys and the price at which he sells. The *floor trader* engages in transactions on the floor of the exchange only for the accounts of other dealers. Finally, the *arbitrage broker* buys shares in order to sell them on another exchange; thus, while he makes a profit on the price differences, at the same time his operations reduce these differences to a minimum. On the Montreal and Toronto exchanges arbitrage operations with each other and with New York and London are very important. In 1962, for example, they made up a quarter of all operations on the Montreal Stock Exchange.

The *investment dealer* not only may deal in outstanding issues but also may act as the underwriter for a new issue. In this case he buys a company stock issue at a discount and then sells the shares to the public. Formerly these various functions of the dealers were kept scrupulously separate. Today a brokerage house usually performs several roles at once. To prevent this mixing of roles from being detrimental to the interests of shareholders, the exchanges usually insist that members give the orders of their customers priority over the orders of their brokerage houses.

---

the first of these being carried out without condition, the second at a stipulated minimum or maximum price. The client may speculate on a rise in price (*bull*) or on a fall (*bear*); he may buy for cash or on margin, or he may sell short. *Margin* is the allowable proportion of the current price that the client-buyer may owe to the broker. The buyer in this case is buying on credit. *Selling short* consists of selling stock that one does not own and that one will buy later when the market has dropped. The *stop order* is a limit order that stipulates neither a minimum price (for a sale) nor a maximum price (for a purchase) but the actual price. *Over-the-counter* trading takes place in unlisted stocks. Shares not sold in 'board' lots are sold in odd (broken) lots. 'Odd-lots are blocks of fewer than 100 shares for most industrial securities selling below $25 a share, fewer than 25 shares of securities selling between $25 and $100 and fewer than 10 shares if the stock sells at $100 or more.' *Report of the Royal Commission on Banking and Finance*, p. 340.

The stock exchange regulates credit by establishing the percentage of margin with which the buyer must comply. At the present time margin is set by the stock exchanges at 50 per cent in Canada. This means that the buyer can buy a share for $10 by paying $5 cash and borrowing $5 from the dealer. If the price of the share goes down to $8, since the allowed credit margin is now only $4, the buyer must then cover by paying $1 to his dealer. In other words the percentage of cover must be constantly maintained. The dealers lend the money required for these transactions, and the stock exchange sets the rate of interest to be charged. The present rate is fixed at 1 per cent above the prime rate of the chartered banks.[1] The margin allowed on the purchase of bonds is only from 1 to 10 per cent. No margin is given on shares selling for less than $1. It is estimated that in Montreal 20 per cent of the shares are traded on margin.

The Canadian stock exchanges do not often make changes in their margin requirements. In the United States, the Federal Reserve Board controls stock margins and uses them to regulate credit. The margin on shares was set at 70 per cent for a fairly long period of time. Today it is fixed at 50 per cent as in Canada, but is required only at the time of purchase and is not maintained afterwards.

3. THE TRANSACTIONS

The Montreal and Toronto stock exchanges are small exchanges in comparison with those in the main financial centres of the world such as London, New York, Chicago, and Paris. At the end of 1963, 785 stocks were listed on the Montreal Stock Exchange and 1,100 on the Toronto Exchange; but 10,000 and

---

1. The Bank of Canada, contrary to what is often said, exercises an influence on stock exchange credit in two ways: (a) by its loans to authorized investment dealers; (b) by changing the liquidity reserves of the chartered banks, which leads to a change in the prime bank interest rate and hence in the cost of stock exchange credit. Moreover, the chartered banks affect exchange credit by their loans to stockbrokers and investment dealers, by their day-to-day loans, and, of course, by the interest rate charged. Finally, banks also loan directly to investors.

2,800 were listed on the London and Paris exchanges respectively. The current value of the stocks listed on the two Montreal exchanges and in Toronto is almost the same ($52 billion each at the end of 1961), but the Toronto exchange is twice as active as the Montreal exchanges. The value of shares traded in Montreal was $1,251 million, in Toronto $3,199 million, during the year 1965. (The current value on the New York exchange was $307 billion in 1959.) But as the price of shares keeps changing constantly, so does the total value. In Montreal the $52 billion at the end of 1961 had become $45 billion six months later, and reached $100 billion at the end of 1965.

The activity of a stock exchange is measured by the volume or the value of the securities traded on it. Table 10:2 gives the value of the shares that changed hands in each of the years 1960 to 1965.

The trading in shares in Canada reached $4.4 billion in 1965. It should again be pointed out, however, that this trading is subject to very wide fluctuations. On the New York Stock Exchange, trading amounted to about $83 billion in 1965.

TABLE 10:2

**Value of shares traded, based on monthly averages
Montreal and Toronto,* millions of dollars, 1960-65**

1960	1,704
1961	3,376
1962	2,887
1963	3,018
1964	4,174
1965	4,450

*Trading on the four other exchanges in Canada amounts to about 3 per cent of total Canadian trading.

SOURCE: *Canadian Statistical Review.*

In a study carried out by the Montreal stock exchanges for the month of June 1962, it was found that half the investors on the two Montreal exchanges were individuals, 30 per cent were members of the exchanges acting for their own account, and 20 per cent were other financial institutions. This is one among many indications of the importance of the financial intermediaries in the capital market. The members' relatively large share of stock exchange transactions (for arbitrage and investment purposes) is a sign that the market is both rather narrow and also strongly influenced by the exchanges of neighbouring cities (hence the importance of the arbitrage operations). Table 10:3 compares the Montreal and New York stock exchanges in these respects.

TABLE 10:3

Number of Shares Traded as a percentage of the total

	Individuals	*Member institutions*	*Other institutions*
Montreal	50.4	29.8	19.8
New York	51.4	22.4	26.2

SOURCE: Submission of the two Montreal exchanges to the Royal Commission on Banking and Finance, 1962.

What part does speculation play on a stock exchange? This question may be answered by showing for how many months

TABLE 10:4

Motivations of Individual Investors expressed as a percentage of shares held for certain periods of time

	6 months and more	*1 to 6 months*	*30 days and less*
Montreal	35.2	35.7	29.1
New York	62.0	28.5	9.5

SOURCE: Submission of the two Montreal exchanges to the Royal Commission on Banking and Finance, 1962.

investors hold on to their shares. In comparison with New York, the Montreal market is much more speculative.

4. THE STOCK MARKET

At this point a few observations on the capital stock market in Canada are called for. These observations, however, will necessarily be incomplete since very little is known about the capital structure of corporations.

During each of the four years 1961 to 1964, corporations, institutions, and governments issued in Canada $2.5 billion to $3 billion worth of securities of all categories (on a net basis: issues less retirements). About 90 per cent of these securities were bonds (borrowings) and 10 per cent were preferred and common stocks (equities). Table 10:5 shows the net stock issues for seven of the years 1956 to 1964.

TABLE 10:5

Net New Issues of Corporate Stocks, Canada, selected years, millions of dollars

	Preferred stocks	Common stocks	Total
1956	175	367	689
1958	25	287	312
1960	37	183	220
1962	66	275	341
1963	48	−103	55
1964	43	250	293

NOTES: When the figure is negative the issues are lower than the retirements.

In 1963 the figures are affected by the redemption of $345 million worth of common stocks and $55 million worth of preferred stocks through the nationalization of the Quebec electric companies.

SOURCE: *Bank of Canada Statistical Summary.*

The major part of new issues in Canada is bought nowadays by the financial institutions. As we shall see later when we deal with the investment companies, three-quarters ($300 million) of the net issues for 1959 ($404 million) were acquired by financial institutions and non-residents, leaving about $100 million for other Canadian investors. Among financial institutions, the investment companies and the pension funds absorbed a very large portion of these stocks. In good times, however, the public usually buys a larger proportion than in this instance (50 per cent of the net issues in 1956 and 1957).

Three hundred million dollars' worth of stock issues in a year is small compared to the $100 billion already in circulation, compared to the $42.5 billion worth of assets held by the financial institutions, and compared to the productive capacity of the country as a whole. Moreover, the life insurance companies estimate that they can buy only about a hundred different Canadian stocks. The reason is that only three hundred stocks fulfil the legal condition of having produced dividends for seven years and two hundred of these are not offered on the market. The capital stock market in Canada is obviously quite narrow and lacking in diversity.

The capital stock issues assume a new significance when they are considered in relation to all the sources of funds on which corporations are able to draw during a certain period of time. According to the Montreal exchanges' study, two-thirds of the funds acquired for net investment (gross investment less depre-

TABLE 10:6

Sources of Funds of
603 Corporations Listed on the Montreal Stock Exchange,
1936-61, as a percentage of the total

Non-distributed profits	66
Bonds	16
Preferred stocks	2
Common stocks	16
Total	100

ciation) come from non-distributed profits, 16 per cent from bond issues, and 18 per cent from stock issues.

If calculations are made on the basis of gross rather than net investment, non-distributed profits contribute 82 per cent of the funds. The proportion contributed by non-distributed profits tends, on the whole, to be larger when the corporations are smaller. These figures call into question the commonly accepted capital theory, for they lend support to the view that investment is more dependent upon profits already realized than upon expected profits. Moreover, they reduce the importance that we should attach to the market as a provider of funds.

One could say a good deal about the individuals who invest: about the influence of income and assets on individual investment, about motivations, about attitudes to security and to risk, and so forth.

We shall content ourselves with reporting the conclusions of several studies on the subject. The proportion of the total population that acquires financial assets is quite low and depends essentially on income. In the United States it is 14 per cent, and in Canada, 9.2 per cent. In Quebec it is 5.4 per cent. Quebec investors own more stocks relative to other investments than Ontario investors, a fact that appears to indicate that the Québécois are less afraid of risk. This conclusion is based on the ratio of dividend income to total investment income. In Quebec 37.8 per cent of investment income is made up of dividends; in Ontario, 33.8 per cent. Dividends plus rents collected make up 58.8 per cent of investment income in Quebec, 48.3 per cent in Ontario.[1]

5. THE BOND MARKET

Mention is often made of the 'over-the-counter market'. This expression covers all buying and selling of securities elsewhere than on the stock exchange. Most of the securities so traded are bonds: bonds of the federal, provincial, and municipal govern-

---

1. Brief to the Royal Commission on Banking and Finance, submitted by the two Montreal stock exchanges, pp. 49 and 163.

ments, and bonds and debentures of private corporations, all of which could be traded on the exchange but are not. Numerous stocks are also traded 'over the counter', but for stocks, the Canadian over-the-counter market is much smaller than the exchange market, in contrast to the situation in the United States where the opposite prevails.

Table 10:7 provides some figures on the importance of the bond market in Canada.

TABLE 10:7

**Net New Issues of Bonds,
Canada 1956 and 1964,
millions of dollars**

	1956	*1964*
Government of Canada	−766	456
treasury bills and notes	(−616)	(−100)
bonds	(−150)	(556)
Provincial governments	540	929
Municipalities	224	428
Corporate bonds	791	695
Other bonds	6	2
Finance companies paper	94	292
Total	889	2,801

SOURCE: *Bank of Canada Statistical Summary.*

Let us consider first the net issues of bonds. In 1964 financing through borrowing totalled $2.8 billion. Of this total $989 million went to the private sector; the rest served to finance current deficits and investments of the public sector. A comparison of the figures for the years 1956 and 1964 in Table 10:7 enables us to measure the influence of economic conditions on the very different cash needs of the two sectors. The figures for 1964 also reflect the immense needs of the public sector for equipment.

The net issues do not take into account either total issues or trading on the secondary market. In 1961, for example, the member dealers of the Investment Dealers Association alone sold $15 billion of bonds of all categories.

A better idea of the importance of the bond market may be gained by totalling the value of bonds in existence at a given moment than by noting the total bond issues for any one year.

TABLE 10:8

**Outstanding Bonds, billions of dollars,
Canada 1964**

Treasury bills	2.1
Government of Canada marketable bonds (direct and guaranteed)	13.0
Canada Savings Bonds	5.6
Provincial (direct and guaranteed)	11.1
Municipal (direct and guaranteed)	5.1
Corporate	8.6
Institutional	0.3
Total	45.8

SOURCE: *Bank of Canada Statistical Summary.*

Plainly the public sector predominates in total bonds on the market. In 1964, 80 per cent of all bonds outstanding were government bonds. To be sure, bonds are not the only way of borrowing money. In section K of this chapter the figures of Table 10:8 will be completed so that the economy's total indebtedness can be examined. Nevertheless, these figures are significant as they stand.

On page 187 the principal holders of Government of Canada bonds were listed. Perhaps at this point we should indicate briefly who are the holders of corporate bonds. In 1963, 38 per cent were held by non-residents and 47 per cent by financial institutions. Among the institutions, the life insurance companies had the largest portfolio: one-quarter of all corporate bonds.[1] Before the war, non-residents held 56 per cent, but this important source of debt capital has markedly declined. The decline, however, has been largely compensated for by a rise in the holdings of stocks by non-residents. It is this switch in the holdings of Canadian securities by non-residents that has caused concern among Canadians.

C. The Investment Companies

1. CONCEPT

Investment companies are 'institutions which, by the sale of their own shares, accumulate the financial resources of several subscribers in a single fund, the purpose of which is to acquire for investment purposes a diversified and regularly supervised portfolio of financial assets of which all the associates share in the profits according to the extent of their participation'.[2]

An investment company combines the savings of investors and buys securities without taking over control of any enterprise. To the investors it offers its own shares at a price that varies according to the return on the whole of its investments.

A distinction should be made between the two main kinds of investment companies:

The mutual funds (or open-end investment companies)[3] will issue or redeem their shares at any time. The mutual funds generally are non-leverage companies in the sense that they do not have priority-claim capital in the form of preferred stocks or

---

1. *Bank of Canada Statistical Summary.*

2. Jean-Claude Faffa, *Les Sociétés d'investissement et la gestion collective de l'épargne*, Paris, Edition Cujas, 1963, p. 351. It deals with American companies. See also William C. Hood, *Financing of Economic Activity in Canada*, Ottawa, pp. 319-31.

3. In England, the mutual funds are sometimes called unit trusts.

bonds (see page 190). The shares vary in price from day to day according to the numbers sold and redeemed.

The investment trusts (or closed-end investment companies) have a relatively fixed amount of capital stock and do not redeem their shares. In general, investment trusts increase their resources by the issue of bonds or preferred shares.

The share certificate of an investment company must not be confused with the guaranteed savings certificate issued by trust companies (see page 237) and other financial institutions. Like a bond, the latter guarantees payment on a certain due date. The share of an investment company is a true share with constantly changing value.

2. HISTORICAL

Investment companies probably originated when William I founded the Société Générale de Belgique in 1822. But it was the English trust companies promoted by Robert Fleming in 1873 that really gave investment trusts a firm footing. The certificates of a typical investment trust of that time bore interest at 6 or 7 per cent and the portfolio, which contained from thirty to fifty different bonds, divided the risks and brought in a return of 8 or 9 per cent. At an early date the investment trusts began to issue bonds in order to benefit from the difference between the return on the portfolio and the cost of the bonds.[1] Then the share certificates were exchanged at par or at a discount on the open market. By combining his own funds with those of others in an investment trust, the small investor had the advantage of a diversified portfolio administered by 'experts'. In addition to obtaining a superior return on his investment, the investor could

---

1. This is what is called 'gearing' in England, 'leverage' in the United States. It is a common practice in Canadian investment clubs. A share worth 100 brings in 10 per cent at the end of a year. The company borrows another 100 at an interest rate of 5 per cent, using the original share as security, and lends it at 10 per cent. The share of 100 therefore finally produces a return of 15 per cent.

also consider that he had a security almost equal to that provided by government bonds.

The founding of the Boston Personal Property Trust in 1893 introduced the investment trust into the United States. In Canada, where such companies appeared about 1920, the most important was the Canadian Power and Paper Investments Limited. The closed-end investment trusts, patterned on the original English trusts, had a very promising and rapid development towards the end of the nineteenth century in England and during the 1920s in the United States and Canada. In 1929, Canada had forty-nine investment trusts controlling assets worth $265 million.

The progress of the investment trusts was of short duration, however. Although today they still lead a quiet and comfortable existence, they have given way to the exuberance of the mutual funds. From 1941 to 1962 investment trusts in the United States multiplied their assets by three, to $1.7 billion, and mutual funds by fifty-five, to $21.2 billion. The first mutual fund dates back to 1924 when the Massachusetts Investors Trust was founded in the United States; the first in Canada began in 1932.

3. FUNCTIONING

The main purpose for the existence of investment companies is to permit the savings of individual investors to be managed by professional administrators. It is 'investment by proxy'. But unlike trust companies, which invest separately the savings of each contributor, the investment companies create common funds that offer the security of all the financial assets that the funds were used to purchase. The risk is spread over the whole portfolio. Investment companies are also different from trust companies in that their portfolios hold mainly *common stocks* rather than mortgages or bonds.

The Income Tax Act (Section 69) reveals an additional characteristic of investment companies: they are not taxed like other enterprises. The Act recognizes that an investment company is to a certain extent only an intermediary and that the dividends received should not be taxed twice.[1] But in order to benefit by this statute, the investment company must fulfil certain conditions, of which these three are the most important:

1. at least 80 per cent of its assets must consist of shares, bonds, marketable securities, or cash;
2. at least 95 per cent of its gross revenue must come from investments;
3. at least 85 per cent of the gross income less taxes must have been distributed to shareholders before the end of the year.

Other conditions provide that the portfolio must be diversified, that the number of shareholders must be at least fifty, and that preference must be given to Canadian securities.

Rule 3 prevents these companies from accumulating large reserves; the rule is a logical one, since the reason for the tax concessions is that the companies operate only for and in the name of their shareholders.

The techniques of subscription to mutual funds and to investment trusts are completely different. The mutual funds sell their shares to the public through brokers or through their own sales agents (like the insurance companies). The buyer pays a commission varying between 8 and 10 per cent of the price of the shares. The shares of the investment trusts, on the other hand, are bought on the stock exchange at the much lower exchange-commission rates. The costs of subscription to the mutual funds, and the general management costs of all investment companies, are a serious handicap: they can amount to more than a year of the subscriber's revenue from his investment. Attempts have been made in the United States to reduce such costs, but with little apparent success.

Investment policies vary markedly between companies: it has

1. The Act does not eliminate double taxation completely. In 1964 the investment companies were taxed at a reduced rate of 21 per cent of the profits.

been said that formerly an investor used to ask a broker's advice on what shares to buy, but now he must ask a broker's advice on what broker to use. The large companies usually offer the investor a choice between participating in a common fund of stocks, a common fund of bonds, or a combination of both. Generally, the greater the risk the higher the return will be on the investment. Some companies concentrate their investments in certain industries, for instance the 'new' industries, the 'mining' industries, the 'growth' industries. But whatever the label of the concentration, the corporations favoured by the investment companies are often the same. In a study of 175 investment companies in the United States in 1960, fifty favourite stocks were found in forty portfolios, thirty favourite stocks were found in fifty portfolios, ten favourite stocks were found in seventy portfolios.[1] The fifty favourite stocks are the most important and best-known corporations in the country. This heavy concentration of investments is explained by the necessity (particularly for the mutual funds) of holding highly liquid securities and of being able to win and keep the confidence of their customers. In Canada the major portion of such investments is divided among seventy Canadian and a few American companies.

Some shrewd persons have suggested – and their observations have been confirmed by rigorous analyses – that if the investment companies that consult the best financial experts, the most scientific research specialists, and the most experienced analysts all end by concentrating their investments in the largest enterprises, then perhaps individual investors should simply do this in a systematic way without the preliminary analyses. The fact is that on the whole the investment companies have not realized returns any higher than the average rate of return as given by the common indices of stock prices; this indicates that the experts' portfolios are no more profitable than the average portfolios as given by the market. Certain studies even indicate that

1. J.-C. Faffa, *op. cit.*, p. 161.

the experts have sometimes built portfolios from which the return was lower than the average return of the aggregate of all securities.[1]

4. IMPORTANCE

Information is badly lacking concerning the investment companies operating in Canada. We do know that there were twenty-three recorded investment trusts and sixty-five recorded mutual funds at the end of 1962.

TABLE 10:9

Assets of Certain Mutual Funds, 1964

	In millions of dollars	As a percentage of the total
Cash and bills receivable	73	6.4
Bonds and debentures	159	14.0
Canadian preferred shares	72	6.3
Canadian common shares	623	54.7
Foreign preferred and common shares	178	15.6
Other assets	35	3.0
Total assets	1140	100

NOTE: Portfolio at cost. The market value at the end of 1964 was $322 million over cost.
SOURCE: *Bank of Canada Statistical Summary.*

There are a great many mutual fund shareholders – the number in Canada in 1962 was nearly 300,000.

Tables 10:9 and 10:10 give the distribution of the assets of

---

1. Jean-Claude Faffa cites in support of this two research studies of the United States Securities Exchange Commission and the periodical studies of the *Forbes Financial Review, op. cit.*, pp. 184-97. It appears that the investment companies show returns higher than the stock indices in periods of falling prices and lower than the indices during periods of rising prices.

TABLE 10:10

Assets of Certain Investment Trusts (closed-end funds) 1964

	In millions of dollars	*As a percentage of the total*
Cash and bills receivable	8	1.8
Bonds and debentures	14	3.2
Canadian preferred shares	33	7.5
Canadian common shares	295	66.7
Other assets	92	20.8
Total	442	100

NOTE: Portfolio at cost. The market value at the end of 1964 was $333 million over cost.
SOURCE: *Bank of Canada Statistical Summary.*

certain mutual funds and investment trusts. Investment in common stocks is the main feature of their activity, representing about two-thirds of the total assets in 1964. The two categories together totalled assets of $1.6 billion at cost and $2.2 billion at current market prices.

Since the investment companies are the only financial institutions to invest mostly in common stocks, they exercise a definite influence on the securities market and hold first place among the financial institutions in the size of their stock holdings and in the extent of their trading on the stock exchanges.

In 1959 private financial institutions in the United States held 13.4 per cent of the common stocks outstanding, and among these institutions the investment companies were in first place with 4.5 per cent. In the same year, financial institutions acquired three-quarters of the net issues, with the investment companies accounting for one-third of this, or one-quarter of the total. It is estimated that from one-quarter to one-third of all trading on the New York Stock Exchange is attributable to the investment companies.[1]

1. Figures taken from J.-C. Faffa, *op. cit.*, pp. 244 ff.

According to fragmentary information, investment companies in Canada seem to share with the pension funds the honour of being the main institutional shareholders in the economy. In 1959, for example, the financial institutions acquired nearly $300 million worth, or 73 per cent, of the $404 million value of the net issues of stocks. Among the Canadian institutions,[1] investment companies come first with $77 million, which represents 18 per cent of the issues. The portfolios of the investment companies represented 3.26 per cent of the Canadian common stocks listed on the Montreal and Toronto exchanges in 1959. In this respect the investment companies are twice as important as the pension funds (1.65 per cent in 1959).[2]

D. Development Corporations

The purposes of development corporations as the term is used here are to extend medium- and long-term loans and to create or acquire enterprises. In recent years a substantial number of development corporations have been established. RoyNat Limited (1962), a joint venture of the Royal Bank of Canada, La Banque Canadienne Nationale, and three trust companies, is a good example taken from the private sector. Another is Canadian Enterprise Development Corporation Limited (C.E.D.). But most of the others in this category of institutions were started at the government's initiative. So it was with the Industrial Development Bank and with Quebec's General Investment Corporation, both of which will be described below.

Crown corporations of this type or related types were to be found in eight provinces in 1966: Alberta Investment Fund (1966), the Saskatchewan Economic Development Fund (1963), the Manitoba Development Fund (1959), the Ontario Development Agency (1963), the New Brunswick Development Corporation (1963), the Industrial Estates in Nova Scotia

---

1. Non-residents purchased $140 million.

2. Figures quoted from the brief of the Investment Dealers Association of Canada to the Royal Commission on Banking and Finance.

(1958), and Industrial Enterprises in Prince Edward Island (1965), as well as the General Investment Corporation in Quebec (1962) already mentioned. In addition to these, the federal government proposed on April 26, 1965, to set up a $100-million Canada Development Corporation. At the time of writing this corporation has not yet been established.[1]

1. THE INDUSTRIAL DEVELOPMENT BANK

Object. The Industrial Development Bank is a public enterprise, a wholly owned subsidiary of the Bank of Canada. The Bank of Canada subscribed all its outstanding stock, buys all its bonds and debentures, and has the same board of directors.

Founded in 1944 to aid small and medium-sized business firms, the Industrial Development Bank got off to a slow start. Even today its operations are modest: in 1962 its net advances of funds did not exceed $42 million and in 1964 they amounted to $23 million. It is not that few small businesses need loans, but that the original policy was to make the Bank a lender of last resort, as it were. Thus it must never advance a loan until it has made certain that no other source of credit is available. This rule, which reflects the existence in Canada of particularly strong feelings against the involvement of government enterprises in business, has the unfortunate effect of preventing small businesses from having ready access to long-term credit.[2]

1. For a discussion of the proposal, and an assessment, see the twenty-one-page pamphlet by E. P. Neufeld, *The Canadian Development Corporation*, Canadian Trade Committee, Private Planning Association of Canada, Montreal, February 1966.

2. The Industrial Development Bank and to a lesser extent the Central Mortgage and Housing Corporation are two examples of an unfortunate tradition in this country. Initially, private enterprise is incapable of providing certain important services because of a restricted market. The government then sets up enterprises to provide these services, but it limits their activities in many ways: for instance, by placing a ceiling on the interest rates they can charge, by strictly defining their services, by reducing their sources of funds from time to time. Thus, the state prevents them from making a vigorous response to existing needs, while at the same time, through the very existence of these enterprises with the competition they represent, preventing or discouraging private business firms from later entering markets that have become attractive with the passage of time.

The principal activity of the Industrial Development Bank is the granting of medium-term loans to provide fixed capital (the average term in 1962 being seven years), while the chartered banks generally provide loans for working capital. The large corporations, already known to the investing public, issue stocks and bonds to raise their capital funds; but small and new businesses find it difficult to do this, not only because their securities are almost unsaleable but also because the costs of floating a small issue are extremely high. The Industrial Development Bank therefore provides an almost indispensable form of credit. It does not seek to acquire a controlling interest in the debtor companies. Other sources of credit sometimes do.

TABLE 10:11

Industrial Development Bank Loans, millions of dollars, selected years, financial year ending September 30

	Number of loans made	Value of loans	Net disbursements*	Value of loans out-standing
1956	349	39.4	8.1	52.2
1959	599	30.6	8.0	96.9
1962	2,085	92.0	41.7	164.9
1964	2,083	88.2	23.3	224.2

*Disbursements less repayments.

SOURCES: *Bank of Canada Statistical Summary* and Annual Report of the I.D.B.

The factor determining the granting of credits is the present and future profit-earning potential of the business firm requesting the loan. Until July 1961, the Industrial Development Bank Act forced the Bank to limit its loans to manufacturing and other stipulated industries, but since then all restrictions on the nature of the borrowing enterprise have fortunately been lifted. There are no regulations regarding regional distribution of the funds. Consequently, almost two-thirds have gone to Ontario and

Quebec, where manufacturing industry is concentrated. In 1964, Ontario obtained 32 per cent (by value) of the loans granted by the Bank, Quebec received 28 per cent, the three prairie provinces 21 per cent, and British Columbia 12 per cent. In 1957 the corresponding percentages were Quebec, 33 per cent; Ontario, 30.4 per cent; prairie provinces, 11.1 per cent; British Columbia, 16.4 per cent.

Half of the loans made in 1962 were less than $25,000. The Bank rarely grants loans in excess of $1,000,000.

The Act places no ceiling on the interest rates to be charged by the Industrial Development Bank; they must be sufficiently high to cover all expenses and ensure a fair return on the investment. In practice they have been traditionally fixed at ½ to 1 per cent above the prime interest rates of the chartered banks. They are therefore higher than the rates charged by other government lending institutions, but generally lower than or equivalent to those on ordinary mortgage loans. Table 10:12 provides figures for comparison.

TABLE 10:12

Interest Rates of the I.D.B. compared with those of other institutions

	I.D.B.	Chartered banks	C.M.H.C.	Farm Credit Corporation	Mortgage loans
Nov. 1944	5	4½	4½	5	5
Apr. 1952	6	4½	4½	5	6
Sept. 1956	6½	5¼	5½	5	6¼
Oct. 1959	7	5¾	6	5	7
Sept. 1960	7	6	6¾	5	7¼

SOURCE: Report of the I.D.B. to the Royal Commission on Banking and Finance, 1963.

Sources of funds. The Industrial Development Bank obtains its funds from its capital, from its reserves, and from the issue of bonds. The capital has been provided by the Bank of Canada. The amount authorized by law is $50 million and the paid-up capital was $35 million on September 30, 1964. The accumulated profits constitute the reserves; capital and reserves reached $58 million on December 31, 1964. Since 1951 the Industrial Development Bank has been obtaining supplementary funds in accordance with its needs through the issue of bonds; up to the present, issues have been sold to the Bank of Canada. At the end of 1964 outstanding bonds amounted to $180 million. The Act fixes the maximum amount of bonds that can be issued at five times the net worth (capital plus reserves).

The Industrial Development Bank pays to the Bank of Canada an interest rate on its bonds that is slightly higher than that on federal bonds of the same maturity. As the I.D.B. increases its operations and as it obtains more of its financing from bonds, the weight of its interest charges becomes heavier: see Table 10:13.

TABLE 10:13

Interest Charges of the Industrial Development Bank

	Average interest rate of bonds issued	*Average interest rate of loans granted*	*Interest charges on loans as a percentage of total expenditures*
1956	3.35	6.04	12
1959	4.81	6.34	34
1962	4.78	6.54	46

SOURCE: Report of the I.D.B., *op. cit.*

This writer believes it unwise for the Industrial Development Bank to continue to supply itself with funds exclusively from the Bank of Canada. The bonds of the Industrial Development Bank are an additional constraint on the Bank of Canada in its role as regulator of the money market. This constraint, added to several others, limits the freedom of action of the Bank of Canada. More important, by identifying itself more with the private financial institutions, the I.D.B. could play a more active role without being accused of unfair competition.

2. THE GENERAL INVESTMENT CORPORATION

The General Investment Corporation (G.I.C.) was founded on July 6, 1962, on the initiative of the government of Quebec. It is a semi-public or mixed institution: both public and private capital participate. Among the subscribers of private capital the *caisses populaires* have a privileged place. On condition that they each hold at least a third of the common shares, the government and the *caisses populaires* are each permitted to name three out of the twelve members of the Board of Directors.

The share capital authorized by the Act is $150 million; $25 million is deferred dividend shares reserved for the government, and $125 million is in common shares (or 12.5 million shares at $10 each).

The government initially subscribed $5 million of the deferred dividend shares and paid up $1 million. A stock issue of $10 million was then offered on the market and bought up by the *caisses populaires* ($5 million) and other financial institutions.

The G.I.C. may also issue bonds. The first issue was fixed at $5 million and reserved for the public in $100 amounts so that public participation in the activities of the corporation could be as wide as possible.

The G.I.C. is both a credit-granting and a controlling corporation. It grants medium- and long-term credit with or without guarantees, and buys the common shares of certain companies in order to participate in their management or to gain a controlling interest. In its role as a controlling organization it differs completely from the Industrial Development Bank; as a credit organization it provides the same kind of funds but does not reserve them for small businesses.

The G.I.C. will influence the Quebec economy primarily through its participation in management and in the eventual success of the new enterprises it helps to create. Indeed, its main purpose, as set forth in the preamble to the Act of Incorporation, is 'to stimulate and promote the formation and development of industrial undertakings and, accessorily, of commercial undertakings in the province, so as to broaden the basis of its economic structure, accelerate the growth thereof and contribute to full employment; to induce the people of Quebec to participate in the development of such undertakings by investing a part of their savings therein'.[1] As noted earlier, the G.I.C. is not an ordinary private company: it is one of several weapons or devices aimed at giving Quebec a definite control over its economy and at reducing the province's chronic unemployment by accelerating the rate of growth of the manufacturing industry.

The G.I.C. has selected and announced the means by which it hopes to promote the development of Quebec. Mention is made of the secondary sector, and, within the secondary sector, of the durable-goods industries. The Corporation will probably give preference to the industries using lumber, electric power, and steel. The first two resources are abundant in Quebec; as regards steel, the government of the province proposes to create an iron-and-steel industry, and no doubt the G.I.C. will wish to recruit customers for it. The early decisions of the G.I.C., as a result of which it has entered the fields of machinery and heavy equipment, newsprint, and lumber processing, are significant, and in this writer's view make a good beginning.

With respect to industrial organization, the G.I.C. is committed to carrying out mergers and various regroupings of existing enterprises and to transforming traditional family companies into joint-stock companies. For example, it has brought together, with financial assistance, three old, established firms in closely related activities in the field of heavy equipment, Forano Ltd., Volcano Ltd., and Marine Industries Ltd.

On October 31, 1964, the common and preferred shares of the G.I.C. amounted to $7.8 million, and loans to subsidiaries or other enterprises came to $5 million. In addition, it had $8.3 million in portfolio investments available for further transactions.

---

1. An Act to incorporate the General Investment Corporation of Quebec. Statutes of Quebec 1962, Chapter 54.

E. Life Insurance Companies

There can be few Canadians today who are unacquainted with life insurance. The nine million insured persons make up over half the population. Life insurance not only affords financial protection against premature death; it also accumulates savings, the earnings of which are paid out to the policyholder in accordance with a variety of conditions. After first describing the activities of life insurance companies, we shall examine the ways in which they use the savings deposited with them. It is in this latter respect particularly that they reveal themselves to be extremely active and important financial intermediaries between savers and investors.

1. THE LIFE INSURANCE INDUSTRY

At the end of 1960 life insurance in force in Canada amounted to almost $48 billion.

TABLE 10:14

Value of Life Insurance in Force, millions of dollars

	Ordinary and industrial	As a percentage	Group	As a percentage	Total
1945	8,894	89	1,070	11	9,964
1960	32,128	68	14,739	32	46,867

NOTE: Insurance of the mutual aid societies ($989 million in 1960) is not included.

Group insurance has increased much more rapidly than individual insurance since the war. This is largely a result of the increase in 'fringe benefits' in employment (often by union contract) and the tendency of self-employed people who belong to professional or business groupings (doctors, accountants) to combine to get better terms. It also indicates an increasing preference for a clearer separation between the insurance services properly speaking and the savings-investment services, since group insurance is always term insurance. Group insurance rose from

11 per cent of the total insurance in force in 1945 to 32 per cent in 1960. This tendency is still more evident in the value of new policies issued.

More than $6 billion worth of life insurance was sold in 1960, with group insurance accounting for 25 per cent.[1] But more important, 42 per cent of the ordinary insurance was term insurance. We can say, then, that 67 per cent of life insurance sold in 1960 was term insurance. The existence of a significant trend is obvious: Canadians are devoting a large part of their savings to insurance, but progressively less with a view to investment and more for purposes of protection.

TABLE 10:15

Annual Sales of Life Insurance, millions of dollars

	Ordinary and industrial	As a percentage	Group	As a percentage	Total
1945	991	94	66	6	1,057
1950	1,642	86	258	14	1,900
1955	2,763	80	691	20	3,454
1960	4,576	75	1,553	25	6,129

Canadians are probably the most heavily insured people in the world. Three-quarters of all families have life insurance and the average value is $10,400. This amount is equal to 2.2 times the average per capita income; in the United States the corresponding figure is 1.7. The Quebec population is the most highly insured in Canada in relation to income (2.5 times the average

1. The statistical information on the life insurance companies is taken principally from the submission of the Canadian Life Insurance Officers Association to the Royal Commission on Banking and Finance, Toronto, 1962. A description of these institutions may also be found in *The Financing of Economic Activity in Canada*, by W. C. Hood, already quoted.

income in the province; the Ontario figure is 2.2, the same as the national figure).

Life insurance companies also sell life annuities, about 90 per cent of which are purchased through group contracts; they amounted to $736 million in 1960. A quarter of the companies' reserves are set aside to guarantee payment of these annuities. In addition, life insurance companies administer (and insure) pension funds with total assets that in 1960 amounted to $1.2 billion, and they are heavily engaged in the field of health insurance.

Of the one hundred and twenty-one life insurance companies in Canada, ninety-nine have federal charters and have written 95 per cent of the total insurance in force. Forty-one are 'mutual' and eighty are stock companies. The mutual companies belong to the policyholders; profits are distributed to them in the form of rebates on premiums or as additional insurance. Since 1957 the stock companies have been permitted to convert themselves into mutual companies by the repurchase of their outstanding shares. In 1962 there were eleven federally chartered mutual companies and two others in the process of conversion.[1] In 1960 mutual companies accounted for 59 per cent of the total life insurance in force; this percentage is likely to increase.

Foreign life insurance companies are numerous in Canada and are playing an important part. They make up half of all companies in the business and have written nearly half of the total insurance in force. However, Canadian companies are doing so much business in foreign countries that on the whole, the exports of life insurance services are almost equivalent to the imports. In 1960 Canadian companies had $13 billion of life insurance business outside the country and foreign companies had $14 billion of business in Canada.

Competition is intense in the life insurance business: twenty-five new companies were founded between 1935 and 1960,

1. One of the aims of 'mutualization' of a company is to prevent the purchase by interests considered undesirable by the present management of sufficient stock to control the company.

causing a decrease in concentration. In 1963 life insurance companies in Canada held assets of $10.8 billion. In 1960 foreign companies held $2.2 billion. Canadian companies had an additional $2.8 billion in assets abroad.

TABLE 10:16

Assets in Canada of Life Insurance Companies,*
millions of dollars, selected years

1945	3,125
1950	4,304
1955	6,043
1962†	9,950
1963†	10,780

*Includes federally chartered companies, provincially chartered companies, and fraternal societies registered in Ontario and Quebec.
†The figures for 1962 and 1963 are estimates.

SOURCE: *Report of the Royal Commission on Banking and Finance*, p. 271, for 1945 to 1962. For 1963, the *Bank of Canada Statistical Summary*, federally chartered companies (whose Canadian assets amounted to $9,943 million).

Assets in Canada increased by 7 per cent per annum between 1945 and 1962. This rate is markedly higher than that of national income.

2. SAVINGS THROUGH LIFE INSURANCE

In the National Income and Expenditure Accounts the insurance companies are deemed to act as agents for their policyholders. The companies' investment income is considered as consumer income; their expenses and profits are regarded as expenses for the consumers. These three items, plus the cash premiums received from policyholders, less the cash claims paid out, equal the item in the Accounts called *policyholder saving*. In other words, this is the savings consumers make through the life insurance companies. Obviously savings thus defined will be lower than the cash premiums paid by the policyholders.

TABLE 10:17

Consumer Saving in Life Insurance, selected years

	Premiums paid in millions of dollars	Savings in millions of dollars	Savings as a percentage of personal disposable income	Savings as a percentage of total personal savings
1951	502	227	1.54	17.1
1956	726	343	1.70	26.0
1959	942	444	1.83	25.3
1960	967	450	1.79	26.9

Taking into account the insured pension funds, savings through life insurance doubled from 1951 to 1960, rising from $227 million to $450 million. The share of personal disposable income that goes to life insurance, however, remains almost constant at about 1.75 per cent. The relation to total personal saving is also almost constant: life insurance has been absorbing about one-quarter of personal saving since the end of the war. In periods of severe economic fluctuations these proportions vary considerably, because while income and total savings fluctuate, premiums and cash payments are relatively stable owing to the fact that the contracts are long-term.

3. INVESTMENTS

Where do the life insurance companies invest their funds? Of their total assets 46 per cent are invested in bonds, about 40 per cent in mortgages, and barely 3 per cent in common stocks. The exact distribution in 1963 is given in Table 10:18.

The life insurance companies have greatly diversified their investments since the end of the war. They first reduced their holdings of federal bonds in order to increase their purchases of provincial, municipal, and corporate bonds; then they seriously went into the mortgage loan business. (Mortgage loans increased from 9.7 per cent of their assets in 1945 to 40 per cent in 1963.)

TABLE 10:18

**Distribution of Canadian Assets of
Federally Chartered Life Insurance Companies, 1963**

	In millions of dollars	*As a percentage of the total*
Government of Canada bonds	670	6.7
Provincial bonds	1,023	10.3
Municipal bonds	676	6.8
Corporate and other bonds	2,099	21.1
Foreign bonds	147	1.4
Total bonds	*4,615*	*46.3*
Mortgage loans	4,043	40.6
Real estate	321	3.2
Policy loans	385	3.9
Preferred and common stocks	311	3.1
Other assets	268	2.7
Total	9,942	100

SOURCE: *Bank of Canada Statistical Summary.*

On the other hand the figure of around 3 per cent in common stocks has remained constant.

Legislation has a great influence on the nature of the investments, but this influence may not be as decisive as the companies claim. Canadian legislation in fact authorizes a wide range of investments and the restrictions are on the whole quite few. In brief, fixed-income securities are allowed,[1] while variable-income securities are subject to two restrictions: (a) the common shares must have produced a dividend of at least 4 per cent in each of the preceding seven years, and (b) the holding of common

---

1. In 1961 the ceiling on mortgages was raised from 60 per cent to 66⅔ per cent of the value of the property.

shares must be limited to 15 per cent of the insurance company's total assets. Investment in real estate is also permitted up to 10 per cent of the assets. Condition (a) is the most restrictive in view of the very narrow market that exists in Canada. Condition (b) could be quite restrictive, but Table 10:18 shows that, by and large, companies' holdings are much below the 15 per cent limit.[1]

The companies' own deliberate investment policies and the actual supply of securities are at least as important as legislation in explaining the nature of the investments. That the supply of securities is restricted has already been mentioned. In theory, life insurance companies would suffer most from the lack of long-term securities – 40 or 50 years – but in practice they have been acting since the war as if interest rates were always going to rise and have not made great efforts to look for very long-term securities.

In establishing investment policies, the prime factor is the nature of the investor's business. In the life insurance business there is a steady inflow of funds, while withdrawals (policy loans) are low and can be calculated, with the result that the company can allow itself to maintain a fairly low level of liquidity. The fact that contracts are long-term and fixed in value (a $5,000 policy payable in 20 years, for example) gives the security of investment a definite priority over the rate of return. Hence investment in bonds and mortgages is typical. The company thus provides against the danger of a severe depression. In the long run, however, inflation deprives the policyholder of a large part of his savings. Against inflation life insurance as presently organized offers little protection.[2]

1. In 1961 the life insurance companies obtained authority to set up special funds for the payment of *variable pensions* modelled on the common funds of the trust companies. For investment purposes these special funds are not affected by restrictions (a) and (b) above. In a variable pension the insurance element completely disappears.

2. From 1940 to 1962 prices have exactly doubled. A life insurance policy of $5,000 taken out in 1940 is worth $2,500 when it is paid to the policyholder in 1962. When premiums have been paid in annually, it works out that the

4. LIFE INSURANCE IN THE CAPITAL MARKET

We have seen that 25 per cent of consumer savings go into life insurance and insured pensions. Table 10:19 shows what the investments of life insurance companies represent in the market for certain selected kinds of securities. It is evident that they account for almost half of all mortgage loans, a substantial share of the bonds issued by private corporations (38 per cent), and a little less than 20 per cent of all provincial and municipal bonds.

TABLE 10:19

The Share of Life Insurance Companies in the Purchases of Selected Securities, Canada 1961, millions of dollars

	1 *Total supply of securities*	2 *Investment of life insurance companies*	3 *2 as a percentage of 1*
1. Residential mortgage loans	1,358	600	44
2. Non-residential mortgage loans	298	141	47
3. Net issues of provincial bonds	924	132	14
4. Net issues of municipal bonds	262	47	18
5. Net issues of corporate bonds	205	77	38

NOTE: The figures for the total supply of securities given above do not agree exactly with those in the *Bank of Canada Statistical Summary* from which they have been taken. The table is reproduced just as it was submitted in the Report of the Canadian Life Insurance Officers Association to the Royal Commission on Banking and Finance. The differences are very small. It should be added that on a net basis in 1961 the life insurance companies were sellers of federal bonds.

F. The Trust Companies

A trust company is a trustee. Trustees are persons or companies charged with managing property entrusted to them by others.

policyholder has lost half this sum, namely $1,250, if prices have increased at a regular rate from year to year.

The document creating a trust stipulates the conditions to be fulfilled by the trustee. The beneficiaries of the trust are generally third parties. The executor of a will is the best example of a trustee. Necessarily, since they manage the wealth of others, trust companies are reputed for their strict and even conservative policies in financial matters and for the high calibre of their administrators.

The functions of a trust company are, in fact, an extension and development of the functions of an old-time European or Quebec notary.

Among financial institutions, trust companies rank second after the chartered banks in the total amount of funds administered. However, since estates, trusts, and agency funds do not belong to the companies, they are usually omitted in analyses, and only company assets are included.

TABLE 10:20

Funds Administered by Trust Companies, millions of dollars, selected years

	1955	1961	1962	1964
Assets, company funds, and guaranteed funds	714	1,590	1,894	2,789
Estates, trusts, and agency funds*	4,713	8,270		
Total funds administered	5,427	9,860		

*Estates, trusts, and agency funds include the pension funds administered by the trust companies.

SOURCES: Assets 1955 and estates, trust, and agency funds from *Report of the Royal Commission on Banking and Finance*, pp. 181 and 188. Assets 1960-64 from *Bank of Canada Statistical Summary*.

Table 10:20 indicates that the total funds administered in 1961 were almost $10 billion, and that in 1964 the companies' own assets amounted to almost $2.8 billion. The growth of the trust companies (company assets) has been rapid. Since 1950 they have been increasing at a rate of 10 to 12 per cent per annum.

The activities of trust companies are so varied that it is difficult to group them. The following three categories overlap to some extent:

1. ESTATES, TRUSTS, AND AGENCY FUNDS

Since the administration of *estates* is the prime function of trust companies, they become involved in all the fields of economic and social life, for the assets of an estate can include the whole range of things that can be owned – factories, lands, commercial and residential buildings, development rights, stock and bonds, chattels, machinery, life insurance policies, and so forth. An estate administrator may have to do anything from collecting the rent of a cottage to supervising the liquidation of a railroad. The companies manage the assets, sometimes buying or selling if it is to the advantage of the estate, and all must be performed in accordance with a multitude of provisions and restrictions imposed by the terms of the trust and the legislation of all jurisdictions, Canadian and foreign, in which the assets and claims exist.

The term *trust*, as used in this subsection, refers to assets for which the company has been made responsible during the lifetime of the trustor. These are called 'living trusts'. A person, for example, may turn over capital to provide a life income for an incapacitated relative.

Agency funds are those which a company administers under the orders of clients. Such orders deal primarily with investment and property management, but in the end may necessitate a wide variety of financial services, even including the preparation of income tax returns. Among the services to which investment gives rise are, for example, the supervision and safekeeping of securities, collection of interest and dividends, recommendations for sale and purchase, execution of orders for sale and purchase, provision of information for the client on anything affecting his securities, and book-keeping for transactions.

The investment of funds administered on behalf of others is

subject to numerous legal restrictions. Because trusts are governed by civil law, the provinces have jurisdiction; and unfortunately their requirements are not uniform. Investments are allowed in Government of Canada bonds, provincial bonds, municipal bonds, school and hospital bonds, and first mortgages on residential property. Certain provinces (not including Quebec and Ontario) allow investments in corporate bonds; British Columbia and Nova Scotia allow a low percentage of preferred stocks; Nova Scotia allows a low percentage of common stocks.

In order to interpret correctly the figures in Table 10:21, it is necessary to remember that the trust deeds first and foremost determine the type of investment. The law applies only if the deeds do not contain any instructions to the trustee in this regard.

TABLE 10:21

Estimated Distribution of Estates, Trusts, and Agency Funds of Trust Companies, 1962, at market prices, in percentages

Government of Canada bonds	11
Provincial bonds	10
Municipal bonds	3
Corporate bonds and debentures	11
Canadian stocks	48
Foreign bonds	1
Foreign stocks	12
Mortgages	1
Other assets	3
	100

NOTE: These figures do not include Trusteed Pension Plans.

SOURCE: *Report of the Royal Commission on Banking and Finance*, p. 191.

Investment in stocks by estates, trusts, and agency funds, excluding trusteed pension plans, is quite high. This fact was revealed in a special sampling study conducted by the Royal Commission on Banking and Finance, the results of which appear in Table 10:21. Of the assets of these accounts, 60 per cent appear to be in Canadian or foreign stocks, and 24 per cent in government bonds. If this distribution is examined in relation to the investments authorized by legislation, the conclusion must be that, at least in the sample, the terms of the trust are the dominating factor.

Trusts are administered separately. When the block of funds of a trust is small it is difficult to make investments sufficiently diversified to have both a high return and only reasonable risk. To help resolve this problem the Ontario Trustee Act authorized, in 1950, the establishment of 'common trust funds' by the trust companies. Later British Columbia and Alberta adopted similar legislation. By 1961 five companies had created common trust funds. Total assets are still negligible ($15 million in 1961) but they will undoubtedly increase.

2. DEPOSITS AND INVESTMENT CERTIFICATES

The trust companies no longer limit themselves to administering for others. Today they compete with the savings banks, the *caisses populaires*, and the investment companies to attract the savings of the public. They accept savings deposits which may be withdrawn at any time like a bank deposit (and cheques may be drawn) or used as a term investment. In the case of a term investment the company issues in favour of the depositor a Guaranteed Investment Certificate which is redeemable only at maturity. The terms are from three to five years.

In 1964 deposits with trust companies amounted to $1.5 billion, nearly two-thirds of which was in the form of certificates. All these deposits are designated as 'guaranteed funds' since they must not exceed a limit fixed by federal law at 12½ times the trust company assets. In this sense, company assets serve as a guarantee for customer deposits. The trust companies have adopted an active policy of developing their savings accounts. In 1962, they had fifty-two savings branch offices, most of them in the suburbs of large cities and in shopping centres. Their main attraction is the interest rate offered: from 3 to 3½ per cent on

TABLE 10:22

Trust Companies'

Distribution of Assets and Liabilities, 1964

Assets	Millions of dollars	Percentage	Liabilities	Millions of dollars	Percentage
Government of Canada bonds	383	13.7	Chequable deposits	506	18.1
Provincial and municipal bonds	292	10.4	Non-chequable deposits	523	18.7
Corporate and institutional bonds and notes	366	13.1	Investment certificates	1,500	53.7
Mortgages	1,422	51.0	Other liabilities	21	0.7
Canadian stocks	68	2.4	Reserves and equity	240	8.6
Cash	82	2.9			
Other assets	177	6.3			
Total	2,789	100	Total	2,789	100

SOURCE: *Bank of Canada Statistical Summary.*

deposits and around 5 per cent on certificates.

The legislation concerning the investment of the trust company funds is not the same as that which applies to their fiduciary business. Briefly, the investments allowed are the same as those allowed to insurance companies (by the federal government, by Ontario and Alberta). The actual distribution of investments is given in Table 10:22.

Although bonds make up an important part of the investments, conventional mortgages (usually of a five-year term) appear to be the most favoured form of investment for the savings deposits.

Unlike the funds received in trust, in which each client's account is administered separately, the guaranteed funds are grouped together for investment purposes, and so the same interest will be paid on all certificates. This practice is the same in principle as that of the investment companies previously discussed. Because the funds are combined, the trust companies, somewhat erroneously, call the guaranteed funds 'common trust funds'.

3. SPECIAL ACTIVITIES AND SERVICES

The pension funds constitute one important category of trusts. A corporation creates a pension fund in co-operation with its employees, and this fund is deposited with a trust company which assures its management. The pension funds administered by trust companies had assets of $1.2 billion in 1961 and $1.5 billion in 1963. (See page 242.)

Since 1957, when the Income Tax Act for the first time allowed premiums paid into individual pension plans to be deducted from taxable income, the trust companies have created special funds to which individuals may subscribe. In 1961 there were 14,103 participants in these funds. The remarkable thing here is that out of $30 million of assets, $20 million was invested in common stocks.

Similarly, contributions to small pension funds are used to buy units in a 'pooled' or common fund. The units are bought and sold at prices that vary according to the return on the funds, and the pension itself is variable. Certain funds are limited to investments in stocks, others in bonds. Eight hundred pension plans participated in these funds in 1963. Corporate stocks and bonds were the two main categories of securities held. A growing tendency to invest in common stocks is clearly apparent.

As of 1963, three trust companies had established six mutual funds, three of the fixed-income type and three with variable income. In addition, a quarter of the assets of the pension plans were administered as common trust funds. The combined assets of these mutual funds and the common funds reached $286 million in that year.

The trust companies fulfil one other important function – that of registrars and transfer agents for corporate securities. Most stock exchanges demand, for example, that a trust company act as transfer agent for their listed stocks. In this connection the trust company keeps the books, carries out the orders it receives, and assures itself that everything is in conformity with the stipulated prescriptions and agreements. It is estimated that in 1961 the trust companies in their role as transfer agents issued 4,111,000 stock certificates. This service gives rise to a great many others that have already been mentioned.

Trust companies appear to be going through a period of great change. While the greater part of the capital they administer is still being invested in government bonds for the sake of security, they are clearly concerned now with protecting savings against inflation. This concern is causing them to go so far beyond the field of their traditional activities that it will soon become difficult to tell the financial institutions apart. Trust companies provide an example of the general tendency of all financial institutions to enlarge progressively the scope of their activities.[1]

---

1. So it is that the term 'trust' is being interpreted in a wider and wider sense. It includes savings deposits, short term deposits of cash balances of corporations, purchases of shares in mutual funds, contributions to pension funds, etc. As well as speaking prose all his life without knowing it, Monsieur Jourdain of Molière's *Le Bourgeois Gentilhomme* must have also engaged in trust company activities without knowing it.

G. The Pension Funds

Before we arrive at a pensionable age we should all learn to distinguish between the different kinds of pensions. First of all there are the federal government's old age pensions. These are supported by a 'non-capitalized pension fund'[1] – that is, by a fund to which is contributed only what is necessary for the payment of current claims.

Next are the government annuities sold to individuals. In this plan any individual can buy an annuity up to the amount of $1,200. In March 1963, almost 400,000 of these policies were in force. The plan has no distinct pension fund.

Old age pensions and government annuities are not included in the statistics on pension funds (Table 10:23). What these statistics do include are pension plans of the consolidated type in which assets have been accumulated beforehand in order to meet the claims which will have to be paid out later. These plans are in three categories: funds managed as trusts, annuities insured by the life insurance companies, and the federal government group annuities.

The trust companies administer the pension funds entrusted to them but do not guarantee payment of the pensions. This guarantee is given by the sponsors of the plan and by the plan itself. When contributions are paid to a life insurance company they are used to purchase each year a collective annuity, and the final pension of the participant is his portion of the sum of the annuities. The life insurance company therefore guarantees payment of the pensions.

In a developed country such as Canada everyone now wants a retirement pension. Consequently the pension plans have multiplied at an extremely rapid rate in recent years. Legislation contributed to this pension boom in 1957 by lifting almost all restrictions on investment and by allowing the participant to deduct pension plan contributions from his taxable income. From $1.2 billion in 1952, the assets of the trusteed pension plans increased to 5.2 billion in 1963, and the assets of all plans reached $7.6 billion.

1. The expression 'non-consolidated' is also used.

TABLE 10:23

Pension Plans, Canada 1963

	Number of plans	Number of employees (thousands)	Contributions (millions of dollars)	Assets (millions of dollars)
Trusteed plans	1,806	1,261	544	5,180
Life insurance group annuities	9,276	500	178	1,818
Federal government group annuities	1,365	156	13	623
Total	12,447	1,917	715	7,621

SOURCE: Dominion Bureau of Statistics, Trusteed Pension Plans, *Financial Statistics*, 1963.

The pension plans included in Table 10:23 cover nearly two million persons. The larger pension plans are administered as trusteed plans, the smaller by the life insurance companies – a distribution that arises naturally from the different services afforded by these two types of organization.

That the trusteed pension plans are the most important is obvious from the assets shown in Table 10:23. They can be grouped in three main categories according to their administration: by the trust companies, by the pension fund societies, or by independent trustees. Of their $5.18 billion in assets in 1963, $1.5 billion was managed by trust companies, $562 million by pension fund societies, and $3.1 billion by independent trustees.

The investment policies of the trusteed pension plans are highly conservative, if not excessively cautious, despite very liberal legislation. Though there has been some progress in recent years, the plans still directly invest only 12 per cent of their total assets in common stocks. It is true that, through the intermediary of the trust companies' pooled and mutual funds, another portion amounting to 2 or 3 per cent can be added to this. Even so, the proportion of assets in common stocks remains very low. Government bonds then serve as the main outlet for the investments. It is said that the pension funds of provincial government employees have contributed a good deal to the sales of government bonds. Some experts have stated that the rate of return is unfortunately not always the sole criterion for administrators in this regard.[1]

TABLE 10:24

Distribution of Assets of the Trusteed Pension Plans, 1963

	In millions of dollars	As a percentage
Government of Canada bonds	582	11.2
Provincial bonds	1,675	32.3
Municipal bonds	546	10.6
Other bonds	814	15.8
Total bonds	*3,617*	*69.9*
Stocks	617	11.8
Mortgages	484	9.4
Pooled and mutual funds*	286	5.5
Other assets	174	3.4
Total	5,180	100

*The pooled and mutual funds are those of the trust companies themselves.

SOURCE: Dominion Bureau of Statistics, Trusteed Pension Plans, *Financial Statistics, 1963.*

H. The Mortgage Loan Companies

Almost all the financial institutions make mortgage loans. We have already seen that the life insurance companies devoted 40 per cent of their assets in 1963 and the trust companies (company and guaranteed funds) 51 per cent of their assets in 1964 to mortgage loans. Mortgage loan companies are financial institutions that concentrate on this kind of investment.

1. *Report of the Royal Commission on Banking and Finance*, p. 260.

1. NATURE AND IMPORTANCE

The financial structure of the mortgage loan companies is similar to that of the trust companies, and their activities are also quite similar, if we except the trust companies' operations relating to estates, trusts, and agency funds. Thus the mortgage loan companies receive deposits from their clients, issue bonds and savings certificates, and invest the funds in mortgage loans and government bonds. The proportions are, however, somewhat different from the trust companies both in the sources of funds and in investments. The mortgage loan companies have greater recourse to debentures as a means of providing themselves with funds; several companies do not even accept deposits. And of course their concentration in mortgage loans – up to 80 per cent of assets – is higher.

Table 10:25 provides the figures on which these observations are based. It will be helpful to compare it with Table 10:22.

In the value of their total assets the mortgage loan companies rank a little below the trust companies. Since 1945 they have made rapid progress, favoured particularly by a strong demand for ordinary mortgage loans in both industry and housing. The rate of growth of their assets has exceeded the rates of the chartered banks and the insurance companies, but has been slightly lower than that of the trust companies.

The governing legislation is generally the same as for trust companies. Hence they have available a wide range of investments. What mainly distinguishes them from banks (and this also applies to the trust companies) is that they do not have the power to make commercial and personal loans.

In the amount of mortgage credit outstanding, they rank just behind the life insurance companies and level with the trust companies. At the end of 1964 their total mortgage loans outstanding amounted to nearly $1.5 billion.

2. THE CENTRAL MORTGAGE AND HOUSING CORPORATION

The Central Mortgage and Housing Corporation (C.M.H.C.) is the most important corporation in the field of housing in Canada. A federal government Crown corporation, it has been

TABLE 10:25

Mortgage Loan Companies
distribution of assets and liabilities, 1964

Assets	In millions of dollars	As a percentage	Liabilities	In millions of dollars	As a percentage
Government of Canada bonds	120	6.3	Chequable deposits	154	8.0
Provincial and municipal bonds	53	2.7	Non-chequable deposits	166	8.1
Corporate and institutional bonds	33	1.7	Debentures	980	51.3
Mortgages	1,469	77.0	Other liabilities	362	19.0
Canadian stocks	56	2.8	Reserves and equity	247	13.0
Cash	64	3.3			
Other assets	113	6.0			
Total	1,908	100	Total	1,908	100

SOURCE: *Bank of Canada Statistical Summary.*

granted very extensive powers. Among other things it can:

1. insure mortgage loans made by financial institutions for the construction of new housing and for home improvements;
2. make direct mortgage loans to individuals;
3. make loans to provinces and municipalities, or their agencies, for the provision of public housing accommodation, existing or new, for low-income families or individuals;
4. make loans to universities and non-profit companies for the construction of student residences;
5. make loans to municipalities for sewage-treatment projects;
6. buy and sell insured mortgages;
7. make short-term advances to and purchase the debentures of lending institutions;
8. acquire and improve land and construct and manage housing, on its own account or on behalf of the federal government, the municipalities, or the provinces;
9. promote improvement and progress in housing construction and community planning and engage in the research necessary to achieve this.

This long list, although far from complete, illustrates quite well the multitude of possibilities and the vast authority that the C.M.H.C. has to hand. Through its guarantees it encourages private institutions to lend money for housing, but in case of need it replaces the private lenders and makes the loan itself. If lenders wish to make loans but lack the necessary resources to do so, the C.M.H.C. may supply them with funds by purchasing their outstanding mortgages (a safeguard against the dangers of severe depression because construction activity can thus be stimulated). If the demand for loans should fall the corporation can, if need be, transform itself into an entrepreneur and construct the required housing. In collaboration with the municipalities or the provinces it participates in urban redevelopment through sizeable financial contributions that can be devoted to the elimination of slums, to the construction of dwellings, and to subsidies to low-income tenants.

Let us take the year 1964 and examine the activities of the C.M.H.C. under various headings:

1. Insured loans and direct loans, new dwellings. The activities of the C.M.H.C. should be described in comparison with those of the whole housing industry whenever possible. In regard to C.M.H.C.-insured loans from financial institutions and C.M.H.C. direct loans, several bases for calculation may be selected: e.g., loans approved, total money paid out, the number of new housing starts. Table 10:26 gives the number of new housing starts in 1964 and the expenditures for the different sources of financing. Of the 165,658 new housing starts, C.M.H.C. participated in 28,728 through its direct loans and in 26,118 through the guarantees it gave to lenders. Thus its contribution to the construction of new dwellings was 54,846 or 33 per cent of the total. Direct loans amounted almost to $303 million and insured loans to $324 million.

The insured loans, of course, come from private financial institutions. The reason for placing them under the heading of C.M.H.C. in the table is that they differ from conventional loans in a great many ways. Not only are they guaranteed loans, but they apply to new houses subject to certain standards of construction and to houses in places where need has made itself particularly felt. The rate of interest charged by the lender is limited; it cannot exceed by more than 2½ per cent[1] the rate of return on long-term bonds. The maturity date of the loan must be between 25 and 35 years. The amount may be as high as 95 per cent of the first $13,000 of the lending value for the house plus 70 per cent of the remainder. Total payments should generally not exceed 27 per cent of the borrower's income. The maximum loan that may be obtained is $15,600. At the time of writing, the rate of interest on insured mortgage loans is 6¼ per cent.

---

1. The maximum rate is lower than this in loans to builders, municipalities, and universities.

The insurance fee for these loans is paid by the borrowers at a cost of about 2 per cent of the amount of the loan and goes into a mortgage insurance fund established by C.M.H.C. If a lender incurs a loss, the Corporation makes it good by drawing on the insurance fund.

In order to evaluate the role played by the private financial institutions in the field of housing construction, it is better to take as a guide the amounts expended rather than the number of housing starts. There are two reasons for this: housing starts are classified according to the *main* source of financing so that the number of houses credited to financial institutions much exceeds their real financial contribution (in 1964 51.3 per cent of housing starts, but 35.2 per cent of expenditures – see Table 10:26); secondly, the C.M.H.C. figures for the conventional mortgage loans of the lending institutions are a purely arbitrary fiction, for they represent, in fact, only a portion of the lending institutions, since credit unions and pension plans are not included.[1] Item 3 of Table 10:26 accordingly does not account for all dwellings financed mainly by mortgage loans from lending institutions. A good number come under Item 4; this also includes houses built without loans. Total expenditures for new housing exceeded $2.0 billion in 1964; owners contributed 13.7 per cent,[2] and the lending institutions supplied 35.2 per cent in the form of conventional loans (plus the greater portion of the 19.8 per cent of line 4b) and another 15.6 per cent in the form of insured loans. In addition, financial institutions loaned considerable sums on existing residential property and on non-residential property.

1. Usually excluded also are companies 'for whom activity in the mortgage loan field is subordinate to their principal functions', as in *Canadian Housing Statistics*, 1962, Table 50, for example. Here, no doubt, are meant companies that grant mortgage loans only as a sideline. And yet we find the chartered banks included among the lending institutions. Have mortgage loans then become the principal activity of the chartered banks? The credit unions and pension funds, however, are placed among the private lenders. On the whole, the C.M.H.C. classification of lenders is based on no useful criterion.

2. This 13.7 per cent applies only to housing for which the main financing came from mortgage loans.

TABLE 10:26

The Share of C.M.H.C. in New Housing, 1964

	Dwelling units, starts	Percentage of total	Expenditures in millions of dollars	Percentage of total
1. Public housing	4,013	2.4	29.9	1.8
2. C.M.H.C.				
(a) direct loans	28,728	17.3	302.8	14.6
(b) approved lenders	26,118	15.7	324.1	15.6
3. Conventional institutional loans	85,090	51.3	730.7	35.2
4. Other sources of financing	21,709	13.1	—	—
(a) owner equities	—	—	274.5	13.7
(b) other financing	—	—	410.8	19.8
Total	165,658	100	2,072.8	100

NOTE: Errors due to rounding.

SOURCES: *Canadian Housing Statistics*, 1964: Dwelling units, starts, Table 34; expenditures, Table 36.

2. Loans for student residences. Since 1960 C.M.H.C. has been granting loans to universities and colleges for the construction of student residences. In June 1964 the total fund available to it for such purposes was increased from $100 million to $150 million; by the end of 1964 it had granted loans to the value of $110 million.

3. Loans to municipalities for sewage-treatment projects. C.M.H.C. grants loans for sewage-treatment projects up to a total of $200 million. Loans totalling $145 million were made to the municipalities between 1960 and 1964, one-quarter of this amount, plus the accrued interest, being for work to be completed before March 31, 1967.

4. Home improvement loans. C.M.H.C. guarantees loans made by the chartered banks for home improvements, up to a total of $500 million. Loans outstanding in this category totalled $348 million at the end of 1964.

5. Urban redevelopment. Between 1948 and 1964 C.M.H.C. participated in twenty-one urban redevelopment projects to which the federal government contributed about $34 million. Projects approved for 1964 amounted to $10.3 million.

6. Secondary market for mortgages. The total mortgages insured under the National Housing Act reached $5.6 billion in 1964. Mortgages are traditionally lacking in liquidity because they are not readily negotiable. As the total amount increases, however, it becomes both more desirable and at the same time easier to create a market where mortgages can be bought and sold before maturity. This is called a secondary market. The first measures taken in Canada with this end in view date back to 1954 when the National Housing Act permitted the insurance on mortgages to be transferred to new purchasers. C.M.H.C. was authorized to sell its insured mortgages and to make loans on the guarantee of these mortgages. The first to take advantage of the new provisions of the Act were the chartered banks, which in 1954 sold a small number of mortgages to the life insurance companies and pension funds. But it is since 1961 or 1962 that trading has really gained in volume thanks to block sales of mortgages by C.M.H.C. Table 10:27 gives a statement of the 1964 trading.

TABLE 10:27

Sales and Purchases of Insured N.H.A. Mortgages, millions of dollars, 1964

	Sales	*Purchases*
1. Chartered banks	3.1	46.8
2. Life insurance companies	5.2	21.4
3. Trust companies	58.2	26.0
4. Pension funds	—	17.1
5. C.M.H.C.	75.3	3.1
6. Other companies	8.4	35.8
Total	150.2	150.2

SOURCE: *Canadian Housing Statistics*, 1964, Table 40.

This is a development very favourable to the growth of a broader and more efficient capital market in Canada. It should in future contribute greatly not only to increased flexibility in financial policies and to increased investment in mortgage loans but also to lower rates for the borrowers.

In addition to the administrative and regulating duties which it has performed since it was established, the C.M.H.C. is now appreciably stepping up its activities in the mortgage loan field by increasing its intervention in the market. Block sale of insured mortgages is one of the several new methods it is using.

The balance sheet of the Corporation is summed up in Table 10:28. Note that the Corporation has a capital of $25 million and that it sells its debentures only to the federal government. Under 'assets' it is clear that nearly all the resources are devoted to direct mortgage loans.

TABLE 10:28

Central Mortgage and Housing Corporation, balance sheet, December 31, 1964, millions of dollars

Assets		Liabilities	
Cash on hand	7.5	Accounts payable	3.8
Loans under the N.H.A.	1,856.2	Estimated income tax	2.1
Agreements for sale and mortgages	92.7	Borrowings from the Government	
Investment under federal-provincial		of Canada	2,054.0
agreements	114.6	Unrealized profits on sales	38.4
Real estate	64.7	Statutory reserve fund	5.0
Assets of the insurance and guarantee		Excess in reserve fund	8.6
funds	137.3	Capital	25.0
Other items	8.0	Reserves of the insurance and guarantee	
		funds	137.3
		Other items	6.8
Total	2,281.0	Total	2,281.0

SOURCE: *C.M.H.C. Annual Report*, 1964.

3. MORTGAGE LOANS OUTSTANDING

Total mortgage indebtedness in Canada at the end of 1962[1] was estimated at $14.2 billion. About 75 per cent of this indebtedness related to housing and the remainder to commercial or industrial buildings and to institutions. As the stock of residential properties in Canada is evaluated at approximately $45 billion, it can be roughly estimated that, on the average, houses are mortgaged up to 25 per cent of their value.

TABLE 10:29

Mortgage Loans Outstanding, Canada 1962

	In millions of dollars	As a percentage
1. Life insurance companies	4,142	35.0
2. Governments (including C.M.H.C.)	2,466	20.8
3. Corporate lenders	989	8.3
4. Mortgage loan companies	976	8.2
5. Chartered banks	921	7.8
6. Estates, trusts, and agency funds of trust companies	865	7.3
7. Trust companies	836	7.1
8. *Caisses populaires* and credit unions	479	4.0
9. Other institutions	144	1.2
Sub-total, lending institutions	11,818	100
Estimated holdings of individuals and unincorporated firms	2,382	
Total	14,200	

SOURCE: *Canadian Housing Statistics*. The total is given by the *Report of the Royal Commission on Banking and Finance*.

Who are the lucky people who have been able to lend this $14 billion? Obviously the insurance companies dominate this

1. See section K, p. 272.

market. They are followed by the government agencies with the
C.M.H.C. in first place. The chartered banks have made hardly
any mortgage loans since 1959, but they own a block of mortgages amounting to nearly $1 billion which were acquired prior
to that year.

I. Consumer Loan Companies

1. INSTALMENT CREDIT

No down payment, twenty-four months to pay, and you jump
into your new car and drive off. Instalment credit has been much
disparaged, but how useful it is! It involves buying a product and
then paying for it in instalments spread over a certain number of
months. Since it serves as security for the lender, the product
should be durable, at least lasting the repayment period (but this
does not invariably happen). Payments include the purchase
price of the product plus interest and borrowing charges. For
indisputably we are here dealing with a loan. The customer signs
a conditional sales contract in favour of the merchant. The
lender can be the merchant himself, but most often the merchant
discounts the conditional sales contract; that is, he sells it to a
sales finance company. The latter takes over all rights to the
product and the collection of payments, and may assume the
risk of losses.

Instalment credit on consumer goods is used primarily for the
purchase of automobiles and secondly for household appliances.
It is also used for commercial, industrial, and agricultural vehi-
cles and equipment. While instalment credit is particularly widespread at the consumer level for the financing of retail sales, it is
also commonly used by manufacturers and wholesalers for the
financing of automobile sales to retailers. The shiny new cars in
the dealer's window, which dazzle the pedestrian, are bought by
the dealer but in reality belong to the sales finance company. In
everyday speech confusion often arises over the distinction
between the sales finance companies and the 'small loans' companies. The latter also make loans which are guaranteed on personal chattels and repayable in instalments, but are not tied to

one specific use as in the case of instalment credit. In one sense instalment credit is a credit in kind for the borrower, whereas the credit extended by the small loans companies is a credit in cash (or a cash loan). The next section deals with 'small loans'.

The sales finance companies were born at the same time as the automobile and they have closely paralleled its progress. It was primarily the outlay for this costly but durable product that made a financial intermediary necessary. The first Canadian sales finance company was the Continental Guarantee Corporation of Canada, founded in 1916. Soon after, the General Motors Corporation created its own finance company, and in 1919 it established a branch in Canada.

Since then, instalment credit has been extended to other durable consumer products such as radios and television sets, furniture, and household appliances. Since the end of the war its use has expanded considerably.

Although the sales finance companies have increased in number to about 175, the industry remains highly concentrated; the three largest corporations among them hold 70 per cent of the total assets and the ten largest hold 95 per cent. The three main companies are, in order of size, Industrial Acceptance Corporation of Canada, Traders Finance Corporation, and General Motors Acceptance Corporation of Canada.

From 1945 to 1956, instalment credit increased nine times, whereas total consumer credit increased only four times.[1] Since 1956, however, although both total consumer credit and instalment credit have continued to rise, the rate of growth of instalment credit has slowed down. In 1956 the sales finance companies accounted for 30 per cent of consumer credit, in 1958 for 24 per cent, and in 1964 for 16 per cent (see Table 10:33). It is not surprising, then, that these companies should turn more to wholesale financing, particularly of commercial and industrial equipment. In 1953 they had $184 million in loans outstanding on commercial and industrial products; in 1964 these loans had

1. W. C. Hood, *op. cit.*, p. 133.

TABLE 10:30

Instalment Credit – Balances Outstanding, Canada, millions of dollars, 1958-1964

	1958	1962	1964
1. Wholesale financing	191	240	258
2. Retail financing	1,026	1,241	1,549
(a) consumer goods	768	801	967
passenger cars	588	609	779
other	180	192	188
(b) commercial and industrial goods	257	440	582
commercial vehicles	111	151	201
other	146	288	381
Total (1+2)	1,216	1,481	1,806

NOTE: Errors due to rounding.
SOURCE: *Bank of Canada Statistical Summary.*

increased to $582 million (Table 10:30). This is the category of instalment credit that has shown the greatest increase in recent years.[1]

By its very nature instalment credit is short-term credit. For the year 1964 the average term of the loans (which since 1958 has increased by from 2 to 6 months depending on the type of credit) was 29 months for new passenger cars, 24 months for other consumer durables, and 31.7 months for commercial and industrial goods. The contracts on industrial-goods financing varied from a few thousand to $500,000, but the majority were between $5,000 and $15,000.

The cost of instalment credit is quite high for the consumer. He needs to be astute to discover the effective rate of interest he is paying, for the contracts usually only stipulate the amounts to be paid for interest and other charges, and the length of term and the number of payments vary considerably between contracts. In 1961 the majority of credit sales contracts for new cars carried effective interest rates of 12 to 16 per cent. The rates would be higher for used cars. For commercial and industrial goods they varied between 10 and 16 per cent.[2]

2. SMALL LOANS

The other companies specializing in personal loans are the 'Small Loans Companies', as they are called in the federal Act which regulates their operations. In 1963 six small loans companies and eighty licensed money-lenders were operating from 1,574 offices across the country. The largest was the Household Finance Corporation of Canada.

---

1. Loans for the purchase of farm implements belong to this category. Obviously, large corporations do not make purchases on instalment credit.

2. The financing of unsold cars is not as costly for the automobile dealer, who has to pay only 6 to 7 per cent. The sales finance company grants the dealer a rebate of 10 to 20 per cent of the finance charges. It is therefore correct to assume that it is in the dealer's interest to sell on credit rather than for cash, although the advantage of so doing is not very great. This information is taken from the *Report of the Royal Commission on Banking and Finance*, pp. 205 ff.

The Act makes provisions concerning loans not in excess of $1,500. In 1963 the 'small loans' granted in that year came to a total of $770 million, 60 per cent of them being between $500 and $1,000. The average loan amount has been tending to increase each year. One worrisome feature is that about three-quarters of them (by value) are made to borrowers who have not finished paying back previous loans. In 1963 an additional 15 per cent went to former customers. Of the total $770 million granted in the year, $371 million represented amounts loaned previously and carried over. In 1963 the companies loaned $136 million in amounts of over $1,500 which are not controlled by the Small Loans Act. Certain of the small loans companies also provide instalment credit.

The main provision of the Act concerns maximum rates of interest. Since January 1, 1957, they have been as shown in Table 10:31.

TABLE 10:31

Maximum Monthly Interest Rates Permitted by the Small Loans Act

Loans outstanding	*Term of Loans*		
	10 to 20 months	*21 to 30 months*	*31 months and over*
under $300	2.0	1.0	1.0
$300 to $500	1.0	1.0	1.0
$500 to $1,000	1.0	1.0	1.0
$1,000 to $1,500	0.5	0.5	1.0

It is evident that in the great majority of cases the maximum rate (including all charges except insurance) is 1 per cent per month on the unpaid balance. It may be ½ of 1 per cent if the loan is over $1,000 and if the term is 30 months or less.

3. COMPANIES' ASSETS AND LIABILITIES

As Table 10:32 indicates, the assets of the consumer loan com-

TABLE 10:32

Sales Finance and Small Loans Companies – Balance Sheet, 1964, millions of dollars

Assets	In millions of dollars	Percentage distribution	Liabilities	In millions of dollars	Percentage distribution
Accounts and notes receivable by sales finance companies	1,806	48.8	Owing parent and associated companies	452	12.2
Instalment credit and cash loans by small loans companies	901	24.4	Bank loans	234	6.3
Other receivables (net)	495	13.4	Demand and short-term notes	1,153	31.2
Cash and securities	159	4.3	Long-term debt	1,030	27.8
Investment in subsidiary and associated companies	273	7.3	Unearned income and other	183	5.8
Other assets	66	1.8	Paid-in capital and retained income	476	12.8
			Other liabilities	138	3.7
Total	3,700	100	Total	3,700	100

NOTE: Errors due to rounding.

SOURCE: Bank of Canada Statistical Summary.

panies amounted to $3.7 billion at the end of 1964. As should be expected, almost three-quarters was in the form of loans. No deposit institution could permit its cash holdings to be at the low levels maintained by the consumer loan companies. Also notable is the size of the investment in subsidiary and associated companies, almost all of which is investment of the sales finance companies in the small loans companies.

On the 'liabilities' side what is particularly striking is the debt structure. Short-term borrowings are very high, while borrowing through bonds and debentures (under long-term debt), a more usual method of company financing, represents scarcely more than one-quarter of the total liabilities.

Since the contracts of the sales finance companies and the small loans companies are short-term, the companies resort to short-term sources of financing to reduce the cost of their borrowings. Until the end of the war in 1945, the chartered banks were the exclusive source of short-term capital for instalment finance companies. In 1946 some of the larger companies began to sell 'notes' to the financial institutions. These notes are securities guaranteed in the same way as bank loans, by pledging the company's accounts receivable as security. Their term is set according to the wishes or needs of prospective buyers. Short-term notes vary from 30 to 365 days and long-term notes from 5 to 15 years. Until recently the short-term notes of instalment finance companies were the only private short-term securities traded on the market.

For the companies themselves these notes tend to take the place of bank loans whenever buyers can be found. From 1953 to 1964, bank loans dropped from 23 per cent to 6 per cent of the instalment finance companies' liabilities, while short-term notes rose from 13 per cent to 31 per cent, representing a very large outstanding indebtedness of $1,153 million, as may be seen in Table 10:32.

Since some of the large companies are subsidiaries of American companies, the contracting of loans in the United States is common practice. In 1964, 24 per cent of the short-term notes and

TABLE 10:33
Consumer Credit, Balances Outstanding, 1958-1964

	1958		1962		1964	
	Millions of dollars	*Percentage*	*Millions of dollars*	*Percentage*	*Millions of dollars*	*Percentage*
Chartered Banks*	553	17.0	1,183	24.9	1,793	29.6
Retail dealers	897	27.6	1,088	22.9	1,206	20.0
Sales finance companies	768	23.6	801	16.8	967	15.9
Small loans companies	401	12.3	714	15.0	901	14.8
Credit unions and *caisses populaires*	320	9.8	579	12.1	770†	12.7
Life insurance companies, policy loans	305	9.4	372	7.8	397	6.5
Quebec savings banks	6	0.2	13	0.2	15	0.2
Total	3,250	100	4,750	100	6,050	100
Total as a percentage of disposable income	14.2		16.9		19.0	

*All personal loans other than those secured against securities and other than home improvement loans.
†Estimated.
SOURCE: *Bank of Canada Statistical Summary and National Accounts, Income and Expenditure.*

28 per cent of the long-term notes and debentures were payable in foreign currency, mostly American dollars.

4. TOTAL CONSUMER CREDIT

In order to estimate the importance of the roles of the sales finance companies and small loans companies, their activities must be compared with the whole field of consumer credit.

The figures in Table 10:33 indicate that in 1964 consumer credit amounted to $6 billion, or 19 per cent of personal disposable income, a considerable increase since 1958.

Although the table does not go back that far, consumer credit has in fact been increasing steadily since 1945, except for the year 1951. It is also higher now than it was before the war. An adequate economic analysis of consumer credit would take into account not only income but also consumer assets, not only the influence of the general economic situation (which no doubt explains the increase in credit since 1956) but also the composition and nature of the demand. Such an analysis is not possible here, but chapter 2 of the *Report of the Royal Commission on Banking and Finance* gives the results of a study which showed that consumers' debts were not more than one-fifth of their assets and that the greater portion of these debts were more than guaranteed by equities in residential dwellings. In the opinion of the Commission, consumers generally are not in a difficult financial situation.

The chartered banks are the largest suppliers of consumer credit, and are followed by the retailers, the sales finance companies, and the small loans companies in that order. Since 1958 the proportions of total consumer credit provided by the banks, the credit unions, and the *caisses populaires* have increased, while the proportions represented by retail credit and instalment credit have decreased.

J. The Caisses Populaires and the Credit Unions

Among the movements for economic and social reform, few, if any, have had as remarkable a success as the *caisses populaires* in the province of Quebec. From 1940 to 1963 the number of members increased by thirteen times from 124,000 to 1,660,500, or from 3.7 per cent to 30 per cent of the total population; at the same time the assets increased by fifty-four times to more than $1 billion. Since personal disposable income in the province, which constitutes the source of savings, increased by only 6.2 times, these figures clearly represent a tremendous growth.[1]

The *caisses populaires* were founded in Quebec in 1900 by Alphonse Desjardins. The new idea rapidly crossed the borders. Known as the credit union movement, it is now, with certain modifications, spread across all of North America. This is an early example, rare in those days, of a new venture organized by French Canadians and as such it merits attention. In the other Canadian provinces, having started later than in Quebec, the credit union movement is of less consequence in relation to total population. The number of members in these nine provinces represents about 10 per cent of the population. On the other hand, progress since the end of the war has been twice as rapid in the other provinces as in Quebec. In 1963 the total assets of the *caisses populaires* and the credit unions in Canada amounted to nearly $2 billion.

1. FUNCTIONS

The *caisses populaires* and the credit unions are savings and credit co-operatives. Being co-operatives, they carry on their activities only among their own members, who are at once the owners of the enterprise and the consumers of its services. For this reason the administrative and financial structure is highly decentralized. Each union is autonomous, because it belongs to its own members. The functions it performs are individual or personal services because of the fact that it is a co-operative.

The *caisse populaire* or credit union receives savings deposits and uses them to make personal loans to its members – either

---

1. Unless otherwise indicated we are following quite closely the excellent study of Gilles Mercure, *Credit Unions and Caisses Populaires*, a working paper prepared for the Royal Commission on Banking and Finance, November 1962, 218 pages.

short-term loans on promissory notes or mortgage loans. One can draw cheques on the deposits or withdraw them on demand. From the economic point of view they are, like the banks, financial intermediaries with the essential function of transmitting disposable savings to those who need them. In performing this function they create 'money', as do the banks and other financial institutions, if by money is meant the deposits resulting from advances of credit. Unlike banks, however, they do not grant credit of a commercial or industrial nature.

Although both are savings and credit co-operatives, the *caisses populaires* differ from the credit unions sufficiently to make a comparison necessary. In each, the member's interest is that of both a saver and a borrower, but in the *caisses populaires* the emphasis is clearly on savings, whereas in the credit unions it is on the needs of the borrower. This difference in emphasis leads to three main results: in the *caisses populaires* the deposits are much more important than the shares, whereas the reverse is true for the credit unions; for the protection of the depositors the *caisses populaires* do not lend more than 50 per cent of their assets, while the credit unions may lend up to 80 per cent; and the *caisses populaires* favour mortgage loans, while the credit unions engage primarily in consumer loans. Another important difference is that the *caisses populaires* are generally organized on a territorial basis (the parish), while the credit unions are organized on an occupational basis or according to other social ties which unite the members. A typical credit union in the United States or in Ontario, for example, will group together the employees of the same business or of the same institution.

Credit unions as described above are on the American model. Except in Ontario, where this model is followed rather closely, Canadian credit unions display several divergencies. Those in Nova Scotia resemble more closely the *caisses populaires*. Both the territorial and the occupational organization are found in the western provinces.

Mainly for the above reasons the *caisse populaire* is usually larger than the credit union. There are about two hundred *caisses populaires* in Quebec that have assets of more than $1 million each. In all the rest of the country there are not more than a hundred credit unions of this size.

The *caisses populaires* are affiliated with regional unions, and for each of these there is a *centrale*. The regional union concerns itself mainly with organization and education. The *centrale* is a financial organization which acts as a clearing-house for cheques, receives some investment funds from the local *caisses*, and makes loans to them if need be. In 1963 the assets of the Quebec *centrales* reached $153 million. Similarly, most of the credit unions are grouped together in 'leagues' which also have corresponding central unions. The assets of the central unions were $115 million in 1963. The credit unions are affiliated with the National Association of Credit Unions (C.U.N.A.) in the United States, and most *caisses populaires* are members of a federation with a head office at Lévis, Quebec.

2. SAVINGS DEPOSITS

The success of a financial institution depends upon its capacity to issue attractive liabilities in competition with other financial institutions. *Caisses populaires* and credit unions, as well as the char-

TABLE 10:34

Savings in *Caisses Populaires* and Credit Unions, and in Chartered Banks, Canada 1946-1963, millions of dollars

	1 *Chartered banks,* *personal savings*	*2* *Shares and deposits* *in local C.P. and C.U.*	*3* *2 as a percentage* *of 1*
1946	3,179	179	5.6
1951	4,296	334	7.8
1959	6,900	1,056	15.3
1961	7,618	1,387	18.2
1963	8,443	1,704	21.3

SOURCE: *Bank of Canada Statistical Summary* and *Credit Unions in Canada.* Department of Agriculture, Ottawa.

tered banks and the trust companies, compete with each other to attract (or sell) savings deposits. Deposits are just a particular form that savings may take and a particular kind of liability for the financial institutions.

To attract savings the financial institutions offer different services which correspond to a great variety of needs. Some offer security for the future (the insurance companies, the pension funds), some consumer credit, and others a higher return.

The *caisses populaires* and the credit unions have met with great success in this competition for the savings of the public. Its extent can be measured by a comparison with the chartered banks, their immediate competitors in the field of savings (Table 10:34).

In 1963 the savings deposits in the *caisses* and the credit unions reached $1.7 billion, an amount equivalent to 21.3 per cent of the savings deposits with the banks, which had grown to $8.4 billion. The figures in Table 10:34 indicate that since 1946 the growth of savings in the former has been nearly four times as rapid as that in the banks.

Velocity (rapidity of turnover) is an excellent indication of the nature of deposits. According to fragmentary information it appears that the deposits of the credit unions have a turnover rate of 20 to 40 times per annum, while that of their registered shares is 0.5 per annum. On the other hand, the turnover rate of the deposits of the *caisses populaires* is 2.7 per annum. Since the velocity of the current accounts and the savings deposits of the chartered banks are respectively 60 and 1.5, it is possible to conclude that the deposits of the credit unions are not true savings deposits, whereas the shares of the credit unions and, to a lesser degree, the deposits of the *caisses populaires*, may be considered as such.

The *caisses populaires* and the credit unions had available, in 1963, $127 million in the form of reserves and non-distributed surplus; this amount, together with the deposits and shares, made up the available capital assets of these institutions.

We shall next examine how these capital funds are used in

order to define more precisely the functions that the credit unions and *caisses populaires* perform on the financial market. The utilization of funds appears on the assets side of the balance sheet. Among the main items are loans and investments.

3. LOANS

It has already been mentioned that the *caisses populaires* and the credit unions differ in their credit and investment policies. Table 10:35 sums up in a few figures the over-all situation as it appeared in 1961. Of the assets of the credit unions, 65.4 per cent went into personal loans; the corresponding figure for the *caisses populaires* was 8.5 per cent. Inversely, the *caisses* had much more in mortgage loans. The *caisses populaires* keep a much higher proportion of their assets in securities and have a higher cash reserve, partly as a result of the fact that a mortgage loan is for a longer term than a personal loan.

TABLE 10:35

Utilization of Funds by the local *Caisses Populaires* and Credit Unions, Canada 1961, as a percentage of total assets

	Credit unions %	Caisses populaires %
Cash	8.2	16.6
Investments	11.1	30.0
Personal and other loans	65.4	8.5
Mortgage loans	12.7	41.2
Fixed and other assets	2.5	3.3
Total	100	100

SOURCE: Gilles Mercure, *Credit Unions and Caisses Populaires*, Working Paper prepared for the Royal Commission on Banking and Finance, Appendix II, Table II-A and Table VI.

As the next section will show, the *caisses populaires* and the credit unions do not loom large in the national picture of the residential mortgage market, though in Quebec the presence of the *caisses* makes itself strongly felt in that market. Indeed, it is estimated that the *caisses populaires* contribute a third of all the conventional mortgage loans for housing in Quebec. Furthermore, from 1960 to 1962 interest rates in Quebec were lower than elsewhere, and they were still below the national average in 1963; and the average term of a mortgage is longer in Quebec than in the country as a whole.[1] The average size of mortgage loans granted by the *caisses populaires* varies between $3,600 and $3,900, and the major portion of these loans are made on existing housing.

Since the *caisses* devote much of their resources to mortgage loans, they have not yet really touched the consumer credit market. This is to be regretted both because the *caisses*, as originally established, were intended to combat usury and to lower interest rates and because consumer credit is still excessively costly. Various indications, however, suggest that the *caisses* will have to turn more in this direction in the future, for competition in the mortgage loan market is becoming increasingly intense. Personal loans made by the *caisses* in the cities vary between $500 and $1,500; more than 50 per cent are for amounts of $1,000 and over. These loans have no guarantee except for the signature of an endorser, and even this is not always required. The interest rate is very low for this kind of loan: it varies from 6 to 7½ per cent net, and 44 per cent of the *caisses* charge only between 6 and 6½ per cent. Insurance premiums are usually required of the borrower in addition to the interest charges. Apparently the *caisses* turn down very few personal loans requests. Under these circumstances it seems rather extraordinary that there is not a greater demand.

The credit unions, on the other hand, are obviously operating in the field of the small loans companies and the sales finance companies. Almost two-thirds of their loans are consumer loans. The interest rates are higher than those of the *caisses populaires*. They vary from 6 to 12 per cent, the majority being between 8½ and 11 per cent, though in well-established rural

1. *Canadian Housing Statistics*, 1964, Table 45.

unions rates tend to be slightly lower. The loans are generally guaranteed either by the borrower's shares in the union, by real estate, or by chattel liens. (This last guarantee is not allowed under the Quebec civil code.) They are larger on the average than the personal loans made by the *caisses populaires*.

The preference shown to the credit union member as borrower rather than as depositor again becomes evident from the fact that, depending on the province in which they live, 35 to 75 per cent of the members are borrowers, whereas in the *caisses populaires* the proportion is only about 10 per cent.

4. INVESTMENTS

Investment performs a very precise function in a deposit institution such as a *caisse populaire*, a credit union, or a bank. Since it is always possible for withdrawals to be made, a certain proportion of the assets must be maintained in the form of securities easily negotiable on the market. In other words, investment must first answer a need for liquidity. An investment is preferable to the ordinary cash reserve inasmuch as it bears interest.

It is in respect to these two characteristics, liquidity and return, that the security holdings of an institution are usually judged.

In 1963 the total investments of the locals of the *caisses populaires* and the credit unions in Canada amounted to $373 million,

TABLE 10:36

Bond Holdings of the *Caisses Populaires*, percentages, 1961

	Locals %	Centrales %
Government of Canada	10.0	20.0
Government of Quebec	14.3	26.6
Municipalities and school boards	65.3	40.0
Religious institutions	10.0	13.3
Total	100	100

SOURCE: Gilles Mercure, *op. cit.*, p. 168.

of which the Quebec locals accounted for $275 million. The investments of the central offices totalled $91 million in Quebec and $123 million in Canada as a whole. Thus in the country as a whole, a grand total of about $500 million was invested, while Quebec's share of this very considerable sum was $366 million. Table 10:36 shows how the investments of the *caisses populaires* were distributed in 1961.

Two-thirds of the investments are in the bonds of municipalities and school boards. The *caisses* consider it a moral obligation to help with the financing of public institutions of a local or regional nature, the rule being that the capital should remain in the local area. The cost of such a policy is excessively high in terms of liquidity. Since many of these securities are not easily negotiable, the *caisses populaires* cannot sell them before maturity: the loss in capital would exceed the return they could obtain from new loans. Also they very rarely borrow money, even though they are permitted by law to do so up to a maximum of twice the paid-up capital plus the net worth of the *caisse*. Thus in periods of heavy demand the clients must wait patiently for funds to come in. In addition, the portfolios of the *caisses populaires* are, on the average, of a long-term nature, as might be expected from the rules they observe. The growing importance of the *centrales*, however, will probably lead to the adoption in future of less rigid and more rational policies.

Quebec law permits the *caisses populaires* to make more diversified investments out of their accumulated surpluses than on their other funds. (Fifty per cent of this surplus is free of any restriction.) Certain resources can therefore be allocated to the establishment of various institutions that will contribute indirectly to the progressive widening of the scope of *caisse* operations. Already the *caisses* have their own general insurance company – La Société d'Assurance des Caisses Populaires (1946); a life insurance company – L'Assurance-Vie Desjardins (1950); and a trust company – La Société de Fiducie du Québec (1963). In 1962 an important life insurance company, La Sauvegarde, came under control of the *caisses*. As already pointed out, they have participated as shareholders in establishing the General Investment Corporation.[1]

K. Some General Observations

At the conclusion of a rather tedious examination of a good many different financial institutions, the reader, like the author, must be feeling that it is high time to leave the particular and return to the general. In the course of the previous pages there have been many references to Government of Canada bonds, provincial government bonds, mortgages, consumer credit, and similar types of credit. A proper financial accounting system would put together in a single table all these dispersed items of information concerning the different kinds of credit. Let us refer for a moment to the first section of this chapter and, in particular, to the nomenclature of Table 10:1. All the securities mentioned are placed at the left as line headings, while the financial institutions are indicated in column headings across the top. Instead of recording in the appropriate spaces the changes that have taken place in the course of a year, as this table of financial transactions seeks to do, we could quite easily record the stocks held at a given time. The table would then become a balance sheet. The column for financial institutions can also be disaggregated to show the details of each category of financial institution, such as banks, insurance companies, and so forth.

As stated earlier, there is not yet a national balance sheet for Canada that is complete and drawn up in this form. Certain portions of an eventual balance sheet have, however, been made provisionally available, thanks to the *Report of the Royal Commission on Banking and Finance*.

1. PRIMARY DEBT OUTSTANDING

One section that could be included in a final balance sheet would be one indicating the outstanding *primary debt*. By primary debt is meant the debt contracted by non-financial borrowers with a

1. The total assets of *caisses populaires* including the subsidiaries amounted to $1.36 billion at the end of 1965 (Lévis Federation only).

view to engaging in transactions on the goods market. In comparison, the financial institutions, in their role as intermediaries between the savers from whom they borrow funds and the consumers of funds to whom they lend them, could be said to contract 'secondary' debt. Money in circulation and deposits (in banks, trust companies, etc.) are excluded from the primary debt; life insurance companies' debt to their policyholders (accumulated insurance premiums) is also excluded, as are the liabilities of the pension funds.

TABLE 10:37

Primary Debt Outstanding, Canada 1962

	In billions of dollars	As a percentage of the total
Government of Canada	19.4	27.0
Provincial governments	9.0	12.5
Municipal governments	4.0	6.0
Business debt	14.5	20.2
Trade credit (accounts payable)	5.4	7.4
Mortgages	14.0	19.5
Other personal debt	5.3	7.3
Total	72.0	100

NOTES: Interpersonal debt and equities are not included.

The figure for trade credit applies to 1960.

Except for the figures concerning trade credit which we have not mentioned elsewhere, the above figures should correspond to those of the other tables in this chapter: Government of Canada obligations and other obligations, Table 10:8. It should be noted that the bonds issued by corporations constitute only a fraction of the corporations' total debt. Mortgage credit, Table 10:29. The other personal debts include mainly consumer credit recorded in Table 10:33.

SOURCE: *Report of the Royal Commission on Banking and Finance*, p. 6.

In a complete balance sheet it is obvious that debt would not include equity or the accumulated surplus of business.[1] A rereading of the types of securities in circulation as given in Table 10:1

1. Foreign inheritances and gifts, like savings, are an addition to the existing stock of wealth.

would now be helpful for an understanding of the significance of Table 10:37.

The main aspects of these figures which should attract attention are the size of the total indebtedness and the relative size of its various categories.

To interpret and evaluate the total indebtedness would be easy if we knew the real and financial assets (on the assets side) and the country's net worth (on the liabilities side). Not having this information we can only make a comparison with the G.N.P. or the national income. A total indebtedness of $72 billion in 1962 was equivalent to 178 per cent of the G.N.P. Contrary to the claims of certain writers, the national debt has not increased appreciably in proportion to the national product since 1950. Indeed, it has decreased in comparison with 1945, when it was 219 per cent of the G.N.P., and is far below what it was in the 1930s[1] (in 1933 the proportion exceeded 300 per cent). Canadian prosperity in the post-war period is therefore not founded on an excessive indebtedness.

Clearly the public sector is the big spender, for government bonds account for nearly half (45.5 per cent) of the total debt. The federal government contracted the major part of its debt during the war, whereas the provincial and municipal governments tripled theirs after 1950, mainly to finance social investments. However, public indebtedness on the whole has decreased relatively since 1935: at that time outstanding government bonds comprised 58.7 per cent of the over-all indebtedness.

Borrowings by business and mortgage loans each accounted for one-fifth of the total debt in 1962. These have increased very rapidly since the war.

Finally, as we have seen in Table 10:33, private individuals are tending to borrow more, both in total and in proportion to income.

2. DISTRIBUTION OF FINANCIAL CLAIMS

For every debtor there is a creditor. For the *debt* of the borrow-

1. *Report of the Royal Commission on Banking and Finance*, pp. 6 and 7.

er there is an equivalent *investment* by the lender. Who are the creditors who hold the $72 billion of debt listed above? The answer given in Table 10:38 is for the year 1961, when primary debt amounted to $66.8 billion (compared with $72 billion in 1962).

The lenders are classed in two groups only: the non-financial units and the financial institutions. In the first group are individuals (such as all those worthy citizens who buy government bonds), non-financial business, and the rest of the world. This group held 48 per cent of the claims, while the financial institu-

TABLE 10:38

Distribution of Financial Claims, billions of dollars, 1961

	Primary debt outstanding	Non-financial units	Financial institutions
Government of Canada	18.6	9.3	9.3
Provincial governments	8.2	4.9	3.3
Municipal governments	4.1	2.0	2.1
Business	13.1	4.0	9.1
Trade debt	5.4	5.4	—
Mortgage debt	12.4	5.6	6.9
Other Personal debt	5.0	1.0	4.0
Total	66.8	32.3	34.6

SOURCE: *Report of the Royal Commission on Banking and Finance*, p. 90.

tions held the other 52 per cent. This percentage gives a very good idea of the importance of the financial institutions to the economy. They held 50 per cent of the stock of federal bonds, 40 per cent of provincial bonds, and 50 per cent of municipal bonds. In the private sector the financial institutions play an even more important role. They held 70 per cent of business debt, 56 per cent of mortgage debt, and 80 per cent of other personal debt. An explanation could be found for each of these percentages by examining the nature and characteristics of the borrowers and of the securities sold to obtain the funds, and also by examining the nature and characteristics of the lenders, whether individuals or financial institutions. Such an analysis would then reduce itself to the factors determining the supply and demand of financial capital. Thus, for example, governments and large corporations have direct access to the investors and so are not obliged to use the services of the financial institutions to the same extent as small businesses and individuals are. For their part, the financial institutions buy securities (or make investments) that investors would not readily buy, and have their own special preferences among the securities offered on the market.

TABLE 10:39

Assets of Financial Institutions, Canada 1962

	In billions of dollars	*As a percentage of the total*
Bank of Canada	3.2	7.6
Chartered banks	14.8	34.9
Quebec Savings Banks	0.3	0.8
Trust companies (company and guaranteed funds)	1.9	4.4
Mortgage loan companies	1.3	3.0
Caisses populaires	1.7	3.9
Sales finance and small loans companies	2.2	5.3
Industrial Development Bank	0.2	0.4
Sub-total	25.7	60.4
Life insurance companies, assets in Canada	9.9	23.4
Pension funds	4.6	10.8
Mutual funds	0.7	1.7
Fire and casualty insurance companies, assets in Canada	1.6	3.7
Total	42.5	100

NOTE: Since these assets include claims on financial institutions held by other institutions, the total includes some duplication.

SOURCE: *Report of the Royal Commission on Banking and Finance*, pp. 106-7.

3. RELATIVE IMPORTANCE OF THE PRINCIPAL FINANCIAL INSTITU-
TIONS

The activities of the institutions have already been described.
This section will attempt to assign to them their proper places in
relation to one another and so to define their relative importance
on the capital market.

The institutions listed here had over-all assets of $42.5 billion
in 1962. The chartered banks are clearly the most important
institutions with 35 per cent of the total assets. Next come the
life insurance companies with almost a quarter, then the pension
funds, the Bank of Canada, the consumer loan companies, and
the trust companies, in that order.

Since the 1930s the relative placings of the financial institutions have changed a great deal. In 1935 the capital market
lacked diversification, being largely dominated by the chartered
banks and the life insurance companies, which together
accounted for 80 per cent of the total assets. The percentage had
dropped to 58 by 1962, owing to the fact that several other
financial institutions had been founded in the interval or had
progressed more rapidly than the banks and the life insurance
companies. Especially noticeable among the new ones are the
pension funds (and the Bank of Canada, which is a special case),
and among the more rapidly growing, the *caisses populaires* and
the consumer loan companies. These three types of institutions
owe their success to the considerable expansion of consumer
credit and also, no doubt, to the slowness or even inertia of the
chartered banks in this new field of credit (and, of course, to the
legal restrictions on the rates of interest that the banks may
charge).

In regard to primary debt, the very large amount in claims held
by financial institutions as a group has already been calculated
(see page 274). Because of the duplication in the total assets
indicated in Table 10:39, our figures are now somewhat different. The financial institutions' assets of $42.5 billion in 1962
represent 59 per cent of the $72 billion of primary debt existing
in that year. By making comparable calculations for previous
years it becomes evident that financial institutions as a group are

increasing in relative importance on the capital market. That this is true also for the United States can be verified by consulting the detailed studies listed in the bibliography.

SUGGESTED READINGS

A. General

CANADA: *Report of the Royal Commission on Banking and Finance,* Ottawa, Queen's Printer, 1964.
The Commission has inquired into the structure and methods of operation of the financial system. Its report covers the financial intermediaries discussed in the present chapter: stock markets, investment dealers, chartered banks, credit unions, trusts, mortgage loan companies, etc. It is the best single reference that can be given in this field.

W. C. HOOD: *Financing of Economic Activity in Canada,* Royal Commission on Canada's Economic Prospects, Ottawa, Queen's Printer, 1958.
A discussion of financial institutions is found in Part IV. Some aspects of the financing of consumers and businesses are analysed in Part III.

R. W. GOLDSMITH: *The Share of Financial Intermediaries in National Wealth and National Assets, 1900-1949,* New York, National Bureau of Economic Research, Inc., 1954.

R. W. GOLDSMITH: *Financial Intermediaries in the American Economy since 1900,* Princeton University Press, 1958.

R. W. GOLDSMITH: *The Flow of Capital Funds in the Post-War Economy,* New York, Columbia University Press, 1965.

The Flow-of-funds Approach to Social Accounting, National Bureau of Economic Research, Conference on Research in Income and Wealth, vol. 26, Princeton University Press, 1962.
A series of papers discussing the flow-of-funds approach. The system developed in Canada is discussed on pp. 103-32.

R. FRISCH: *A Generalized Form of the REFI Interflow Table*, and *A Macroeconomic Interflow Table with Specification of Competitive Imports*, memoranda from the Institute of Economics, University of Oslo, 1959.

B. *Particular markets or financial institutions*

C. A. ASHLEY AND J. E. SMYTH: *Corporation Finance in Canada*, Toronto, Macmillan, 1957.
A description analysis of structural aspects and financing techniques in Canadian corporations.

E. SCHWARTZ: *Corporation Finance*, New York, St. Martin's Press, 1962.
A theoretical study of corporate finance.

THE FINANCIAL POST: *The Financial Post Survey of Investment Funds*, Toronto, 1964.

G. D. SUTTON: *Corporate Finance*, Ottawa, Queen's Printer, 1962.
A study prepared for the Royal Commission on Banking and Finance.

J.-C. FAFFA: *Les Sociétés d'investissement et la gestion collective de l'épargne,* Paris, Editions Cujas, 1963.
A survey and analysis of the American experience in mutual funds and investment trust companies.

B. E. SCHULTZ: *The Securities Market and How it Works*, revised edition, edited by Albert P. Squier, New York, Harper, 1963.

J. P. WILLIAMSON: *Securities Regulations in Canada*, Toronto, University of Toronto Press, 1960.

A. H. FULLERTON: *The Bond Market in Canada*, Toronto, The Carswell Company, 1962.
A study of the institutions, machinery, techniques, and problems involved in the issuing and marketing of bonds and debentures in Canada.

S. TURK: *The Foreign Exchange Market*, Ottawa, Queen's Printer, 1964.

A study prepared for the Royal Commission on Banking and Finance.

J. POAPST: *The Residential Mortgage Market*, Ottawa, Queen's Printer, 1962.

A study prepared for the Royal Commission on Banking and Finance.

THE CANADIAN LIFE INSURANCE OFFICERS ASSOCIATION: *Submission to the Royal Commission on Banking and Finance*, Toronto, July 1962.

G. CLAYTON AND W. T. OSBORN: *Insurance Company Investment; Principles and Policy*, London, George Allen & Unwin Ltd., 1965.

Certain chapters of this book are of general application. Chapter II deals with insurance companies as financial intermediaries, chapter III with the role of accumulated funds in insurance, chapter IV with the theory of the portfolio choice. The conclusion in chapter X evaluates the global impact of insurance companies' policies on the economy.

J. V. POAPST: *Consumer Survey*, Ottawa, Queen's Printer, 1965.

A study prepared for the Royal Commission on Banking and Finance.

CANADIAN ECONOMIC RESEARCH ASSOCIATES: *Sales finance companies in Canada*, Toronto, Ryerson Press, 1959.

A two-part study devoted to the costs and profits of sales finance companies, prepared for the Federated Council of Sales Finance Companies of Canada.

G. MERCURE: *Credit Unions and Caisses Populaires*, Ottawa, Queen's Printer, 1962.

A study prepared for the Royal Commission on Banking and Finance.

Part three

PUBLIC FINANCE

_____

CHAPTER

11

TAXATION

This chapter is devoted to the taxes that are levied by governments. In an introductory section government activity will be put into the perspective of the general economy.

A. Public Finance in the Canadian Economy

The expenditure of the federal, provincial, and municipal governments in 1963 constituted 31.7% of the gross national product. Since in that year all governments taken together incurred a deficit, revenue was less than expenditure; revenue rose to 30 per cent of the G.N.P. Total taxes represented a quarter of the G.N.P. The relative importance of the public finances in the economy of the country today may thus be estimated as being about 30 per cent of the national product. Table 11:1 provides a time perspective that demonstrates the increasing participation of governments in the country's economic activity. Although the figures are not exactly comparable, it is worth adding that in 1870 government expenditure did not represent more than 7 per cent of the G.N.P. and that in 1910 it came to about 14 per cent.[1] Since 1929, the importance of government activity in the economy has almost doubled.

The increase in government expenditure is not primarily due to the two world wars as some people seem to believe; it is just as much due to the increase in social security payments and in gov-

1. Taken from O. J. Firestone, *Canada's Economic Development,* London, Bowes & Bowes, p. 72.

TABLE 11 : 1

Revenue and Expenditure of All Governments as a Percentage of Gross National Product

	Expenditure*	Revenue*	Direct and indirect taxes†
1929	15.9	15.7	13.1
1933	26.6	21.1	18.7
1947	23.7	29.4	25.2
1956	26.1	27.3	22.8
1961	32.4	29.7	24.6
1963	31.7	30.0	25.0

*Exclusive of inter-governmental transfers.
†Not including employer and employee contributions to social insurance and government pension funds.

SOURCE: Canadian Tax Foundation, *The National Finances*, *1964-65*, Tables 5, 6, and 8.

ernment expenditure on goods and services. The rise in these expenditures on goods and services is found in the categories of both current and capital expenditure.

The increase in government expenditure, on the other hand, has not been continuous as a percentage of the national product. The war years apart, it was not until 1952 that the percentage of 1933 was again reached. These variations stem from the fact that the percentages reflect variations not only in the expenditure but also in the gross national product. Thus the percentage increase between 1956 and 1961 was caused primarily by the very small increase in the G.N.P. The same situation prevailed in the 1930s.[1]

1. Government expenditure and revenue is one among many bases by which to measure the importance of government in the economy. Another one, producing more striking results perhaps, is government contributions to total capital formation. If we refer again to Table 2:5 we see that the share of government departments was 13.6 per cent in 1962. To this proportion must be added investments in schools, hospitals, and universities, some of the investment in public utilities, and so forth. These categories increase the share of governments to about 30 per cent of total capital formation. In

Table 11:2 shows how the tax revenues are divided among the different levels of government.

TABLE 11 : 2

Direct and Indirect Taxes as a Percentage
of Gross National Product, by Level of Government

	1956		1963	
	As a percentage of G.N.P.	*As a percentage of total taxation*	*As a percentage of G.N.P.*	*As a percentage of total taxation*
Federal	16.1	70.6	14.2	57.1
Provincial	3.6	15.6	6.5	26.1
Municipal	3.1	13.8	4.2	16.8
All governments	22.8	100	24.9	100

NOTE: These figures are exclusive of inter-governmental transfers and of employer and employee contributions to social insurance and government pension funds.

In 1963 the federal government levied 57 per cent of the total taxes, the provinces 26 per cent, and the municipalities nearly 17 per cent. These proportions are not constant. Immediately before the war the federal government levied barely 50 per cent of the taxes. Since 1952 the federal government's share has been declining while that of the provinces and municipalities has been rising. As will be seen in the next chapter, federal expenditures are now lower than provincial and municipal expenditures together. *There is nothing immutable or sacrosanct about the relative importance of the provinces, the municipalities, and the federal government in the fiscal domain.*

addition to this, governments contribute directly (through loans) to a quarter of housing construction and indirectly (through guaranteed loans) to another 20 per cent so that a further 8 to 9 per cent is added to the previous 30 per cent of capital formation. On the whole, governments contribute a good 40 per cent to capital formation in Canada.

B. The Tax Structure by Level of Government

1. FEDERAL TAXES

A distinction may be made between direct taxes, which bear on income, and indirect taxes, which bear on expenditures.[1] The principal direct taxes are the personal income tax, the corporation profits tax, and succession duties. This last one must be classed as a tax on wealth or capital. Customs tariffs and the general sales tax are examples of indirect taxes.

Direct taxes found greatest favour with the federal government during the two world wars. Since the end of World War II in 1945 they have represented approximately 60 per cent of all taxes levied by the federal government. In 1926, in comparison, they were only 14 per cent. Moreover, as Table 11:3 shows, the personal income tax has been increasing in importance relative to the corporation profits tax.

Among the indirect taxes, customs tariffs are relatively less important than before World War I, although since 1945 they have increased more rapidly than the other indirect taxes.

Excise duties and taxes are sales taxes paid by the manufacturers. The excise taxes consist mainly of the general sales tax of 11 per cent (of which 3 per cent goes to pay for old age pensions) and other particular *ad valorem* taxes (tax expressed as a percentage of value). They are applied to both imported and domestic commodities. Excise duties are mainly applied to liquor, tobacco, cigars, and cigarettes; they are calculated on quantity rather than value and are not levied on imports. The excise taxes are much more important, as Table 11:3 illustrates.

2. PROVINCIAL TAXES

Taxes differ from one province to another. From 1957 to 1962, Quebec was the only province to levy a tax on personal income,

---

1. The distinction that we draw between direct taxes and indirect taxes is of a 'statistical' order. In economic analysis the direct tax is that whose burden is borne by the taxpayer himself and the indirect tax is that whose burden is transmitted to others. The sales tax is paid by the manufacturers or the retailers, but these taxpayers may transmit part or all of this tax to the consumers in the form of price increases.

TABLE 11 : 3

Federal Government Direct and Indirect Taxes, 1950 and 1963

	1950		1963	
	Millions of dollars	*As a per- centage of the total*	*Millions of dollars*	*As a per- centage of the total*
1. DIRECT TAXES				
Personal income tax	612	23.48	2,102	35.05
Corporation profits tax	837	32.12	1,353	22.57
Succession duties and estate taxes	35	1.34	89	1.48
Miscellaneous	7	0.26	2	0.04
Total direct taxes	1,491	57.21	3,546	59.14
2. INDIRECT TAXES				
Customs import duties	257	9.86	577	9.62
Excise duties	226	8.67	393	6.56
Excise taxes	620	23.79	1,462	24.38
Miscellaneous	12	0.46	18	0.30
Total indirect taxes	1,115	42.78	2,450	40.86
Total taxes	*2,606*	*100*	*5,996*	*100*

NOTE: To obtain total revenues, withholding taxes paid by non-residents, employer and employee contributions to social insurance and government pension funds, and investment income must be added to taxes. The total revenue of the federal government in 1963 was $7,154 millions.

SOURCE: *National Accounts, Income and Expenditure, 1926-56* and *1963*.

and only Quebec and Ontario levied taxes on corporation profits and on estates (successions). These taxes were deductible from the corresponding federal taxes by virtue of the fiscal agreements. As we shall see later, all provinces have levied their own direct taxes since 1962.

In 1945 direct taxes accounted for 21 per cent of provincial taxes.[1] At that time Quebec and Ontario collected succession

1. Hospitalization insurance premiums and driving licences are considered direct taxes for special reasons.

Federal Taxes, 1963

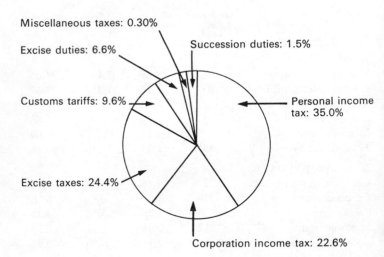

Miscellaneous taxes: 0.30%

Excise duties: 6.6%

Succession duties: 1.5%

Customs tariffs: 9.6%

Personal income tax: 35.0%

Excise taxes: 24.4%

Corporation income tax: 22.6%

duties but left the two other income taxes to the federal government. In 1963 direct taxes made up 40 per cent of provincial taxes, mainly because the provinces had taken back part of the tax rights they had yielded during the war to the federal government. In spite of these recent changes in policy, by and large the provinces employ indirect taxes and the federal government direct taxes. Among the indirect taxes, the retail sales tax and the gasoline tax are the most productive. Details appear on p. 289.

3. MUNICIPAL (INCLUDING SCHOOL BOARD) TAXES

The principal source of revenue for the municipalities is the property tax, which is an indirect tax generally classed among the taxes on wealth. A lesser but well-known municipal source of funds is the water tax. Certain towns or municipalities levy a retail sales tax and various other business taxes of less significance.

TABLE 11 : 4

Provincial Government Direct and Indirect Taxes, 1950 and 1963

	1950		1963	
	Millions of dollars	As a percentage of total	Millions of dollars	As a percentage of total
1. DIRECT TAXES				
Personal income tax	—	—	385	13.76
Corporations profits tax	128	18.90	420	15.01
Hospital insurance premiums	18	2.65	120	4.29
Succession duties	31	4.58	82	2.93
Mining and logging profits tax	8	1.18	37	1.32
Private-motor-vehicle licences and permits	24	3.54	76	2.72
Miscellaneous	9	1.32	24	0.86
Total direct taxes	228	33.67	1,144	40.89
2. INDIRECT TAXES				
Gasoline	158	23.33	521	18.62
Retail sales tax	87	12.85	576	20.59
Miscellaneous taxes on natural resources	51	7.53	152	5.43
Business motor vehicle licences and permits	42	6.20	120	4.29
Corporation tax (not on profits)	23	3.69	23	0.82
Licences, fees, and permits	25	3.69	34	1.22
Amusement	19	2.80	27	0.96
Miscellaneous	38	5.61	201	7.18
Total indirect taxes	449	66.32	1,654	59.11
Total taxes	*677*	*100*	*2,798*	*100*

NOTE: To obtain the total revenue of provincial governments, investment income, social insurance contributions, and federal government subsidies must be added. The total revenue of provincial governments in 1963 was $4,740 million.

SOURCE: *National Accounts, Income and Expenditure, 1926-56* and *1963*.

C. The Rates of Taxation

In the fiscal domain, as in several other fields, Canada follows

Provincial Taxes, 1963

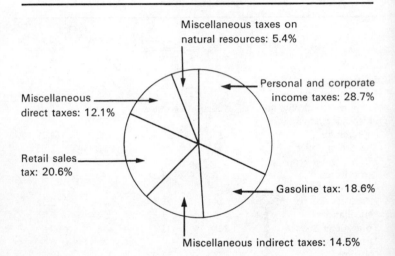

Miscellaneous taxes on
natural resources: 5.4%

Personal and corporate
income taxes: 28.7%

Miscellaneous
direct taxes: 12.1%

Retail sales
tax: 20.6%

Gasoline tax: 18.6%

Miscellaneous indirect taxes: 14.5%

English rather than United States practices. Thus the general
criterion for taxation is residence rather than citizenship, and
capital gains are not taxed. Canadian residents are liable for
Canadian income taxes on income from all sources, domestic or
foreign. Non-residents are liable on income arising from employment in Canada or from business activities carried on in Canada.

1. PERSONAL INCOME TAX

*For purposes of this tax, income includes all categories of income
of domestic or foreign origin with the exception of family
allowances, unemployment insurance benefits, and several other
transfer revenues. From the total income the standard exemptions are subtracted in order to obtain the taxable income.* It is
on the concept of taxable income that the rates quoted below are
applied. Exemptions are (broadly speaking) $1,000 for a single
person, $2,000 for a married taxpayer (if his wife is not earn-
ning), plus $300 for each child qualified for family allowances

and $550 for any other dependant. Other exemptions are also allowed, for instance in respect of medical expenses and charities.

TABLE 11 : 5

Municipal Government Direct and Indirect Taxes, 1950 and 1963

	1950		1963	
	Millions of dollars	*As a percentage of total*	*Millions of dollars*	*As a percentage of total*
1. MISCELLANEOUS DIRECT TAXES	4	0.79	30	1.66
2. INDIRECT TAXES				
Real property	407	80.91	1,479	81.98
Retail sales tax	24	4.77	59	3.27
Licences, fees, and permits	15	2.98	36	2.00
Miscellaneous (including water tax)	53	10.53	200	11.09
Total taxes	503	100	1,804	100

NOTE: To obtain the total revenue of municipal governments, investment income, contributions to social insurances, and federal and provincial subsidies must be added. The total revenue was $3,331 million in 1963.

SOURCE: *National Accounts, Income and Expenditure, 1926-56* and *1963*.

By virtue of the fiscal agreements of 1962 between the provinces and the federal government (and subsequent revisions), the provinces now levy a tax on personal income, which is expressed as a percentage of the tax that would otherwise be collected by the federal government. This percentage is as follows:

16 per cent for 1962
17 per cent for 1963
18 per cent for 1964
21 per cent for 1965
24 per cent for 1966

Since 1962 Manitoba and Saskatchewan have added a differential, introduced to finance health services, so that in 1964, for

TABLE 11 : 6

Federal and Provincial Marginal Personal Income Tax Rates, 1964*

Taxable income exceeding $	1 Federal rates after abatement for provincial taxes† %	Provincial taxes, marginal‡ rates			Total marginal rates, federal and provincial		
		2 Quebec %	3 Man. and Sask. %	4 Other provinces %	5 Quebec %	6 Man. and Sask. %	7 Other provinces %
1	9.02	2.50	2.64	1.98	11.52	11.66	11.00
1,000	11.48	2.80	3.36	2.52	14.28	14.84	14.00
2,000	13.94	3.20	4.08	3.06	17.14	18.02	17.00
3,000	15.58	3.20	4.56	3.42	18.78	20.14	19.00
4,000	18.04	3.60	5.28	3.96	21.64	23.32	22.00
6,000	21.32	4.70	6.24	4.68	26.02	27.56	26.00
8,000	24.60	5.40	7.20	5.40	30.00	31.80	30.00
10,000	28.70	6.30	8.40	6.30	35.00	37.10	35.00
12,000	32.80	7.20	9.60	7.20	40.00	42.40	40.00
15,000	36.90	8.10	10.80	8.10	45.50	47.70	45.00
25,000	41.00	9.00	12.00	9.00	50.00	53.00	50.00
40,000	45.10	9.90	13.20	9.90	55.00	58.30	55.00
60,000	49.20	10.80	14.40	10.80	60.00	63.60	60.00
90,000	53.30	11.70	15.60	11.70	65.00	68.90	65.00
125,000	57.40	12.60	16.80	12.60	70.00	74.20	70.00
225,000	61.50	13.50	18.00	13.50	75.00	79.50	75.00
400,000	65.60	14.40	19.20	14.40	80.00	84.80	80.00

instance, the income tax was equivalent to 24 per cent of the federal tax, thus adding in that year 6 per cent to the burden of the residents of these provinces. The situation of the province of Quebec in relation to the other provinces is much improved as a result of the 1962 agreements. In fact, the abatement of 16 per cent that the federal government granted to all provinces in that year represented for Quebec an abatement 3 per cent higher than 1961 and was nearly equal to the tax that Quebec had already had in force since 1954. The elements of double taxation were

Municipal Taxes, 1963

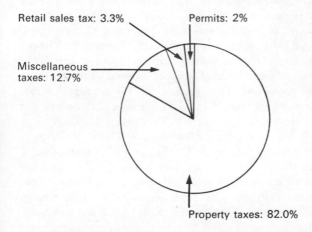

Retail sales tax: 3.3%   Permits: 2%

Miscellaneous taxes: 12.7%

Property taxes: 82.0%

For Table 11:6:

*Excluding Old Age Security tax of 4 per cent with ceiling of $120; also excluding surtax of 4 per cent on investment income from non-Canadian sources.

†Abatement is 18 per cent of tax payable under federal rates before abatement. These federal rates before abatements are given in the last column. If 18 per cent of each of the rates is deducted, the net federal rate is obtained as given in the first column. For example, with taxable income exceeding $1, 18 per cent of 11 per cent is 1.98%; 11% minus 1.98% is 9.02%.

‡For explanation of 'marginal' see p. 294.

SOURCE: Canadian Tax Foundation, *The National Finances, 1964-65*, Table 19.

thus progressively eliminated. The task was completed in 1965 when Quebec adjusted its tax rates to the federal abatements. Compared to Manitoba and Saskatchewan the Quebec tax is lower.

This is shown in Table 11:6. Column 1 indicates the 1964 rate of the federal income tax – that is, the former rate after the subtraction of the 18 per cent abatement. Columns 2 and 4 show that the federal abatement applicable to 'other provinces' is almost equivalent to the Quebec tax. Columns 5, 6, and 7 give the sum of the federal and provincial taxes and indicate the total rate to be paid by the taxpayers.

Let us consider the other aspects of the personal income tax. *First of all the progressive character of the rates should be noted. By progressive is meant that the rates increase with income.* They rise from 11 per cent for a taxable income of less than $1,000 to 80 per cent for an income exceeding $400,000. For 1965 and 1966, the basic tax payable was reduced by 5 per cent and 10 per cent respectively with maximum reductions of $300 and $600. Table 11:6 gives some selected marginal tax rates, that is, rates that apply to successive layers of income. The average tax rate also increases with income, but at a slower pace. Let us take, for example, a taxable income of $2,000. On the first $1,000 the rate is 11 per cent and on the second 14 per cent. The tax to be paid, then, is $110 + $140 = $250, or 12.5 per cent of income. The 11 per cent and the 14 per cent are two marginal rates; 12.5 per cent is an average rate. Such a tax structure is equalitarian, since it obviously hinders the citizen from accumulating great wealth. In the United States personal income tax is higher and more progressive still.

2. CORPORATION INCOME TAX

The fiscal agreements of 1962 prescribe that taxes on corporation profits be shared between the provinces and the federal government according to a rule similar to that pertaining to the personal income tax. The arrangement consists of the federal government's granting an abatement to take account of the tax levied by the provinces. However, the abatement is expressed not as a percentage of the tax payable as is that on the personal income tax, but as a percentage of taxable income.

Let us first consider the tax rates from the point of view of the taxpayer.

TABLE 11 : 7

Marginal Rates of Corporation Income Taxes, Combined Federal and Provincial, 1965

| | *Taxable net income* | |
	up to $35,000 %	over $35,000 %
Quebec and Ontario	23	52
Saskatchewan and Manitoba	22	51
Other Provinces	21	50

NOTE: Including 3 per cent as the Old Age Security Tax.

SOURCE: Canadian Tax Foundation, *The National Finances, 1964-65.*

There are three different rates in the country. On a profit of more than $35,000 the Quebec or Ontario taxpayer pays 52 per cent, the Manitoba or Saskatchewan taxpayer 51 per cent, and the others 50 per cent. The greater part of this goes to the federal government. The federal tax on a profit of $35,000 and more is 41 per cent (making for provincial rates of 11 per cent in Ontario, 10 per cent in Manitoba and Saskatchewan, and 9 per cent in other provinces) except in Quebec where it is 40 per cent (making for a Quebec rate of 12 per cent). It is 12 per cent and 11 per cent respectively on a profit of less than $35,000. The federal government grants an additional 1 per cent to Quebec in order to compensate for the federal university grants that are paid to the other provinces.

The rates have varied quite considerably at times since the early forties. In 1939 profits were taxed at a uniform rate of 15 per cent plus 2 per cent on the profits of the consolidated return of the company. In the middle of the war the average rates rose by from 40 per cent to 80 per cent depending on profits. After the war, the rates were reduced until 1949 and since that time they have remained at approximately the present rates. In the United States the rate of the corporation tax is lower than in Canada: in 1965 it was 22 per cent of profits up to $25,000 and 48 per cent of profits in excess of this figure.

3. ESTATE TAX

According to the federal Estate Tax Act, the net value of an estate must exceed $50,000 in order to be taxable. The taxable value is the net value less a minimum exemption of $40,000, plus an additional exemption of $20,000 for a widow and $10,000 for each dependent child. The taxable value is taxed according to progressive rates rising from 10 per cent on the first $5,000 to a maximum of 54 per cent. Ontario, Quebec, and British Columbia have their own estate tax and the federal government grants a 75 per cent abatement of the federal estate tax collections in a province.

4. WITHHOLDING TAX

Canada levies a 15 per cent tax on dividends paid to non-residents. The tax rate was raised in 1963 to 20 per cent unless foreign firms became 'Canadianized' to the extent of being 25 per cent Canadian-owned before 1967. This provision was abolished in 1964.

5. OTHER INCOME AND CAPITAL TAXES

There are a number of other income and capital taxes levied by provinces. It is impossible to describe them all here in detail. Following are a few:

    (a) Taxes on logging operations.

            Ontario and Quebec levy 10 per cent on net income in excess of $10,000; British Columbia levies 10 per cent on net income in excess of $25,000. These taxes are fully deducted from the total taxes paid under the corporation income tax. Three-quarters is deducted from the federal portion and one-quarter from the provincial portion. The net result is that the provinces get three-quarters of the tax from the federal government, the reason being that logging operations are a use of natural resources, which come under provincial jurisdiction.

(b) Taxes on mining operations.

Seven provinces levy a tax on revenue from mining operations.

(c) Taxes on capital.

Quebec levies a tax of one-tenth of 1 per cent on the net worth plus the long-term debt of business firms; Ontario levies similarly one-twentieth of 1 per cent but only when the amount involved exceeds the income tax.

(d) Taxes on business premises.

Only Quebec and Ontario levy this tax. In Quebec it is set at $50 when the paid-up capital is $25,000, and $25 when the paid-up capital is less. Ontario levies the tax only under certain conditions.

(e) Taxes on insurance premiums.

All provinces levy 2 per cent on the value of premiums received by insurance companies. This is an income tax of a sort on the insurance companies.

6. COMMODITY TAXES

(a) The principal federal excise tax is the general sales tax which is 8 per cent (plus 3 per cent for old age pensions). A 1963 amendment made the tax applicable to building materials and machinery, which it previously did not affect. It is collected from the manufacturers. The provincial and municipal retail sales taxes vary between 2 and 6 per cent according to region. They are collected from the retailers. In 1965, the provincial rates were 6 per cent in Quebec, 3 per cent in Ontario (raised to 5 per cent afterwards) and New

Brunswick, 4 per cent in Saskatchewan, and 5 per cent in British Columbia, Newfoundland, Nova Scotia, and Prince Edward Island.

(b) Customs import duties are commodity taxes treated in Chapter 15.

(c) Ontario, Manitoba, and Saskatchewan levy a special tax to cover hospital insurance. The premiums are respectively $39, $24, and $20 for single persons. The family rate is double.

(d) Tobacco and alcoholic beverages are heavily taxed at both the federal and provincial levels. The federal taxes on tobacco amount to about 1c per cigarette. In Quebec there is an additional tax of 4c per 20 cigarettes and in Ontario of 1c per 20 cigarettes.

(e) Amusement taxes. The rate varies from 5 to 13 per cent of the admission prices in eight provinces.

(f) Taxes on gasoline and diesel fuels. The rates in 1965 ranged from 12c in Alberta to 19c in Newfoundland and Nova Scotia per gallon of gas for automobiles and trucks, and from 14c in Alberta to 27c in Nova Scotia per gallon of diesel fuels.

(g) Motor vehicle licences and driving permits are taxed in all provinces.

(h) Taxes on transfers of real estate and on securities transactions. Alberta and Ontario levy a tax on the first, at rates based on prices. Ontario and Quebec tax the second.

(i) Municipalities generally levy a water tax calculated on the property assessment.

7. REAL PROPERTY TAX

Municipal taxes are based on property values and are levied against property owners. The assessment represents a certain percentage, which varies considerably from one municipality to another, of the 'real value' of lands and buildings. For certain

special purposes the tax also depends on the size of the property
(e.g. the foot frontage on sidewalks).[1]

D. Federal-Provincial Fiscal Relations

At the beginning of World War II the federal government proposed and concluded a fiscal agreement by virtue of which the
provinces rented out their constitutional rights to levy direct
taxes. In exchange for the proceeds of these taxes the federal
government paid various grants to the provinces. This was the
essential feature of those famous agreements in which Quebec,
at heavy financial sacrifice, has refused to participate since the
beginning of 1947. During this period federal-provincial relations
progressively worsened until 1963. The provincial demands
reflect growing needs for revenue, needs that are linked to the
increasing importance now being attached to provincial fields of
activity such as health and education. The federal government
has not been in a position to reduce its own activities since the
war, not only because of defence expenditures but also because
in certain matters it found that the negligence of the provinces in
carrying out their responsibilities was causing serious injury to
the country as a whole. The fact that the federal government
found it necessary to intervene in matters outside its jurisdiction
has led to political conflicts. Furthermore, between 1957 and
1961 Canada went through a period of economic stagnation
which resulted in heavy budgetary deficits and a pressing need to
maintain a high level of expenditure. A worsening of the general
economic situation never facilitates the sharing of revenues or of
responsibilities. Some writers will say that this enterprising spirit
on the part of the federal government arose not because of circumstances but rather as the expression of a renewed desire for
the centralization and unification of the country. Whatever the
reason, the trend has since been reversed, as will be seen later.

Let us briefly examine the nature of the fiscal agreements.

1. On tax rates see Dominion Bureau of Statistics, *Principal Taxes and Rates,
Federal, Provincial and Selected Municipal Governments*, 1964, cat. 68-201.

1. TAX-RENTAL AGREEMENTS, 1941 AND 1947

The first agreement was made in 1941. In exchange for grants the provinces agreed not to levy personal and corporation income taxes and succession duties. All the provinces were parties to this agreement, which expired at the end of 1946.

In 1947 a second tax-rental agreement was entered into for the period 1947 to 1952. Quebec and Ontario refused to participate in this agreement. They both continued to levy succession duties and they introduced their own corporation income tax. They did not at this time levy a personal income tax. The main terms of the agreement as concluded in 1947 were as follows:

(a) The participating provinces had the right to levy royalties and rents on the use of natural resources according to certain norms established by the agreement.

(b) The provinces could levy income taxes from logging and mining operations when calculating federal taxable income.

(c) The federal government allowed these royalties, rents, and taxes to be deducted when calculating federal taxable income.

(d) The federal government granted an abatement of 5 per cent on corporation profits to Quebec and Ontario and 50 per cent of the succession duties levied in the same two provinces.

(e) The federal government paid to the participating provinces annual grants based on population and tax yields.

Statutory subsidies (subsidies paid to the provinces by the federal government according to a 1907 amendment to the constitution) were also included.

These provisions produced a certain degree of equalization of revenues. The corporation income taxes of Quebec and Ontario were set at 7 per cent, and since the federal abatement was only 5 per cent, taxes paid were higher in these two provinces for the duration of the agreement.

2. THE 1952 AGREEMENT

The 1952 agreement made few changes in the former arrangements except to increase the federal compensations. Ontario entered into this agreement in respect of personal income tax and corporation income tax, but continued to impose its own succession duties. Quebec maintained its 7 per cent tax on corporation profits but the federal abatement was increased to the full 7 per cent. Because Quebec, not being a party to the fiscal agreements, did not receive the federal grants, it decided to enter the personal income tax field as it had done for a very short period in 1939 and 1940. In February 1954 Quebec introduced a provincial tax on personal income that was roughly equivalent to 10 per cent of the federal income tax. The federal government allowed first an abatement of only 5 per cent, but after a few months of controversy the abatement was increased to 10 per cent in the fall of 1954 to prevent the double taxation that was involved.

Both Quebec and Ontario maintained their succession duties with a 50 per cent federal abatement.

3. TAX-SHARING AGREEMENT, 1957

The 1957 agreement, significantly, was called a tax-sharing rather than a tax-rental agreement. It continued from 1957 to the end of 1961. Ontario participated in the agreement in respect of the personal income tax but reserved the other two taxes for itself. Quebec continued to collect its own taxes.

The grants to the provinces were now calculated on the basis of three component elements: a grant covering the rental of the three direct taxes, an equalization payment, and a stabilization payment to bring the provincial revenue up to a certain minimum.

The rental rate was set at 10 per cent of the personal income tax levied in each province, 9 per cent of the taxable corporation incomes, and 50 per cent of the inheritance tax. In 1958 the rental rate for personal income tax was increased to 13 per cent.

To take advantage of this, Quebec increased its tax rate to the same level. In 1960 the abatement on corporation income taxes was increased by 1 per cent to 10 per cent for provinces that preferred the abatement to the grant of $1.50 per capita to universities. Quebec increased its own corporation income tax while the other provinces accepted the payment.

The purpose of the equalization payments is to make fiscal receipts by provinces more uniform and to compensate for the inequality of returns from the three direct taxes. The payments are based on the yield per capita of the three taxes in the two provinces where this yield is the highest, namely Ontario and British Columbia. For example, if the average per-capita yield in British Columbia and Ontario is $30 and if in one province the per-capita yield is $10, the equalization payment to that province is $20 per person.

The purpose of the stabilization payments is to maintain the federal grants at the level they would have reached under the previous arrangements and at a level equal to at least 95 per cent of the grants of the previous two years.

The 1957 agreement also included payments for the Atlantic provinces and various other secondary arrangements.

4. FISCAL ARRANGEMENTS, 1962

The 1962 arrangements differed from previous agreements. All the provinces took back the personal income tax and the corporation income tax, and the equalization payments were considerably reduced. This was a victory for provincial autonomy at the expense of equalization. The principle of granting a federal abatement in respect of provincial taxes, which had been more or less imposed by Quebec, was henceforth extended to all the provinces. In place of an agreement on the rental of tax *rights*, an agreement concerning the *costs* of collection of taxes was substituted, by which agreement the federal government would collect the tax on behalf of the provinces. No change was made in respect of the estate tax except that British Columbia adopted a tax of its own for the first time. A province that collected this tax had the right to an abatement of 50 per cent and a province that did not collect it received an equivalent federal grant.

The equalization payments were reduced because the yield on the taxes from the whole of the country was now to be used as the basis of calculation rather than the yield from the taxes of the two most prosperous provinces. On the other hand, in order to establish the *per-capita* yield of the standard taxes, 50 per cent of the natural-resources revenue based on the average over the last three years was added to the direct taxes. This addition has caused Alberta in particular to receive lower grants, but has increased the payments to the eastern provinces, including Quebec. Since it is of less importance than the change in the basis of calculation, however, total equalization payments in 1963 were nearly $40 million less than in 1962. If, in fact, federal grants were not reduced, it was because of the stabilization clause in the agreement which provided that no province would receive less than it would have received under the former system.

The 1962 agreement also provided for an increasing reduction of the federal personal income tax. We mentioned previously that the abatement was fixed at 16 per cent in 1962 and that it was to increase by 1 per cent each year until 1966. This clause is very important, since it reflects the federal government's progressive retreat from what is the most important taxation field at the present time. Further evidence of this trend is given in the remainder of this chapter. The subsidies to the Atlantic provinces were continued.

5. CURRENT SITUATION

Federal-provincial agreements change very rapidly nowadays. In November 1963, the 50 per cent abatement of the federal estate tax was increased to 75 per cent effective from April 1, 1964. The equalization payments were tied once again to the weighted average of the top two provinces. In the spring of 1964, another conference resulted in an additional 2 per cent abatement on the federal personal income tax in favour of the provinces, for each of the 1965 and 1966 fiscal years. The total federal abatement in respect of personal income tax thus became 21 per cent for 1965 and 24 per cent for 1966.

Quebec is entitled to two other abatements. One has been mentioned already: the 1 per cent abatement on its corporation income tax in lieu of university grants of $2 per capita (from $1.50 previously). The other is in lieu of the federal family allowances for 16- and 17-year-olds who remain at school, and consists of a 3 per cent abatement on the personal income tax effective since the 1965 tax year. The 'youth allowances' program was initiated by Quebec and adopted later on by the federal government.

Tables 11:8 and 11:9 show the federal government's unconditional grants to the provinces. Table 11:8 draws attention to the differences between the 1961, 1963, and 1965 fiscal arrangements. It will be noted that the rental payments for the two income taxes have disappeared as a result of the 1962 agreement.

TABLE 11 : 8

Federal Unconditional Grants to the Provinces
Fiscal Years 1960-61, 1962-63, and 1964-65

| | *Millions of dollars* | | |
	1961	*1963*	*1965*
Tax rentals	288.7	—	—
Equalization	189.7	161.9	215.1
Stabilization	2.3	—	—
Share of estate taxes	*	15.3	40.1
Atlantic provinces	25.0	35.0	35.0
Newfoundland	8.0	8.0	8.0
50 per cent share of income tax on power utilities	4.2	6.5	10.6
Statutory subsidies (fixed by the constitution)	20.7	23.5	29.6
Other			6.0
Total	538.6	250.2	338.4

*Included in the figure for tax rentals.

SOURCE: Canadian Tax Foundation, *The National Finances*, *1962-63* and *1964-65*, Table 66.

TABLE 11 : 9

Federal Unconditional Grants to the Provinces
Fiscal Year 1964-65

| | *Millions of dollars* | |
	Total unconditional grants	*Estimated value of abatements*
Newfoundland	39.4	8.7
Prince Edward Island	8.9	1.3
Nova Scotia	41.5	15.8
New Brunswick	36.1	11.5
Quebec	116.9	213.2
Ontario	20.8	376.4
Manitoba	24.5	32.7
Saskatchewan	29.2	23.8
Alberta	12.9	53.7
British Columbia	2.2	95.2
Total	338.4	832.5

NOTES: The figure for Quebec excludes 1 per cent abatement in lieu of university grants and 3 per cent abatement in lieu of youth allowances.

SOURCE: Canadian Tax Foundation, *The National Finances, 1964-65.*

The equalization payments were increased again in 1965 as a result of the 1963 change in the formula. Since the grants give only an incomplete picture of the situation in so far as abatements are substituted for direct payments, Table 11:9 gives an estimated value of abatements. The table shows that in addition to the $338 million in direct grants, the federal government in the 1964-5 year reduced its tax collections by $833 million in the form of abatements allowed to the provinces. Whereas in 1961 the direct grants amounted to $541 million and the abatements to $327 million, in 1965 the abatements increased considerably: this of course meant a net increase in provincial tax resources.

It should be pointed out that, contrary to an opinion widely held in Quebec, the province of Quebec is not treated unfairly by the tax agreements but instead derives a great deal of benefit from them. This is mainly because of the equalization payments, which for Quebec alone amounted to $100 million in 1965 and were paid for by the provinces of British Columbia and Ontario.

Only the unconditional grants are covered in this chapter. Other grants are discussed in the next chapter.

SUGGESTED READINGS

The National Finances, Toronto, Canadian Tax Foundation, annual.
An annual publication studying the role of federal government activities in the economy.

J. H. PERRY: *Taxation in Canada*, sponsored by the Canadian Tax Foundation, University of Toronto Press, 3rd edition, revised, 1961.
A comprehensive view of the Canadian methods of taxation at all levels of government.

J. F. DUE: *Provincial Sales Taxes,* Canadian Tax Papers No. 7, Toronto, Canadian Tax Foundation, 1953.
An analytical report on a survey of retail sales taxes in Canada.

Corporate Management Conference: Eight Papers on Business Tax Problems, Canadian Tax Papers No. 15, Toronto, Canadian Tax Foundation, 1959.
Papers dealing with profits taxation and other topics related to business tax problems.

G. MCGREGOR: *Business Deductions Under the Income Tax*, Canadian Tax Papers No. 13, Toronto, Canadian Tax Foundation, 1958.
Background of theory, statute law, and jurisprudence on the nature of an expense chargeable in the determination of net profit.

Corporate Management Conference, Canadian Tax Papers No. 19, Toronto, Canadian Tax Foundation, 1960.
See especially the paper by J. H. Perry on federal and provincial profits taxes.

I. J. GOFFMAN: *The Burden of Canadian Taxation*, Canadian Tax Papers No. 29, Toronto, Canadian Tax Foundation, 1962. A study of the allocation of federal, provincial, and local taxes among income classes.
Comprehensive studies on taxation were published in five provinces in 1964 and 1965: New Brunswick, Manitoba, Nova Scotia, Saskatchewan, and Quebec.

A. M. MOORE AND J. H. PERRY: *Financing Canadian Federation: The Federal-Provincial Tax Agreements*, Canadian Tax Papers No. 6, Toronto, Canadian Tax Foundation, 1953.

J. H. PERRY: *Federal-Provincial Tax Negotiations: An Interim Report*, Canadian Tax Papers No. 10, Toronto, Canadian Tax Foundation, 1956.

D. V. SMILEY: *Conditional Grants and Canadian Federalism: A Study in Constitutional Adaptation*, Canadian Tax Papers No. 32, Toronto, Canadian Tax Foundation, 1963.
Three essays on federal-provincial tax agreements.

J. F. DUE: *Government Finance, An Economic Analysis*, Homewood, Ill., R. D. Irwin, Inc., 1963.
A standard textbook with several illustrations taken from the Canadian situation.

R. A. MUSGRAVE AND C. S. SHOUP (EDS.): *Readings in the Economics of Taxation*, American Economic Association, Homewood, Ill., R. D. Irwin, Inc., 1959.

Reports of the Proceedings of Dominion-Provincial Conferences, Ottawa, Queen's Printer.
Dominion and provincial submissions and plenary conference discussions.

CHAPTER

12

PUBLIC EXPENDITURES

At the beginning of the previous chapter we indicated that from 1929 to 1963 public expenditures increased from 15.9 per cent to 31.7 per cent of the G.N.P. Let us now see how these expenditures are distributed among the different levels of government.

1. TOTAL EXPENDITURES BY LEVEL OF GOVERNMENT

We see from Table 12:2 that the federal government is responsible for 46 per cent of the total expenditures and that the provincial and municipal governments share the remainder about equally. It should be particularly noted that municipal expenditures are as large as provincial expenditures, as the fact is easily forgotten. The federal government's share has been decreasing since 1956.

2. PRINCIPAL CATEGORIES OF EXPENDITURES, ALL GOVERNMENTS

Public expenditures may be classified in four large categories:

TABLE 12 : 1

Total Expenditures, Calendar Year 1963, millions of dollars

Federal government	6,267
Provincial governments	3,574
Municipal governments	3,791
All governments	13,632

NOTE: Inter-governmental transfers excluded; deficits included.

TABLE 12 : 2

Government Expenditures by Level of Government, 1956 and 1963

	1956		1963	
	As a percentage of G.N.P.	*As a percentage of total*	*As a percentage of G.N.P.*	*As a percentage of total*
Federal government	14.9	56.86	14.6	45.97
Provincial governments	5.4	20.60	8.3	26.22
Municipal governments	5.9	22.13	8.8	27.81
All governments	26.1	99.59	31.7	100

NOTE: Exclusive of inter-governmental transfers.
SOURCE: Canadian Tax Foundation, *The National Finances, 1964-65*, Table 8.

expenditures on goods and services; capital expenditures; transfer payments, including subsidies; and the interest on the public
debt. *Expenditures on goods and services, whether for consumption or investment, represent actual production on the part of
governments. On the other hand, transfer expenditures merely
represent a redistribution of revenue or wealth and do not absorb
any real resources.*[1] An example of a transfer is the family
allowance. The government levies a tax on some citizens and
passes on the product of this tax to other citizens without causing
any increase in the government sector's production or any
decrease in the private sector's production, since the allowance
is spent by the citizen himself. This does not mean, of course,
that the transfer has no effect. Expenditures or prices do increase
when, on the average, those paying the tax consume a smaller
portion of their incomes than those receiving the transfer allowance.

The distinction between consumption and investment is impor-

---

1. Francis Bator, in a very interesting book, *The Question of Government
Spending: Public Needs and Private Wants* (see Suggested Readings), designates expenditure on goods and services as 'exhaustive expenditure', and
transfer expenditure as 'non-exhaustive expenditure', which illustrates the distinction quite well.

tant in the public sector just as it is in the private sector. Unlike consumption, investment creates productive resources for the future. Roads, schools, and hospitals, for example, represent investment.

The interest on the public debt is kept separate from the other items. In Canada it is considered a transfer payment.

Expenditures on goods and services (including capital formation, i.e. investment) amount to about 60 per cent of public expenditures in Canada. In 1963 the investment part of expenditures on goods and services made up 13.3 per cent of the total, transfers and subsidies 30.4 per cent, and interest on the public debt 10.4 per cent, as may be seen in Table 12:3. The differences shown between 1950 and 1963 reflect tendencies that have become more and more marked in the last three or four decades. Transfer payments have shown the most rapid increase. In 1926 such payments represented only 9.3 per cent of total expenditure. This trend is a measure of the increased importance that modern society attaches to social security. The interest on the public debt now absorbs a much smaller proportion of the expenditures. On the other hand, expenditures on goods and services follow general economic conditions. For example, their share of the total amount was 61.4 per cent in 1926, 49.5 per cent in 1933 (a time of depression), and 73.5 per cent in 1945. Note that in 1963 debt charges represented only 10.4 per cent of total expenditures, compared with 29 per cent in 1926. We shall return to this question in chapter 14.

3. FEDERAL GOVERNMENT EXPENDITURES

In order to examine government expenditures from the point of view of particular functions we must now set aside the national accounts and pass on to other concepts specific to the public finances. First we find the *budgetary accounts* proper, the revenue and the expenditure that are included in the federal budget; then the *extra-budgetary accounts,* the special funds, of which the Unemployment Insurance Fund and the Old Age Security Fund are the best known. In Canadian statistics we designate as

TABLE 12 : 3

Expenditures by All Levels of Governments, 1950 and 1963

	1950		1963	
	In millions of dollars	*As a percentage of total*	*In millions of dollars*	*As a percentage of total*
Purchase of goods and services	1,756	44.1	6,259	45.9
Gross fixed capital formation	588	14.8	1,817	13.3
Transfer payments and subsidies	1,093	24.7	4,142	30.4
Interest payments on the public debt	545	13.7	1,414	10.4
Total	3,982	100	13,632	100

general expenditures the total of the budgetary and extra-budgetary expenditures (whether consumption or investment expenditures). These various terms are frequent sources of confusion. Two other sources of confusion are the difference between actual disbursements and appropriations, and the difference between the fiscal year and the calendar year: unfortunately the distinctions are not always clearly indicated. These various bases of calculation are not of much importance when one is concerned only with very general information, but they present great difficulties in making any detailed comparative examination.

Table 12:4 classifies federal expenditures by function. These are net general expenditures – that is, gross expenditures less revenues deriving from these expenditures (think of the Post Office as an example). Payments to other governments are included in the table in two different forms. First, the figure of $567 million on line 10 represents the unconditional grants (largely resulting from the fiscal agreements). Included in other items are $619 million for conditional grants, of which the purpose is stated in advance.[1]

TABLE 12 : 4

Net General Expenditure of the Federal Government
Fiscal Year Ending March 31, 1962

	Millions of dollars	As a percentage of total
Defence services and mutual aid	1,649	23.5
Veterans' pensions and other benefits	337	4.8
General government	287	4.1
Transportation	394	5.6
Health	366	5.2
Social welfare	1,424	20.3
Natural resources and primary industries	403	5.7
Debt charges (excluding retirement)	690	9.8
Payments to government enterprises	171	2.4
Payments to other governments	567	8.1
International co-operation and assistance	67	0.9
Postal service	215	3.1
All other expenditures	453	6.4
Total	7,023	99.9

SOURCE: Dominion Bureau of Statistics, *Financial Statistics of the Government of Canada, 1961.*

National defence is the largest item of federal expenditure even if one does not include veterans' benefits. Including veterans' benefits it represents 28.3 per cent of the total. Health and social welfare, added together, follow very closely with 25.5

---

1. Table 12:4 cannot be compared with Table 12:3 for several reasons which need not be given here. The breakdown of the federal payments to other governments is given in Table 12:5. There is a small discrepancy between the figures of Table 12:4 and those of Table 12:5 in this respect. This is negligible.

per cent of the total. It should be stressed that unemployment insurance benefits are not included in the figure for social welfare but only the federal government's contribution to the Unemployment Insurance Fund. Old age pensions and family allowances are the two main expenditures under the social welfare heading. Servicing of the federal debt represents 9.8 per cent of the total expenditure, and the unconditional grants to other governments 8.1 per cent (the conditional grants included in other items represent 8.8 per cent). Payments to government enterprises include $76 million to the Canadian Broadcasting Corporation and $77 million to the Canadian National Railways (of which $67 million went to make up the deficit for the calendar year 1961). Observe Canada's very meagre contribution to international co-operation and assistance: $67 million, or 0.9 per cent of the total expenditures.

Although it is not felt necessary to reproduce here all the relevant statistics for past years, it should be noted that the proportion of total expenditures devoted to national defence in the budget is decreasing, while the proportion for health and social welfare shows a considerable increase.

Because of the growing interest in federal grants to provincial and municipal governments, Table 12:5 has been included to provide figures in respect of these grants.

Unconditional grants should not be compared directly between one province and another because federal tax abatements[1] *have to be taken into account.* The reader is referred to chapter 11 for a discussion of this matter. It will be noted that the figures for Table 12:5 are equivalent to those of Tables 11:8 and 11:9 but for different years.

The conditional payments, on the other hand, may be compared directly between provinces. These are the grants (the notorious shared-cost programs) that have justly aroused the vehement opposition of the province of Quebec because they

1. When corrected for abatements and related to population, the unconditional grants are quite equally distributed among the provinces, except that the Atlantic provinces receive a larger than proportional share.

TABLE 12 : 5

Federal Government Amounts Paid to Provincial and Municipal Governments Fiscal Year Ending March 31, 1962

	Atlantic provinces	Quebec	Ontario	British Columbia	Total
			Millions of dollars		
1. Unconditional grants	123.4	66.5	125.9	76.9	541.1
2. Conditional grants for specific purposes:	79.1	175.7	204.3	75.3	642.5
(a) to provinces:					
transportation	12.6	3.3	16.4	14.2	52.6
health	35.2	86.1	121.0	29.6	332.2
social welfare	16.2	58.0	29.3	19.7	143.6
education	5.9	8.8	12.1	2.8	35.9
natural resources	2.2	3.7	1.2	1.9	12.8
others	1.5	11.1	6.4	3.6	27.7
(b) to municipalities	5.3	4.8	17.2	2.8	36.0
3. Total payments	202.5	242.2	330.2	152.2	1,183.6

NOTE: Excluding Yukon and Northwest Territories. Payments to the Prairie provinces may be found by subtracting from total.

SOURCE: Dominion Bureau of Statistics, *Financial Statistics of the Government of Canada, 1961.*

were distributed in a very inequitable manner. Ontario, for example, received more than twice as much from them as Quebec did in 1960-1.[1]

Since upon reflection this last observation appears more and more significant, the author has calculated the conditional grants on a per-capita basis, then checked to see whether the year 1960-1 was exceptionally unfavourable for Quebec by making the same calculations for 1958-9, 1960-1, and 1961-2. Table 12:6 gives the results.

TABLE 12 : 6

Conditional Grants Per Capita, Selected Provinces, fiscal years ending 1959, 1960, 1961, and 1962

	1958-9 $	1959-60 $	1960-1 $	1961-2 $
Atlantic provinces	25.87	35.27	37.00	41.06
Quebec	8.63	9.98	13.70	32.75
Ontario	13.84	25.03	27.00	32.21
British Columbia	29.02	35.65	41.00	45.34
Canada	16.00	23.13	26.00	34.67

SOURCE: Dominion Bureau of Statistics, *Financial Statistics of the Government of Canada*, 1958, 1959, 1960, and 1961.

For the three fiscal years ending 1959, 1960, and 1961, Quebec was obviously in an unfavourable position. British Columbia received three times as much as Quebec, and Ontario twice as much. The national average was double that of Quebec. Whatever the reasons given for this state of affairs, such a distribution of the federal expenditure was clearly inequitable and required correction. The correction occurred in the fiscal

1. A shared-cost program is an agreement between a province and the federal government by virtue of which each government usually pays half the cost of financing a certain program of activities. These programs apply particularly to public works and social security measures: e.g., the Trans-Canada Highway and hospital insurance.

year 1961-2. Quebec's per-capita grant then reached the level of Ontario's. British Columbia, however, still received more.[1]

For some people at least, the improvements of 1962 came too late, for Quebec still remembered its previous experience with shared-cost programs. The final result was an opting-out formula introduced in 1964, which allows Quebec to cease to participate in or to stay out of many shared-cost programs in the future and to receive compensation in the form of cash and additional abatements on the federal personal income tax. Abatements totalling 20 per cent were offered by the federal government in August 1964 and Quebec accepted them all. Twenty-nine programs were involved, the most important being the hospital insurance.[2]

One last lesson is to be drawn from all this: *The regional incidence of all federal expenditures should be subjected to a detailed analysis (as is done in other countries) as soon as these expenditures become of any size, because the incidence is a matter for political as well as economic decision.*

---

1. It may be interesting to see how Quebec caught up in 1962 relative to 1961. Let us compare the two years on the basis of the categories given in Table 12:5.

Conditional Grants to Quebec in millions of dollars

	1961	1962
Transportation	0.8	3.3
Health	28.0	86.1
Social Welfare	34.6	58.0
Education	—	8.8
Natural resources	1.6	3.7
Other	1.7	11.1
Total	66.7	171.0

2. As a result of this new formula, the 20 abatement points on the federal personal income tax must be added to the 24 percentage points discussed in the previous chapter. Add to this the 3 points allowed to Quebec for the youth allowances and you realize that Quebec became entitled to collect 47 per cent of the 1966 federal personal income tax levied in the province.

TABLE 12 : 7

Net General Expenditures of Provincial Governments, fiscal years ending March 31, 1961, and March 31, 1962

	1961		1962	
	In millions of dollars	*As a percentage of total*	*In millions of dollars*	*As a percentage of total*
Health	509	17.7	600	19.3
Social welfare	258	9.0	275	8.9
Education	700	24.4	841	27.0
Transport and communications	713	24.8	659	21.2
Natural resources and primary industries	201	7.0	202	6.5
Debt charges (exclusive of retirement)	67	2.3	84	2.7
Unconditional grants to local governments	70	2.4	72	2.3
General government and other expenditures	355	12.3	376	12.1
Total	2,873	100	3,108	100

NOTE: Figures rounded.

SOURCE: Dominion Bureau of Statistics, *Financial Statistics of Provincial Governments*, 1960.

TABLE 12 : 8

Gross Current Expenditures of Municipal Governments, 1961 and 1963 (estimated)

	1961		1963	
	In millions of dollars	As a percentage of total	In millions of dollars	As a percentage of total
General government	140.1	7.12	164.2	7.4
Public works	268.3	13.65	293.4	13.2
Sanitation	68.9	3.50	77.2	3.5
Health	38.3	1.94	42.5	1.9
Social welfare	96.8	4.92	105.9	4.8
Education	672.5	34.21	770.6	34.7
Debt charges	221.1	11.25	268.1	12.1
Recreation and community services	68.5	3.48	80.1	3.6
Other expenditures	390.5	19.86	415.4	18.8
Total	1,965.3	100	2,217.4	100

SOURCES: Dominion Bureau of Statistics, *Financial Statistics of Municipal Governments*, 1961 and 1962; *Financial Statistics of Municipal Governments*, 1962 and 1963.

4. PROVINCIAL GOVERNMENT EXPENDITURES

The provincial government expenditures shown in Table 12:7 are comparable to those of the federal government. They are net general expenditures, including payments to other governments, and apply to the fiscal year.

The provincial governments devote nearly half their resources to education and highways, and another quarter to health and social welfare. Thus, the distribution of expenditure is relatively simple. The provinces differ little in the manner of this distribution, though Quebec spends a great deal more than the others on social welfare and relatively less on health.

Since 1950 the provincial governments have appreciably increased the proportion of their expenditures devoted to education and transportation, while the proportion devoted to the servicing of debt has decreased.

5. MUNICIPAL EXPENDITURES

The municipal expenditures shown in Table 12:8 are gross general expenditures exclusive of capital outlays, and they pertain to the calendar year. They include grants received from the federal and provincial governments.

Unlike the previous tables, this one includes both repayments and interest under debt charges. Interest charges on the debt of school boards are, however, included under education.

Education costs make up the greater part of municipal budgets. In 1963 they accounted for 35 per cent of total expenditures. Next come public works and debt charges. Total expenditures exceeded $2 billion in 1963.

SUGGESTED READINGS

The National Finances, Toronto, Canadian Tax Foundation, annual.
   An annual publication studying the role of government activities in the economy.

320 / *Public Finance*

F. M. BATOR: *The Question of Government Spending: Public Needs and Private Wants*, New York, Harper, 1960.

J. K. GALBRAITH: *The Affluent Society*, Cambridge, Mass., Riverside Press, 1958.
Government expenditure viewed in a broader scope. An influential book.

CHAPTER

13

SOCIAL SECURITY

A. General Considerations

The Magna Carta of modern social security is the Beveridge Report published in England in 1942. In Canada the principles and the general rules of this charter were adopted and applied in the Marsh Report of 1943.

Social security aims at protecting the individual against certain risks at the expense of the whole of society. This idea involves a transfer of responsibilities from the personal to the collective domain because of the need for some equalization of burdens. The increased awareness of such collective responsibility is the distinguishing feature of contemporary social security. The attitude towards unemployment is the most obvious example. Formerly considered a purely individual concern, unemployment has become a collective responsibility. Similarly, it is agreed today that people normally do not become sick, crippled, or disabled through their own fault. Consequently, society as a whole assists with the expenses of the illness or the disability. The same principles apply to assistance to old people. They also apply through extension to family costs and education costs. It is recognized that the benefits accruing from a healthier and better-educated population are not only individual but also collective; hence society agrees to share the expenses on a correspondingly collective basis. In principle, social security is the concrete expression of people's aspirations to greater security and greater equality.

What aspects of this phenomenon concern the economist? Let us group them under three principal headings:

First, the redistribution of income. Social security helps to reduce the inequality of income; for this reason it probably decreases savings and increases consumption. Moreover, certain programs have a secondary effect in that they stabilize the economy. For instance, the government collects unemployment insurance contributions during times of prosperity and pays out benefits when times are bad.

Second, the influence of social security on the demand for certain products and services and hence on the allocation of resources. For example, the introduction of hospital insurance doubtless causes people to seek more and better medical care. The demand for hospital and medical services markedly increases; prices of medical supplies go up; fees and salaries of doctors, nurses, and other medical and para-medical personnel all go up. The upward movement is halted when ways and means are found to increase the supply of services and personnel to a level corresponding to the initial increase in demand. The effect of other social security measures on demand may be more diffused and in some cases may be reduced to the general over-all effect resulting from the redistribution of income. Thus Old Age Assistance and Family Allowances do not affect the demand for particular products as hospital insurance does.

Third, the problem of financing the social security programs. Such questions as whether hospital care should be paid for by the personal income tax or by specific insurance premiums and whether or not old age pensions should be financed out of consolidated revenue are extremely important from the economic point of view.

It is unfortunately not possible to examine these three aspects of social security in an outline such as this because the answers differ for each social security measure. Accordingly, we shall limit ourselves to describing the provisions of existing measures.

First, however, we must call attention to the difference between social insurance and social assistance. *Social insurance is a protection against certain possible and known risks.* The beneficiary of such insurance receives a payment when the risk materializes. For his part he has paid a premium or contribution into a government institution, which in turn does a statistical balancing of contributions and benefits. Generally this balancing consists of redistributing revenues in favour of those who have the greatest need. Social insurance is a precautionary measure; it has the advantage of making the individual contribute to the eventual aid that he may receive.

Social assistance, on the other hand, plans nothing in advance; it attempts to respond to needs as they arise. It is to a certain extent a palliative. The principle of social assistance is very old. Formerly it was left entirely to private initiative, but today the

TABLE 13 : 1

Expenditure on Social Security in Selected Countries, as a Percentage of Gross National Product 1959-60

	%
West Germany	16.1
Belgium	14.2
France	13.9
Italy	12.7
Sweden	12.4
Denmark	11.1
United Kingdom	11.0
Netherlands	11.0
Norway	10.3
Canada	*8.9*
Australia	7.9
Switzerland	7.7
Israel	7.1
United States	6.3

SOURCE: International Labour Office, *The Cost of Social Security, 1958-60*, Geneva, 1964.

state tends more and more to organize all forms of social assistance.

In Canada, as in many countries, social security includes both insurance and assistance measures.

Some idea of the scale of expenditures on social security may be obtained from the fact that in 1962 transfer payments excluding interest reached $3.6 billion, or $196 per capita. The expenditure amounted to 11.9 per cent of a national income of $30.6 billion. In 1913 Canada devoted $15 million to health and welfare – $2 per capita.

Certain critics are beginning to consider current expenditure on social security excessive. Table 13:1, by showing levels of expenditure on social security in other countries, enables us to see the relative position occupied by Canada.

As might be expected, a good many countries, particularly in Europe, assume a much heavier burden of social security in relation to available resources than Canada does. On the other hand, Canada is considerably in advance of the United States in this respect.

In the remainder of this chapter the particular programs of social security are described.

B. Federal Programs

1. FAMILY ALLOWANCES

Family allowances are payments made to families to aid in the rearing, maintenance, and education of children.

Date of origin: 1945.

Purpose: Compensation for dependants.

Those eligible: All children born in Canada or recognized as such, from birth to age 16.

Payments: For children under 10 years of age, $6 a month; for children aged 10 or over, $8 a month.

Financing: From consolidated revenue without any specific contribution being required of the beneficiaries.

Because of their difficulties in obtaining supplies Eskimoes and Indians in remote areas are often paid in goods.

TABLE 13 : 2

Net Family Allowances, Canada, selected fiscal years 1947-65

	Millions of dollars
1947	245.1
1950	297.5
1955	366.4
1960	491.2
1963	531.6
1965	545.8

SOURCE: Department of Health and Welfare, annual reports.

2. OLD AGE SECURITY

Old Age Security is intended to insure aged persons against the risk of loss of income. The government therefore pays out pensions to old people to help them meet their needs. The principle is one of insurance, since it is presumed that needs exist and each taxpayer pays a premium to the Old Age Security Fund (a premium made up of certain percentages of different direct and indirect taxes).

Date of origin: The Old Age Security Act came into force in January 1952. The original Old Age Pensions Act was passed in 1927.

Purpose: Compensation for old people.

Those eligible: All the Canadian population aged 70 and over. From 1966 to 1970, the qualifying age is being lowered annually by one year until in 1970 everyone of 65 and over will be eligible.

Conditions: Continuous residence in Canada for the preceding ten years or statutory equivalent. The

Payments: reason for this condition is that the beneficiaries must have contributed to the Fund by paying taxes.

Payments: $75 a month, plus an annual upward adjustment for changes in the cost of living.

Financing: From the Old Age Security Fund aided by loans and grants from consolidated revenue. The Fund is built up from three different sources:

    (a) 3 per cent sales tax;

    (b) 3 per cent tax on corporation profits;

    (c) 4 per cent tax on personal income with a maximum of $120 a year (raised from 3 to 4 per cent in January 1964).

TABLE 13 : 3

Old Age Security: Beneficiaries and Payments, Canada, selected fiscal years 1955-65

	Beneficiaries	Net payments (millions of dollars)
1955	745,620	353.2
1958	827,560	473.8
1961	904,906	592.4
1963	950,766	734.4
1965	993,582	885.3

SOURCE: Department of Health and Welfare, annual reports.

In addition to these benefits under the 1952 Act, the Canada Pension Plan, as passed by Parliament in March 1965, will provide retirement pensions equal to 25 per cent of 'average pensionable earnings', as well as disability pensions, death benefits, widows' pensions, and other benefits, subject to compulsory contributions which began on January 1, 1966. For the self-employed these contributions amount to 3.6 per cent of 'contributory earnings'. Employers and employees pay 1.8 per cent each. Contributory earnings are ordinary total earnings up to a maximum of $5,000, less a basic exemption of 12 per cent. The system is universal in the sense that all occupations are covered (except primary and casual employment, and particular cases such as members of the Canadian Armed Forces). Both the contribution base and the benefits payable will increase annually according to the cost-of-living index with a maximum of 2 per cent in any year. Some provinces have their own pension plans, but since they are nicely co-ordinated with the federal plan nobody need be afraid of having to subscribe to more than one. (Private pension plans still remain, however.)

3. UNEMPLOYMENT INSURANCE

The Unemployment Insurance program, one of the most important both from the economic and from the social points of view, consists of insurance for workers against the risk of unemployment.

Date of origin:	1941.
Purpose:	Compensation for the unemployed.
Those eligible:	All wage-earners in insurable employment. Certain kinds of activity considered as stable, or in which the program is difficult to administer, such as the liberal professions, agriculture, and domestic service, are excluded from the scheme.
Conditions:	(a) The claimant must be registered with the National Employment Service.
	(b) He must have paid his contributions (because this is an insurance scheme).
	(c) He must not have left his employment voluntarily or for reasons of misconduct.
Payments:	The amount of the weekly benefit payments which begin five days after the loss of employment depends:
	(a) on the number of the claimant's dependants;
	(b) on his wage prior to being unemployed;

(c) on the average of his weekly contributions in the thirty weeks preceding the claim;

(d) on the duration of the payments.

The maximum rate of benefit is $27 a week for a single person and $36 a week for a person with dependants.

Financing: The Unemployment Insurance Fund is built up from payments by employees, employers, and the government, each party contributing about a third of the Fund's resources.

The National
Employment
Service: The National Employment Service is responsible for the administration of the program. It also conducts an employment service.

TABLE 13 : 4

Unemployment Insurance, Canada, selected fiscal years 1946-64

	Benefit payments (millions of dollars)	Beneficiaries (thousands)	Balance in fund at end of year (millions of dollars)
1946	49.0	101.2	317.0
1950	99.0	127.9	582.6
1955	229.0	222.7	840.7
1960	481.8	430.0	365.9
1962	409.2	414.0	99.0
1964	344.4	357.0	81.4

NOTE: The Unemployment Insurance Fund dropped to $19.9 million at the end of May 1962.

SOURCE: Dominion Bureau of Statistics, *Statistical Report on the Operation of the Unemployment Insurance Act*.

A committee of inquiry into the Unemployment Insurance Act submitted its report at the end of 1962. The following were the principal recommendations:

1. That aid to the unemployed should be given in accordance with three distinct systems:
   (a) *an insurance scheme proper* built up by the contributions of employers and employees (the government contributing only to the cost of administration), for periods of unemployment that would be more limited than obtained at that time;
   (b) *a scheme of prolonged benefit payments* supported by the government. Payments would be made to claimants who have exhausted their benefits under the first scheme and to unemployed persons in other categories such as the seasonally unemployed;
   (c) *a scheme of assistance* to the victims of residual unemployment; this scheme to be based on need and administered by all levels of government.

2. That participation in the insurance scheme should be extended to cover, in principle, all wage-earners without distinction, including, for instance, teachers, white-collar workers, and government employees regardless of the size of salaries.

3. That the bases of calculation under the insurance scheme 1(a) should be more rigorous, but that the rates of payment should be increased from 50 to 60 per cent of earnings for an insured worker with dependants and from about 40 to about 45 per cent for an insured worker without dependants. The maximum weekly payment for the worker with dependants would rise from $36 to $44, and that for the worker with no dependants would rise from $27 to $33. A special classification would be added to include all those with salaries exceeding $80 a week. Their payments would be $48 (with dependants) and $36 (without).

4. That the scheme of prolonged payments 1(b) would entitle a claimant to benefit payments at the same rates as in 3 for a maximum period equal to one and a half times that to which he was entitled under the insurance scheme. Restrictions in respect of eligible employments would be more severe than in the insurance scheme.

5. That the National Employment Service should come under the Department of Labour rather than under the Unemployment Insurance Commission.

4. VETERANS' SERVICES

The social security services affecting veterans come under the Department of Veterans' Affairs.

*Principal
services:*   (a) Free medical, dental, and prosthetic services to eligible veterans.

(b) Land settlement assistance and home construction assistance.

(c) Educational assistance to the children of war dead.

(d) Veterans' life insurance.

(e) Pensions.

(f) Assistance to needy veterans.

(g) Education and training of veterans. Today this service is primarily intended for disabled veterans who were unable to take courses after the 1939-45 war or after the Korean war.

Date of origin: The South African war, the two world wars, and the Korean war created the need for veterans' assistance programs. Certain of the services date from the period between the two world wars; others are more recent.

Purpose: Compensation for veterans.

Those eligible: This depends on the service. All veterans are eligible for certain services. Other services are intended solely for disabled veterans or for the children of veterans.

Payments: For disability the basic scale is the same for all ranks up to and including colonel. For dependants of war dead, pensions are granted to widows and to young children. A large part of the assistance is given in the form of free services.

Financing: Through the budget of the Department of Veterans' Affairs. In 1965 the Department paid out $353 million in benefits of all kinds including the cost of administration of the various programs.

5. WELFARE SERVICES FOR INDIANS AND ESKIMOES

These services are provided by the Department of Citizenship and Immigration and by the Department of Northern Affairs and National Resources. Their purpose is to help the Indians and Eskimoes to adapt themselves to modern living.

Principal services:

(a) Free education.

(b) Placement in employment; aid to agriculture, to handicrafts, and to home industry; assistance in obtaining housing.

(c) Special public assistance.

C. Federal-Provincial Programs

With the exception of hospital insurance, the social security programs administered jointly by the federal and provincial governments are, in general, programs of social assistance. Coverage under this section is limited to federal legislation.

1. THE OLD AGE ASSISTANCE ACT

This is to some extent a supplement to the federal Old Age Security Act.

Date of origin: 1927. The Act, to become effective in a province, required an agreement between the province and the federal government. These agreements were signed between 1927 and 1936.

Purpose: To provide for the needs of aged persons who cannot support themselves after 65.

Those eligible:	Persons aged 65 and over who are in need.
Conditions:	(a) Continuous residence in Canada for the preceding ten years.
	(b) The recipient must not also be a recipient of another welfare allowance.
	(c) The recipient's total annual income, including assistance, must not exceed $1,260 for a single person or $2,220 for a married person.
Payments:	The maximum provincial assistance eligible for federal sharing is $75 a month.
Financing:	50 per cent of the allowance is provided by the province and 50 per cent by the federal government. The provinces administer the program.

In March 1965, 107,354 persons were receiving assistance in Canada under this Act. The federal contribution was $45 million in that year. Four provinces provide supplements on a needs test: British Columbia, Alberta, Ontario, and Quebec.

2. THE BLIND PERSONS ACT

Assistance to the blind is one of the oldest provisions of provincial legislation in the field of social security.

Date of origin:	The federal government entered the field in 1937 and the Blind Persons Act dates from 1952.
Purpose:	To assist blind persons in need.
Those eligible:	All blind persons aged 18 or over who fulfil means-test requirements.
Conditions:	(a) Continuous residence in Canada for the preceding ten years.
	(b) The recipient's total annual income, including assistance, must not exceed $1,500 for a single person and $2,580 for a married person.

| *Payments*: | The maximum provincial assistance eligible for federal sharing is $75 a month. Supplementary payments are made in certain provinces. |
| *Financing*: | 75 per cent of the allowance is provided by the federal government, and the remainder by the province. The provinces administer the program. |

In March 1965, 8,586 blind persons in Canada were receiving allowances under this Act. The federal contribution was $5.6 million.

3. THE DISABLED PERSONS ACT

The Disabled Persons Act provides for federal sharing under agreements with the provinces.

Date of origin:	January 1955.
Purpose:	To assist disabled persons in need.
Those eligible:	Disabled persons 18 years of age and over suffering from major physiological, anatomical, or psychological impairment verified by objective medical findings. The disability must be permanent and prevent the victim from leading a normal life.
Conditions:	(a) Continuous residence in Canada for the previous ten years.
	(b) The recipient's total annual income including assistance must not exceed $1,260 for a single person and $2,220 for a married person.
	(c) The recipient must not be hospitalized in a sanitorium or in a hospital for mental patients or in any charitable institution.
Payments:	The maximum provincial assistance eligible for federal sharing is $75 a month.
Financing:	50 per cent of the allowance is provided by the federal government and 50 per cent by

the province. The provinces administer the program.

In March 1965, 53,103 persons were receiving Disabled Persons' Allowances. The federal contribution was $23.4 million.

4. THE UNEMPLOYMENT ASSISTANCE ACT

The Unemployment Assistance Act supplements the unemployment insurance program. Its aim is to help the unemployed who are not eligible for unemployment insurance.

Date of origin: 1956. The province of Quebec concluded an agreement with the federal government in 1959.

Purpose: To assist the uninsured unemployed who are in need.

Those eligible: Unemployed persons who are not eligible for unemployment insurance payments and who are either employable or only temporarily unemployable.

Conditions: The recipient must not also be a recipient of another welfare allowance.

Payments: Assistance according to need and number of dependants.

Financing: The federal government reimburses the provinces and the municipalities for 50 per cent of the average monthly cost of assistance per person. The provinces and the municipalities administer the program.

In March 1965, 700,000 persons, including dependants, were receiving unemployment assistance allowances. The federal contribution was $107 million. In April 1965, the Prime Minister proposed 'The Canada Assistance Plan' which would replace the four programs reviewed above and extend the federal benefits to persons not covered under them. The proposed plan would share the assistance with the provinces on a fifty-fifty basis.

5. HEALTH INSURANCE

Date of origin: The federal government passed the Hospital Insurance and Diagnostic Services Act in May 1957. The majority of the provinces joined the program in 1958. The province of Quebec was the last to take advantage of it, on January 1, 1961.

Purpose: To share with the provinces the cost of services in hospitals.

Those eligible: Persons hospitalized.

Payments: The insurance covers, for instance:

(a) standard ward accommodation and meals;

(b) necessary nursing care;

(c) laboratory and X-ray services and other diagnostic services provided during the stay in hospital;

(d) medicines prescribed and taken during the stay in hospital;

(e) the use of delivery rooms, operating rooms, and anaesthetic facilities.

Usually the federal and provincial governments, after inspecting the accounts, make direct payments to the approved hospitals in the sums required for their operation.

Financing: The federal government contributes about 50 per cent of the cost of the hospital insurance program from general revenue. Financing and administration vary from one province to another. The revenues that serve to finance the program at the provincial levels come either from general revenue, from provincial sales taxes, or from individual and family premiums. The 1965 federal contribution amounted to $430 million.

6. MEDICARE

The Royal Commission on Health Services (the Hall Commission) submitted an important report in 1964. It proposed adoption of a 'health charter' in which society would set itself an objective 'to make all the fruits of the health sciences available to all our residents without hindrance of any kind'.

Through agreements between the federal and the provincial governments, the provinces would establish a comprehensive and universal medical care program covering all of these: medical services; dental services, for children, expectant mothers, and public-assistance recipients; prescription drug services; optical services, for children and public-assistance recipients; prosthetic services; and home care services.

In addition the Royal Commission proposed a major re-orientation of mental health services and important changes in the system of hospital insurance. It was opposed to state-operated medical services and instead recommended the free, independent, and autonomous functioning of the medical professions in all provinces.

The comprehensive medical care program would cost $470 million in 1971 in addition to projected costs on present services, and would also call for the training of a very large number of additional personnel in all sectors of health services.

SUGGESTED READINGS

I. J. GOFFMAN: *Some Fiscal Aspects of Public Welfare in Canada*, Toronto, Canadian Tax Foundation, 1965.

CANADA: Report of the Royal Commission on Health Services, Ottawa, Queen's Printer, 1964.
The commission has studied health services in terms of existing facilities, methods of improvement, present and future requirements of personnel, projected costs of any changes recommended, methods of financing health care services, research, etc.

L. G. MARSH: *Report on Social Security for Canada*, prepared for the Advisory Committee on Reconstruction, Ottawa, King's Printer, 1943.
A study of the principal matters involved in the consideration of comprehensive social security legislation in Canada.

A. E. GRAUER: *Public Assistance and Social Insurance*, a study prepared for the Royal Commission on Dominion-Provincial Relations, Appendix 6, Ottawa, King's Printer, 1939.
The study deals with the various forms of public assistance in Canada; the author also discusses the principles and applicability of social insurance.

CANADA: Report of the Committee of Inquiry into the Unemployment Insurance Act, P.C. 1961-1040, Ottawa, Queen's Printer, 1962.
History of the Act, analysis of financial operations, and recommendations.

CHAPTER

14

FISCAL POLICY
AND THE PUBLIC DEBT

More than any other field of economic activity, the public finances give rise to the wildest and most absurd opinions. Common sense is a poor guide in these matters; it rarely fails to lead us astray. Thus it can be demonstrated that continuing budgetary deficits do not lead to bankruptcy, that the public debt is not necessarily a burden, that taxes are not only levied to meet expenditures – three propositions that may offend against common sense, but are nevertheless as true as that day is not night.

The facts about the public finances are little known. Let us, then, begin with some facts.

A. Taxes

People everywhere tend to think that their taxes are higher than anywhere else, while commentators are never lacking to warn that the intolerable burden of taxation is harming the whole economy. Table 14:1 shows the percentage of the gross national product paid in taxes to all levels of government in Canada and in nine other countries in the year 1960.

Canada is far from being ranked among the most heavily taxed nations. It is in fourteenth place in a list of forty countries for which figures are available. *With two or three exceptions, the most advanced countries all have higher taxes than Canada.*

As Table 14:1 shows, France and West Germany levy about one-third of the G.N.P. as taxes. According to calculations made by the author, percentages of G.N.P. going to taxes have been increasing since 1950 in Canada, France, and the United States; in the United Kingdom they have decreased in the same period by almost 10 per cent. As no relationship has yet been established between these tax levels and the rise or decline of these particular countries, we do not yet know the magic percentage of the G.N.P. beyond which the tax collectors ought not to be allowed to go. It is certain, however, that very low taxes are in no way a guarantee of prosperity. We can see, in fact, that the richer countries provide themselves with more community services and usually levy higher taxes.

TABLE 14 : 1

Taxes as a Percentage of the Gross National Product, 1960

West Germany	34.0
France	33.2
Sweden	31.3
Italy	28.7
United Kingdom	27.9
United States	27.5
Canada	*24.8*
Belgium	24.2
Australia	23.5
Japan	20.2

SOURCE: Table taken from the United Nations statistics and compiled by Ronald Robertson, in *Tax Aspects of Canada's International Competitive Position*, Canadian Trade Committee, Private Planning Association of Canada, Montreal.

Ronald Robertson, whose tables we reproduce here, has been investigating whether Canadian taxes have raised prices and wages in such a way as to harm the country's exports. In so far as the total amount of taxes is concerned, it is clear that this has not occurred, since Canada's principal trading partners are carrying heavier financial burdens.

Fiscal policy consists, in part, in choosing between the various categories of taxes, from the lottery to the most complicated levies. In this chapter there can be no question of establishing the merits and disadvantages of each tax, but a rough classification may be useful, since some very interesting statistics on this subject are available.

Referring back to Chapter 11, a first distinction is made between direct and indirect taxes. Since the main differences between the two kinds of tax result from the fact that *a tax on income reduces savings more than does a tax on expenditure*, it follows that a direct tax is preferable when there is a strong tendency to unemployment. On the other hand, when savings are inadequate, as in underdeveloped countries, or when inflation rages, it is preferable to tax consumption. A high tax on income may decrease the incentive to work and invest, as some writers believe, but studies on this point are hardly conclusive except in respect of very high incomes. From the point of view of social justice, it is generally admitted that the direct tax is more progressive and fairer than the indirect tax, if not in theory at least in practice. Thus the advantages and disadvantages of these two taxes depend to a great extent on the relative abundance of savings and investment.

Table 14:2 shows the preference given to direct or indirect taxes in nine different countries in 1959. For some years we have been hearing statements that Canada resorts too much to direct taxes and that it ought to follow the example of France in relying more on indirect taxes. To imitate France in this respect would clearly have meant no change in 1959, since in that year the percentages were identical in the two countries. Compared with other countries, Canada is far from being a leader in the field of direct taxation. On the contrary, of the countries listed in the table, only Italy and Australia relied less upon direct taxes. As economic theory might have led us to believe, a positive relationship may be observed between the level of development or income and the extent to which the direct tax is used. According to this criterion, Canada probably does not tax incomes enough. It should be noted that the United States and Sweden levy two-thirds of their taxes in the direct form.

TABLE 14 : 2

Direct and Indirect Taxes as a Percentage of the Total Taxes, 1959

	Direct taxes*	Indirect taxes†
France	46.7	53.3
Sweden	66.0	34.0
Italy	30.4	69.6
United Kingdom	53.4	46.6
United States	66.2	33.8
Canada	*46.7*	*53.3*
Belgium	59.0	41.0
Australia	45.6	54.4
Japan	50.0	50.0

*Taxes on personal and corporation income, succession duties, taxes on capital, and social insurance contributions.
†All taxes on products including customs tariffs plus property taxes.
SOURCE: Robertson, *Tax Aspects of Canada's International Competitive Position*.

Among direct taxes a distinction is made between taxes on personal income and taxes on corporation profits. The latter reduce savings and investment still more if the tax burden is not passed on to the consumers through price increases. For this reason it is often alleged that the tax on profits slows down the rate of economic growth and discourages corporations from embarking on new and risky projects. The argument is valid in a period of full employment when savings are scarce and when competition is very keen (preventing the tax from being passed on to the consumers). This question is still being debated, however. Conclusive studies on the incidence of this tax are lacking. The fact that the government participates as much in the losses as in the profits raises some doubt about the lack of incentive to

risk capital. Table 14:3 shows that Canada is one of the industrialized countries taxing corporation profits most heavily.

TABLE 14 : 3

**Taxes on Corporation Profits and on Personal Income
as a Percentage of the Total Income Taxes, 1959**

	Taxes on profits	*Taxes on personal income*
France	15.8	84.2
Sweden	14.6	85.4
United Kingdom	26.4	73.6
United States	27.1	72.9
Canada	*38.6*	*61.4*
Belgium	14.7	85.3
Australia	34.0	66.0
Japan	41.2	58.8

SOURCE: Robertson, *Tax Aspects of Canada's International Competitive Position.*

The classification of taxes according to the concepts of direct
and indirect taxation often leads to confusion because of the
taxes on capital (or assets). From an economic point of view the
most important thing to know is whether a tax affects decisions
to consume, to invest, or to work, and how, in their turn, these
decisions will affect the stability of the national income. In this
respect it is better to make a straight classification of taxes
according to whether they bear on income, capital, or consumption.

The taxes on consumption are mainly sales and excise taxes,
and taxes on business turnover or on value added. As we said in
chapter 11, these taxes are generally regressive;[1] they favour

---

1. The 'expenditure tax' proposed by the distinguished British economist N. Kal-
dor is not regressive because it is based on total expenditure and not on the
consumption of particular commodities. It is really the only tax that encourages
saving and economic growth without sacrificing equity. The difficulties of
applying it are unfortunately rather great.

savings and increase the inequality of incomes. Consequently they are efficient correctives during periods of inflation; they are not at all recommended in times of unemployment. At all times they are, with good reason, opposed by the poor and advocated by the rich.

One can be rich in several ways – having a nice plump bank account or a trunk full of gold, owning buildings, factories, stocks and bonds, having a great number of debtors. If all these forms of wealth were taxed uniformly – i.e., on the total of assets minus liabilities – such a tax would be as equitable as a tax on income. The transfer of the tax to others would be reduced to a minimum, and although savings would be affected much more than consumption, the incentive to increase one's income would be maintained if not intensified. The basic exemptions would protect small investors with no other source of income. On the other hand, economic fluctuations would be accentuated rather than reduced by the tax on wealth; at a time when the national income was decreasing, this tax would represent a higher percentage of revenue; and conversely during periods of inflation.

In Canada the principal tax on wealth is the tax on real property. Probably its only justification is that municipalities need it and cannot easily find a substitute. As it is now levied, this tax is regressive: it reduces expenditure on socially desirable goods such as housing; it affects the choice of localities for new housing and commercial construction; it is a source of conflict because of arbitrary methods of assessment.

Among the ten countries listed in Table 14:4, Canada has the highest taxes on capital, mainly because of real property tax – a fact that indicates the relative significance of this tax in the Canadian system of taxation.

The United States comes second for the same reason. This table enables us to return to the question of the relative importance of taxes on income and taxes on consumption. It is here that France's fiscal policy differs most from Canada's. Almost half of French taxes are on consumption, compared with hardly more than a third of Canadian taxes. Italy and Belgium pursue

TABLE 14 : 4

**Taxes on Income, on Capital, and on Consumption,
as a Percentage of Total Taxes, 1960**

	Taxes on income	Taxes on capital*	Taxes on consumption
West Germany	62.0	3.2	34.8
France	45.2	5.1	49.7
Sweden	63.3	1.1	35.6
Italy	49.3	3.0	47.7
United Kingdom	51.7	12.6	35.7
United States	63.5	14.2	22.3
Canada	*48.8*	*17.1*	*34.1*
Belgium	52.8	1.5	45.7
Australia	48.8	9.7	41.5
Japan	60.3	6.7	33.0

*Includes taxes on inheritances, gifts, and property.

SOURCE: Robertson, *Tax Aspects of Canada's International Competitive Position.*

policies similar to that of France, whereas in the United States taxes on consumption only amount to 22 per cent of total taxes.

If we set aside questions of social justice and administrative efficiency, the choice between taxes depends essentially on their influence on saving and investment on the one hand, and on consumption on the other. The importance of fiscal manipulations can easily be exaggerated, however. Usually the changes introduced in one or the other direction will not affect the general rate of economic growth, because the fiscal system is only one among several factors that determine whether we shall have prosperity or hard times. We must never consider a tax in isolation, but must examine not only the whole range of the fiscal system but also fiscal policy in its relation to all the other instruments of economic policy, including the monetary and the exchange-rate policies. It is this general appraisal of all the instruments of economic policy that allows us to evaluate the place and merit of one particular measure. Thus low interest rates combined with budgetary surpluses have been recommended as a stimulant for the North American economy in the years ahead: obviously it is the combination that would give effect to the suggested policy.

B. Budgetary Surpluses and Deficits

Essentially, the government levies taxes to prevent the inflation that would otherwise be caused by its expenditures. This means that government expenditures (like private expenditures) are a stimulus to the economy whereas taxation acts as a brake. It will also be agreed that it is advantageous to stimulate activities until full employment is attained, but that it is useless and harmful to go beyond this point since it will only lead to price increases. From these two propositions there follows a third: a budgetary surplus halts expansion and becomes necessary when inflation appears; a budgetary deficit accelerates the rate of expansion and is required when conditions of unemployment exist. *The guiding rule for fiscal policy, then, is not to balance the budget but to achieve full employment in the economy.* And if it was necessary to resort to a budgetary deficit for ten years in succession in order to absorb unemployment, the rule would remain equally valid, unless inflation appeared before full employment was reached.

Although the budgetary deficits and surpluses are not always the result of deliberate policy, they do agree with the above stated principles (except in wartime, of course).

Conflicts in policy may appear between the municipal, provincial, and federal governments. The deliberate deficit on the part of one level of government may be nullified by another's surplus or vice versa. Since 1926 one can count only five years in which this process of nullification has not operated. But this has been due to the municipalities rather than the provinces. The years in which the provinces went in the opposite direction to the federal government were 1926 to 1929, 1946, 1954, 1958, and 1959. (We are not including the war years.)

TABLE 14 : 5

Budgetary Surpluses and Deficits, All Levels of Government, Canada 1926-63

	Surpluses		Deficits	
	In millions of dollars	*As a percentage of government expenditure*	*In millions of dollars*	*As a percentage of government expenditure*
1926-28	138	4.9		
1929-39			1,788	16.0
1940-45			7,712	44.0
1947-53	3,832	10.0		
1954			131	2.0
1955-57	556	2.0		
1958-63			4,833	7.4

SOURCE: *National Accounts, 1926-1956* and *1963*.

From 1929 to 1939 there were eleven successive years of budgetary deficits in times of peace. If the war years are included, the deficits extend from 1929 to 1946 inclusive, with the exception of 1941.

Then, from 1947 to 1957, a period of very rapid expansion for Canada, we find surpluses, except in 1954 which was a year of recession. From 1958 to 1961 governments again showed deficits at a time when the economy was going through a period of stagnation. The deficits were there also in 1962 and 1963 but appreciably reduced. This is not to say that governments have deliberately followed an anti-cyclical policy. For one thing, there are enough 'built-in stabilizers' in the economy to produce the figures shown in Table 14:5.

C. The Public Debt

When the government has a budgetary surplus its debt decreases; when it has a deficit its debt increases. A balanced budget is no proof of the talent or wisdom of the minister of finance, nor is the public debt resulting from the deficits a criterion of good or bad management. There is no cause for rejoicing when the debt decreases; there is no cause for alarm when it increases. Unfortunately, people transfer private experience to the government level, so that they have come instinctively to identify the public debt with the plague. *When a government borrows from its citizens it obtains from some the money to give to others. The country as a whole cannot be poorer for this reason.* Neither are interest payments a burden since again we take from some to repay others. And it often happens that 'some' and 'others' in these contexts are the same people. It is in this essential fact that a government differs from individual citizens.[1]

This, then, means that variations in the public debt are not in themselves either a good or an evil. The debt, like the budgetary surplus or deficit, must be judged in relation to circumstances.

Writers have, of course, long sought to discover the dreadful consequences of the public debt that might explain the instinctive fear it inspires. Some undesirable consequences certainly have been found, but generally they are either pretty harmless or easy to correct. Interest payments, for example, increase the inequality of incomes, possibly encouraging the lenders to consume more. In a depression this is ideal, but during a period of inflation it constitutes an additional pressure on prices and must be opposed. Also, a budgetary deficit causes total investment to increase or decrease according to the way in which the deficit was arrived at and according to its resulting effect on the level of the national income. It is possible that its influence may not have the desired effect at a given moment.

On the other hand, the public debt allows the government to exercise a much more efficient control over economic fluctuations. Fiscal and monetary policy would be reduced to very little importance were it not for the possibility of bringing about variation in the public debt and the debt charges. In this sense, if the debt did not exist it would be necessary to invent it.

---

1. The propositions of this paragraph apply to a debt held by residents of the country, not to a debt held by foreign investors. Almost all the federal debt, however, is held by Canadians. In 1962 the figure was 95 per cent.

Public debt varies enormously from one country to another without any apparent connection between the size of the debt and the prosperity of the country. The Canadian government's debt has fluctuated greatly over a period of time, as Table 14:6 shows.

TABLE 14 : 6

Public Debt, Canada 1929-62

	Gross debt in millions of dollars	Net debt in millions of dollars	Net debt per capita in dollars	Net debt as a percentage of the G.N.P.
1929	2,647	2,225	221.88	36.2
1939	3,711	3,153	279.84	55.9
1945	15,712	11,298	935.88	95.4
1958	18,419	11,046	647.95	34.6
1964	25,923	15,070	783.39	35.0

SOURCES: Dominion Bureau of Statistics, *Public Accounts, National Accounts*; Canadian Tax Foundation, *The National Finances, 1964-65*.

The last column of the table is a good measure of the public debt. In 1964 the debt was a little lower in relation to the gross national product than it was in 1929. The per-capita debt, though a widely used figure, has no particular significance; one might as well compare the debt to the heights of various buildings.

The difference between the gross debt and the net debt depends on the assets (equipment, for example) that it has been possible to acquire, or to create, as a result of the debt.

If the public debt were a real burden, that burden would have to be measured by the net amount that it costs the government each year to keep the funds that have been borrowed. The interest paid on the public debt does not by itself give the true cost. Since a part of the debt goes into productive investments, it is only fitting that we deduct from the interest charges the income earned from these investments (column 2 of Table 14:7). By adding the other expenses related to the debt we obtain the net cost. By comparing the net cost to the national income, we find the percentage of resources that must be devoted to the public debt. In 1964 debt charges absorbed 1.8 per cent of the national income.

TABLE 14 : 7

Net Public Debt Charges, 1940-64, in millions of dollars

	1 Interest paid	2 Interest earned and other investment income	3 Other debt charges	4 Net public debt charges	5 Column 4 as a percentage of the national income
1940	129	14.9	5.3	119.7	2.3
1945	319	60.7	20.9	279.2	2.9
1958	539	169.4	28.2	398.0	1.5
1962	803	308	36.0	531.5	1.7
1964	954	366	39.2	627.3	1.8

SOURCE: Canadian Tax Foundation, *The National Finances*, 1964-65.

To the federal government debt must be added provincial and municipal government debts. In 1959, when the federal debt was $20.7 billion, the provinces owed $3.3 billion and the municipalities $4.3 billion, bringing the total to $28.3 billion.

SUGGESTED READINGS

T. N. BREWIS: 'Fiscal Policy', in Brewis, English, Scott, and Jewett, *Canadian Economic Policy*, revised edition, Toronto, Macmillan, 1965, pp. 262-87.
An introduction to fiscal policy in a Canadian setting.

A. SMITHIES AND J. K. BUTTERS (EDS.): *Readings in Fiscal Policy*, American Economic Association, Homewood, Ill., R. D. Irwin, Inc., 1955.

A. E. BUCK: *Financing Canadian Government*, Chicago, Public Administration Service, 1949.
A study of Canada's system of government finance, showing its development and outlining its essential characteristics as compared with the American system of government finance.

S. BATES: *Financial History of Canadian Governments*, research study prepared for the Royal Commission on Dominion-Provincial Relations, Ottawa, King's Printer, 1939.

I. BRECHER: *Monetary and Fiscal Thought and Policy in Canada, 1919-1939*, University of Toronto Press, 1957.
This study traces the course and interrelationship of Canadian stabilization thought and policy during the period.

J. M. BUCHANAN: *Public Principles of Public Debt*, Homewood, Ill., R. D. Irwin, Inc., 1958.
A complete analysis of economic thought on public debt.

E. NEVIN: *The Problem of the National Debt,* University of Wales Press, 1954.
A discussion of the role of the public debt in the economic system.

UNITED STATES CONGRESS, HOUSE COMMITTEE ON WAYS AND MEANS: *Public Debt Limit,* 88th Congress, 1st Session, House of Representatives, Report No. 885, Washington, 1963.
Papers and discussions relating to the establishment of a ceiling to the national debt.

ABBA LERNER: *The Economics of Control: Principles of Welfare Economics*, New York, Macmillan, 1944.
Analysis of the economic aspects of social organization and social control over the economic system. A classic.

Part four

FOREIGN TRADE

CHAPTER

15

FOREIGN TRADE
AND THE TARIFF POLICY

A. Some International Comparisons

Canada ranks among the great trading nations of the world. In spite of its small population it stands sixth in the size of its foreign trade (sum of exports and imports) after the United States, West Germany, England, France, and the U.S.S.R. Among industrialized countries, generally speaking, the smaller the population, the larger the volume of foreign trade per capita. Thus foreign trade per capita is relatively high in Switzerland, Belgium, the Netherlands, Sweden, and Canada. In 1962 Canada's foreign trade per capita amounted to $632 (Table 15:1).

Table 15:2, however, presents a picture that gives some cause for reflection.

As is generally known, Canada is pursuing a resolutely independent and multilateral trade policy, whereas most other countries have formed or are attempting to form vast groups within which trade is conducted on more or less preferential terms. The Treaty of Rome establishing the European Economic Community (E.E.C.) came into force on January 1, 1959. Its purpose is to abolish barriers to trade between member countries, to protect internal trade by the establishment of a common external tariff, and to create finally an integrated political community. As a result of a remarkable acceleration in the inte-

TABLE 15:1

Foreign Trade, Selected Countries, 1962

	In billions of U.S. dollars	In U.S. dollars per capita
United States	37.7	202
West Germany	25.5	472
United Kingdom	22.7	425
France	14.8	316
U.S.S.R.	13.4	—
Canada	11.7	632
Italy	10.7	213
Japan	10.5	111
Netherlands	9.9	842
Belgium:Luxembourg	8.8	930
Sweden	6.0	798
Switzerland	5.2	925

NOTE: Foreign trade means here the sum of exports and imports.

SOURCES: United Nations, *Yearbook of International Trade Statistics*, 1962, and *Demographic Yearbook*, 1963.

gration process it is estimated that for industrial products (with the exception of refined petroleum) average reduction of customs duties within the community reached 60 per cent in 1964 and the reduction of foreign tariffs to a common tariff was also 60 per cent complete in that year. The European Free Trade Association (E.F.T.A.), set up at the end of 1959, aims at abolishing customs duties and other obstacles to trade between member countries over a ten-year period. Unlike the E.E.C., however, a free-trade zone entails neither a common external tariff nor common political institutions. Now a grouping of the Latin American countries has been carried out on the E.F.T.A. model. The Latin-American Free Trade Association was established in June 1961, with the purpose of abolishing customs duties between members over a period extending to 1973; however Venezuela and Bolivia are not members of the association.

TABLE 15:2

Foreign Trade, Groups of Countries, 1962

	In billions of U.S. dollars
European Economic Community*	69.9
European Free Trade Association†	44.2
United States	37.7
Eastern Europe and China	34.8
Canada	*11.7*
Latin-American Free Trade Association††	11.1

*West Germany, Belgium-Luxembourg, France, Italy, the Netherlands.
†Austria, Denmark, Norway, Portugal, United Kingdom, Sweden, Switzerland.
††Argentina, Brazil, Chile, Colombia, Ecuador, Mexico, Paraguay, Peru, Uruguay.
SOURCE: United Nations, *Yearbook of International Trade Statistics*, 1962.

Lastly, Australia and New Zealand are in the process of establishing preferential trade relations between their two countries.

In a world that has become regionalized in this way, Canada appears as a very small party to international trade. The foreign trade of the E.E.C. alone reached $70 billion in 1962, that of the E.F.T.A. $44 billion. Compared with the combined trade of these two blocs, even that of the United States is only a third as great. *If we take into account the trade of Eastern Europe and China and that of the L.A.F.T.A. countries we come to realize that Canada's isolation in a world of large-scale trading blocs is beginning to be a matter for concern.*

The following were the percentages of world trade for certain regions in 1962: industrialized countries, 63.4 per cent; Eastern countries, 12.0 per cent; non-industrialized countries, 24.5 per cent. Among the industrialized areas, the United States' share of the world total is 14.0 per cent, Canada's is 5.0 per cent, the E.E.C.'s 30.0 per cent, and the E.F.T.A.'s 15.0 per cent.[1]

1. These calculations are based on General Agreement on Tariffs and Trade, *International Trade in 1962*, p. 7 and Table D.

Canada can hardly afford to remain indifferent to this situation because foreign trade provides an important part of its national income. In 1962 its export receipts amounted to 26.8 per cent of its national income (and to 20.4 per cent of its G.N.P.). Several European countries find themselves in a similar position, but far from seeking to withdraw into themselves in order to avoid 'colonization by foreigners', they are seeking an even greater increase in their foreign trade. Consider Table 15:3 for a moment: the United Kingdom, West Germany, and Italy, with domestic markets much larger than Canada's, derive from exports comparable proportions of their gross domestic product.

TABLE 15:3

Exports as a Percentage of the Gross Domestic Product, 1962

Canada	*22.2*
United Kingdom	22.1
Italy	18.9
West Germany	17.5
France	13.9
Japan	11.0
United States	4.6

SOURCE: United Nations, *Yearbook of National Account Statistics*, 1963.

Although the exact figures are not available here, we know that all the countries of the E.F.T.A. are in a similar position (if not to an even greater extent). As a matter of fact, the United States is one of the rare exceptions to the rule that all countries are very 'dependent' on foreign trade. The reasons for the independence of the United States in this respect are very simple – its geographical isolation and the large size of its domestic market both in population and in purchasing power.

Over a long period the importance of foreign trade decreases in relation to domestic demand. This has been happening in most countries over the last fifty years. In 1926 Canadian exports represented 32 per cent of the G.N.P.; today they represent only

20 per cent. This is a considerable decrease.

Table 15:4 indicates recent developments in international trade by showing the changes in volume that have taken place since 1950.

TABLE 15:4

Indexes of the Quantity of Exports and Imports, 1953=100

	1950	*1963*	*Increase as a percentage*
1. EXPORTS			
Canada	*83*	*153*	*84*
United States	73	133	82
E.E.C.	76	268	252
United Kingdom	106	138	30
2. IMPORTS			
Canada	*73*	*131*	*79*
United States	92	163	77
E.E.C.	84	296	252
United Kingdom	90	148	64

SOURCE: Organization for Economic Co-operation and Development, *General Statistics*, November 1964.

It is clear that the E.E.C. countries have had the most rapid increase in foreign trade. Since in the opinion of several economists the year 1950 is non-representative, let us look at a comparison with the year 1953. This is the base year for the indexes we have employed, and so it can be quickly seen from the 1963 column that in the decade 1953-63 Canadian exports increased in volume by 53 per cent, those of the United States by 33 per cent, and those of the E.E.C. by 168 per cent. During that period we have been witnessing in the field of foreign trade a very noticeable reduction in the economic influence of the United States throughout the world and a corresponding rise in that of the European Economic Community.[1]

1. On this observation see H. G. Johnson, *Canada in a Changing World Economy*, University of Toronto Press, 1962.

What is happening is that Europe is beginning to recapture the place it held in world trade before World War II.

B. Structure of Foreign Trade

1. PRIMARY PRODUCTS AND MANUFACTURED PRODUCTS

In the last section of chapter 2 it was stated that the structure of the Canadian economy is still characterized by an intense exploitation of natural resources to serve world markets. Table 15:5 provides justification for this statement by giving the relevant export and import statistics.

Since the classification of products according to manufacturing content is always arbitrary, the calculations have been made on the basis of the international classification now in use, the revised Standard International Trade Classification established by the United Nations. Moreover, since results are difficult to interpret in isolation, Canada has been compared with the United States, the E.E.C., and the E.F.T.A. countries. The table resulting from this comparison is remarkably clear: 74 per cent of Canada's exports in 1962 were primary products, while the corresponding U.S., E.E.C., and E.F.T.A. figures were 38 per cent, 33 per cent, and 31 per cent respectively. These figures leave no doubt about the predominance of the primary sector in our exports and hence in the general economic structure derived from them.[1]

It does not follow, however, that there would be any point in comparing Canada with the underdeveloped countries. The weakness and instability of these countries' exports result mainly from lack of diversification in the products exported. A second examination of Table 15:5 (and of other following information) readily demonstrates that Canada's situation is quite different. The primary products exported by Canada belong to the three main categories in the classification – agricultural, forest, and mining – and within each category are found a great num-

1. Referring again to the main argument of chapter 2, it is necessary to add that if the staple-product theory is to find an indisputable empirical basis, one would still have to prove that it is exports that control the rate of growth of the whole of the economy.

TABLE 15:5

Structure of Exports, Each Category as a Percentage of Total, 1962

	Canada	United States	E.E.C.	E.F.T.A.
1. Food products	22.9	21.1	10.5	10.7
2. Raw materials of agricultural origin	19.6	7.1	4.3	7.3
3. Minerals and metals	26.0	5.7	12.6	10.2
4. Fuel and energy	5.8	3.8	5.9	2.6
Total of primary products	74.3	37.7	33.3	30.8
5. Chemicals	3.3	9.0	9.2	8.6
6. Machinery and transportation equipment	11.3	38.5	33.0	36.2
7. Other manufactured products	11.1	14.8	24.5	24.4
Total of manufactured products	25.7	62.3	66.7	69.2
Total	100	100	100	100

SOURCES: United Nations, *Yearbook of International Trade Statistics*, 1962. General Agreement on Tariffs and Trade, *International Trade in 1962*. The above groups are based on the Standard International Trade Classification, Revised.

ber of producer goods as well as consumer goods. Cereals form the major part of the exports of food products (the proportion is quite close to that of the United States); other materials of agricultural origin include lumber, wood pulp, and fertilizers. But where the export structure differs most between Canada and the other regions selected is in the exceptional place occupied in Canada by the mining products – iron ore, non-ferrous metals, and non-metallic minerals. The category of fuel and power includes crude petroleum, the export of which will certainly increase in the future. About the field of manufactured products, only the following need be said here: in the first place, newsprint makes up about half the total of the exports under the heading 'other manufactured products'; in the second place, the automobile industry chiefly accounts for the other countries' high percentage and Canada's low percentage under 'machinery and transportation equipment'.

Let us now consider the import structure, using the same procedures. Table 15:6 reveals to what an extraordinary extent Canada differs from the three other regions with which it is compared. Manufactured products make up more than two-thirds of Canada's imports but only about two-fifths of the imports of the United States and Europe. The similarity between the United States, the E.E.C., and the E.F.T.A. countries, in this respect is also noteworthy, particularly in imports of primary products. The structure of Canadian imports confirms what has been said earlier about the structure of exports. It is not necessary to dwell any further on this point.

Now let us return to the arbitrary nature of the classification. In the opinion of some, Canadian exports could be presented in a much more favourable light if special-purposes criteria were introduced. For example, statistics have been published showing that raw materials represent only 30 per cent of exports (in 1959), and that another 30 per cent is made up of products that have been completely or 'almost completely' manufactured (this latter category includes aluminum ingots).

A classification according to use would indicate that 70 per cent of the exports are producer goods. *In this writer's opinion,*

TABLE 15:6

Structure of Imports, Each Category as a Percentage of Total, 1962

	Canada	United States	E.E.C.	E.F.T.A.
1. Food products	11.9	24.2	21.7	26.3
2. Raw materials of agricultural origin	5.4	12.1	13.3	11.4
3. Minerals and metals	6.5	14.5	12.9	9.6
4. Fuel and energy	7.9	11.6	11.9	11.1
Total of primary products	31.7	62.4	59.8	58.4
5. Chemicals	6.3	3.2	5.4	5.9
6. Machinery and Transportation equipment	37.8	10.5	18.9	18.6
7. Other manufactured products	24.2	23.9	15.9	17.1
Total of manufactured products	68.3	37.6	40.2	41.6
Total	100	100	100	100

sources: See Table 15:5.

what is important is the comparison between countries as in Tables 15:5 and 15:6 rather than percentages, no matter on what basis, that apply to Canada alone.

2. PRINCIPAL PRODUCTS

Often a good method of resolving the thorny problems of classification is to have no classifications at all. A simple list of the principal products exported and imported will give significant information on the nature of our foreign trade. From Table 15:7 it can be seen at a glance that Canada exports the product of its natural resources, of which there are a great variety, and that it imports equipment goods and durable consumer goods.

What have been the main trends in recent years? In exports, agricultural products show a tendency to lose their former predominant position to forest products and particularly metals and minerals. In the fifties and sixties the exports with above-average rates of growth have been iron ore, nickel, aluminum, and copper. Among export products that have appeared since World War II are iron ore, petroleum, and uranium. Table 15:7 reveals that in 1962 these were among the leading exports, amounting to more than $600 million.

Among manufactured products, chemicals have shown the largest increase since the war, notably synthetic rubber, chemical fertilizers, calcium salts and compounds, plastics, and cellulose products. R. V. Anderson's study for the Royal Commission on Canada's Economic Prospects, the principal study of trends in exports to 1980, forecasts that there will be only minor modifications in the concentration of the leading exports.[1] We should see a relative increase in the exports of aluminum, petroleum, and iron ore and a relative decrease in the exports of wheat, nickel, and copper.

Among imports, past tendencies indicate that the following categories will show increases: equipment goods, durable consumer goods (particularly household equipment), petroleum,

1. R. V. Anderson, *The Future of Canada's Exports,* Study of the Royal Commission on Canada's Economic Prospects, 1957, pp. 111 and 134.

TABLE 15:7

Leading Domestic Exports and Imports, Canada 1962, millions of dollars

Exports		Imports	
Newsprint paper	753	Machinery (non-farm) and parts	676
Wheat	601	Automobile parts (except engines)	392
Lumber and timber	396	Electrical apparatus, n.e.s.*	325
Wood pulp	369	Petroleum, crude and partly refined	304
Nickel and products	322	Aircraft and parts	259
Aluminum and products	293	Automobiles, passenger	153
Petroleum, crude and partly refined	232	Tractors and parts	140
Iron ore and concentrates	220	Plastics and products	119
Copper and products	210	Farm implements and machinery (except tractors and parts)	113
Radioactive ores and concentrates	166	Engines, internal-combustion, and parts, n.e.s.*	113
Aircraft and parts	146	Parcels of small value	85
Asbestos, unmanufactured	135	Apparel and apparel accessories	71
Total as shown	3,843	Total as shown	2,750
Total exports	6,348	Total imports	6,258

*Not elsewhere specified'.
SOURCE: *Canada Year Book, 1963-64.*

and chemical products. Imports now declining as a percentage of the total are food products, textiles, certain raw materials such as rubber and coal, and primary iron and steel (the list is not exhaustive). In 1957, when David Slater's study of imports was published by the Royal Commission on Canada's Economic Prospects, there was no anticipation of major changes in these trends up to 1980.[1]

3. TERMS OF TRADE

It is possible to verify whether a foreign trade structure is favourable or not by means of the terms of trade. This expression currently means *the ratio of the price index of exported products to the price index of imported products*. By representing these two indexes by Px and Pm respectively and using more precise terms we can write:

$$\text{Net barter terms of trade}^2 = \frac{Px}{Pm}$$

It is evident, speaking generally, that a favourable foreign trade structure is one in which export prices remain stable or rise over a period of time while import prices either remain stable, fall, or rise less rapidly than export prices. *If export prices rise while import prices remain the same, the country can acquire a greater quantity of commodities at no extra cost.* It is because such a change in the terms of trade has taken place that inter-

---

1. David Slater, *Canada's Imports,* Study of the Royal Commission on Canada's Economic Prospects, 1957, p. 112. An important conclusion of this study is to the effect that the changes in the structure of imports depend on changes in the composition of the total expenditure rather than on changes in the sources of supply.

2. The exchange rate (which will be defined in the next chapter) enters into this calculation. Prices must be translated into the same currency unit in order to be comparable. If initially Pm are prices in foreign currency we multiply them by the rate of exchange, T, in which T = the price of the foreign currency in terms of the national currency. It follows that a devaluation of the national currency increases Pm and that a rise in value of the national currency decreases Pm.

national trade since World War I has favoured the industrialized countries at the expense of the underdeveloped countries. Does this unfavourable relationship apply to Canada, which, as we have seen, exports primary products and imports manufactured products? The answer is no. Since the beginning of the century Canada's terms of trade have shown no tendency either to rise or fall. Between 1905 and 1950 the fluctuations have not been of more than 5 per cent except for short periods. In 1952, following the appreciation of the Canadian dollar, the average price of imports fell by 12 per cent and Canada's terms of trade accordingly improved by 12 per cent. In 1961 and 1962, again largely because of the inverse movement of the exchange rate, the terms of trade worsened. They stood at the index 95 in 1962 compared to 100 in 1953.

With this information we can better interpret the data of Tables 15:8 and 15:9.

TABLE 15:8

Terms of Trade, 1962, 1951 = 100

	$\dfrac{Px}{Pm}$
Canada	105
United States	123
E.E.C.	118
E.F.T.A.	121

SOURCE: Organization for Economic Co-operation and Development, *General Statistics.*

But the advantage that the country is deemed to derive from increases in commodity terms of trade is a very uncertain one. *When prices of exports go up, one must expect the volume of sales to decrease.* No one can sell unlimited quantities at whatever price he pleases. This being the case, a rise in the terms of trade is not of necessity an advantage nor is a fall in the terms of trade necessarily a cause for anxiety. (To associate a rise in the

TABLE 15:9

Income Terms of Trade and Export Receipts, Canada and Selected Other Countries, 1962, 1951 = 100

A	$\frac{Px}{Pm}$	Qx	$\frac{Px}{Pm} \times Qx$
Canada	105	152	160
United States	123	133	164
E.E.C.	118	263	310
E.F.T.A.	121	154	186
B	Px	Qx	$Px \times Qx$
Canada	104	152	158
Industrial countries	101	183	185
Non-industrialized countries	75	162	121

NOTE: Industrial countries: Western Europe, Japan, and North America. Non-industrialized countries: the rest of the world. The indexes are based on 1953 and moved back to 1951 = 100.

SOURCES: Part A: Organization for Economic Co-operation and Development, *General Statistics*. Part B: General Agreement on Tariffs and Trade, *International Trade in 1962*, p. 11.

commodity terms of trade with a rise in export receipts is postulating a price elasticity lower than unity in the demand for exports.)

In order to take into account both variations in volume and variations in price, the concept of *income terms of trade* must be introduced:

$$\text{Income terms of trade} = \frac{Px}{Pm} \times Qx$$

where Px and Pm again designate the price indexes of exports and imports, and Qx the index of the quantities exported. The expression gives the changes that take place in the export receipts (Px × Qx), when import prices are given. In a more concrete way, perhaps, it indicates the changes that take place in the capacity of the country to import a given volume of products (the possibilities of borrowing being set aside).

Table 15:9 sums up the changes in the income terms of trade of Canada and certain other countries from 1951 to 1962. As the situation of the underdeveloped countries is quite interesting in this regard, part B of the table makes a second comparison which in this case applies only to export receipts.

It becomes evident from these calculations that Canada's 'capacity to import' increased by 60 per cent during the eleven-year period and that this rate of growth, very close to that of the United States, was less than that of the E.F.T.A. countries, and very much less than that of the E.E.C countries. The growth in the volume of exports had much more effect on this result than the commodity terms of trade. For example, the United States had the highest increase in the commodity terms of trade of the four regions considered, but its exports rose so little that its income terms of trade deteriorated in comparison with those of Europe. The opposite applies to the countries of the E.E.C.: two-thirds of the advance in the income terms of trade is attributable to the rise in the volume of exports.[1]

Let us now consider part B of Table 15:9, in which the commodity terms of trade regain their importance. The quantities exported by the underdeveloped countries increased by 62 per cent between 1951 and 1962. This rate of growth is remarkable; it is higher than the Canadian and United States rates. However, because of a drop of 25 per cent in export prices, the total export receipts of the underdeveloped countries increased by only 21 per cent. Canada, in comparison, thanks to more favourable prices for its products, increased its receipts by 58 per cent.

This examination of commodity terms of trade gives at least a partial answer to the question whether Canada's foreign trade structure is favourable or unfavourable, and whether it is well or poorly adapted to the conditions of world demand. In relation

1. 1951 is not an appropriate year for establishing comparisons because of the rise in the price of raw materials brought about by the Korean war. Other base years would give less pronounced variations: they would, however, point in the same direction.

to Europe, and notably in relation to the E.E.C., Canada's development is rather unsatisfactory, and commodity terms of trade have played a certain part in this.[1] On the other hand, if a comparison is made with the underdeveloped countries taken together, it will be seen that Canada's export prices have been very favourable, more favourable, indeed, than the export prices of the industrial countries. *On the whole, then, and in spite of appearances, Canada's import and export structure does not reveal any major weaknesses.*

C. Balance of Trade

From the analysis of commodities we must now turn to an examination of the balance of trade with Canada's principal trading partners.

TABLE 15:10

Commodity Exports and Imports, Canada, millions of dollars

	Exports	*Imports*	*Balance*
1951	3,950	4,097	−147
1956	4,837	5,565	−728
1959	5,150	5,572	−386
1962	6,380	6,203	177
1964	8,238	7,538	700

SOURCE: Bank of Canada, *Statistical Summary*.

In its commodity trade with the rest of the world, Canada recorded a comfortable surplus from the beginning of World War II up to 1950. Then, with the exception of 1952 when there was a surplus of $489 million, it showed an average annual deficit of $325 million until 1960. The largest deficit ($728 million) was that of 1956 when, in a single year, imports increased by

1. We have seen, however, that the fall in the terms of trade was not primarily caused by a defective structure but by the depreciation of the currency, which resulted in turn from the over-all deficit on the current account.

$1 billion. After a deficit of $150 million in 1960, the situation improved in 1961, thanks to a noticeable increase in exports. The surplus for that year was $173 million. From 1962 to 1964, the record was excellent, with sustained increases in exports which led to the very large surplus of $700 million in 1964.

The devaluation of the Canadian dollar in 1961 was the main reason for the re-establishment of a favourable trade balance. The wheat sales to Eastern countries have helped to maintain export receipts. There is no doubt that it is the volume of exports that has contributed primarily to the elimination of the trade

TABLE 15:11

Exports and Imports by Countries, Canada 1964

	Exports as a percentage of total	*Imports as a percentage of total*	*Balance in millions of dollars*
United States	52.7	68.9	−893
United Kingdom	14.8	7.6	625
E.E.C.	6.8	5.4	149
Western Europe, others	2.6	2.1	49
Eastern Europe, including China	7.6	0.5	579
Africa and Middle East	1.6	2.3	−43
Japan	4.1	2.3	155
Other Asia and Oceania	4.2	2.9	127
Latin-American Free Trade Association	2.1	1.4	67
Venezuela	0.8	3.6	−206
America, others	2.7	3.0	−5
	100	100	
Total (in millions of dollars)	$8,094	$7,489	$605

NOTE: The total trade balance is not strictly comparable to that shown on Table 15:10.
SOURCES: Calculations made from Dominion Bureau of Statistics, *Trade of Canada, Summary of Imports*, and *Trade of Canada, Exports by Countries*.

deficit since 1956. In fact, the value of exports increased by 70 per cent and that of imports by 35 per cent in the period from 1956 to 1964, as can be seen in Table 15:10. Since export prices increased less rapidly than import prices in the same period, the result is explained in terms of volume.

The geographical distribution of the external trade reveals, however, that the improvement in the balance of trade remains superficial in that the chronic deficit with the United States has not been affected in the least. But let us first consider a few more general facts.

Canada's leading customers are, first, the United States, which bought 53 per cent of Canadian exports in 1964, and then the United Kingdom, which bought 14.8 per cent. Japan came third, taking 4.1 per cent. It was followed by West Germany with 1.5 per cent. Apart from those to the United States, Canadian exports are relatively dispersed, as is clear from the low percentages in the first column of Table 15:11. The E.E.C. countries (which includes West Germany) took only 6.8 per cent of Canada's exports, or a total of $550 million, in 1964.

In imports into Canada the United States holds a still more dominant position, accounting for almost 70 per cent in 1964; 7.6 per cent came from the United Kingdom and only 5.4 per cent from the E.E.C. countries. Note, however, the relatively large imports from Venezuela: 3.6 per cent or $270 million. This was largely for petroleum.

In the last column of Table 15:11 are the trade balances. The deficit with the United States, although very high, is more than compensated for by the surpluses with other countries.

The most remarkable development in Canadian external trade in this century has been the substitution of the United States for Great Britain as the main outlet for Canadian exports. This transfer was confirmed at the beginning of the 1950s. In 1901, 60 per cent of Canadian exports went to Great Britain and a little less than 30 per cent to the United States. In 1951, the proportion going to Great Britain had fallen to 16 per cent, while the proportion going to the United States had risen to 60 per cent. From 1951 to 1962 the relative proportions to these two countries showed only minor changes, but in the 1964 figures the increasing significance of exports to other countries asserts itself.

TABLE 15:12

Destination of Canadian Exports as a Percentage of the Total

	1901	*1951*	*1962*	*1964*
United States	28	59	59	52
Great Britain	60	16	14	14
Other Countries	12	25	27	34

The present dominance of imports from the United States is not a development of this century, as is the case with exports. In 1901 the United States was already supplying 60 per cent of Canadian imports.

One can deduce from these figures that, apart from very exceptional circumstances, the trade deficit with the United States is as old as Canada itself. Since 1946 the deficit has averaged about $520 million a year and shows no sign of disappearing. Far from it. In 1964 it reached $800 million. The only year in which it was less than $300 million was 1950; the low figure of that year was due to strict import controls.

The year-to-year changes in the over-all balance of trade are largely attributable to the other countries, whereas the deficit with the United States either changes little or changes for the worse (Table 15:13). From 1959 to 1960 the over-all deficit fell by $275 million; the deficit with the United States increased by $141 million. From 1960 to 1961 we passed from a deficit of $148 million to a surplus of $173 million; the deficit with the United States decreased by only $64 million. From 1961 to 1962, by exception, the American deficit fell by $140 million,[1] and this was compensated by a reduction in the surplus with the

---

1. Note that the Canadian dollar depreciated from the end of 1961.

TABLE 15:13

Commodity Trade Balances, Canada 1959-64, millions of dollars

	With the United States		With other countries		With all countries	
	deficits	changes	deficits (–) or surpluses (+)	changes	deficits (–) or surpluses (+)	changes
1959	−538		+115		−423	
1960	−679	−141	+531	+416	−148	+275
1961	−615	+ 64	+788	+257	+173	+321
1962	−475	+140	+630	−158	+155	−18
1963	−488	− 13	+991	+361	+503	+348
1964	−805	−317	+1505	+514	+700	+197

SOURCE: Dominion Bureau of Statistics, *The Balance of International Payments.*

other countries. Again in both 1963 and 1964 the over-all situation improved while the U.S. deficits increased. Trade between Canada and the other countries seems much more sensitive to economic conditions and to the usual policies of adjustment than trade with the United States. Thus when Canada went from a deficit in the general balance of trade of $386 million in 1959 to a surplus of $155 million in 1962, trade with the United States was in no way responsible, since our deficit with that country came to $536 million in 1959 and $555 million in 1962.

The breakdown of trade according to broad categories of commodities and according to countries sheds scarcely any new light apart from showing that agricultural products are exported mainly to Europe rather than to the United States, and that almost 80 per cent of our exports of lumber and paper are sold to the United States. In particular commodities, of course, we would find similar concentrations, but a list of these would be too lengthy to include here.

This brief examination of Canada's customers and suppliers leads us to conclude that the United States is by far our most important trading partner. Let us end with this little note of common sense: If we want to bring about important changes in Canada's external trade, our efforts must first be directed to altering our trade relations with the United States. This applies particularly to the disequilibrium in the balance of trade and more generally to the disequilibrium in the balance on current account. (See the next chapter for the terminology relating to the balance of international payments.)

D. The Tariff Policy

The level and nature of international trade are fundamentally controlled by the differences between countries in cost of production and by world demand for the products. In broad terms these are the market conditions. Market conditions, however, are influenced to a great extent by the customs duties set by the various countries. *A customs duty is a tax levied on imported commodities; the customs tariff of a country is a list of all the duties in force.* The influence of the tariff on foreign trade can considerably affect the country's economic structure, its rate of growth, and the income level of its population. The tariff is therefore, like domestic taxes or the money supply, an instrument of economic policy.

The customs tariff has played a particularly important role in the economic development of Canada. According to certain writers it has been detrimental, but others hold that Canada would not have survived without it. All agree that whatever the final appraisal, the tariff is responsible for creating and maintaining in existence a great number of Canadian industries and for preventing the creation and development of many others. In short, the tariff has profoundly transformed Canada's economic structure. Whether for better or worse need not be discussed here.

1. PAST DEVELOPMENTS

Before outlining the history of the Canadian customs tariff we must agree on several indispensable concepts and propositions. *Free trade is a system in which no deliberate barrier in the form of tariffs or quotas is placed in the way of international trade.* (A quota is a prohibition to import commodities over and above a certain quantity.) The opposite system is *protectionism*, which derives its name from the protection against foreign competition that it affords to national producers through imposition of a tariff. Since certain duties protect no one a distinction is made between a *protective tariff*, which reduces or effectively suppresses imports, and a *revenue tariff*, which aims at procuring revenue for the government. In Canada a duty on the importation of coffee is a revenue tariff because the coffee shrub does not grow here.

One of the main propositions of economics is that under certain conditions of application, the free-trade system procures at a given moment higher gains from trade than any other system and therefore the highest per-capita real national income. Two of the conditions of application are *competition* and *full employment*. In the absence of competition and full employment a particular country may impose a tariff and enforce its payment by other countries, provided the import and export elasticities are of the right kind. But even if a country is short of free competition and has unemployment, the tariff is not a good strategy, for the other countries will retaliate and the country that set up the tariff will find itself as badly off as before. The only real restriction on the rule concerns the expression 'at a given moment'. It is logical that we might be willing to reduce today's national income by imposing a tariff, if we think that thereby tomorrow's national income will be increased. This is the argument for protecting 'infant industry', according to which an industry is *provisionally* protected in the hope that it will be able to meet foreign competition a little later. Such a tariff is compatible with the objective of maximizing world national income. The other tariffs are not compatible with such an objective; in fact they have the opposite effect.

As a general rule the customs tariff raises the cost to the consumer, allocates resources in an inequitable manner, and channels production within industries in an inefficient way so that on the whole a protected country is less prosperous than it would otherwise be. Most people, unfortunately, tend to be less concerned about the general prosperity than about their own. Many would cheerfully permit the impoverishment of the country if this were the price of maintaining the protected positions of particular industries and special groups. Thus it is claimed that restrictions on imports will create jobs in the garment industry, but the fact that they will also reduce the number of jobs in the export industries is ignored.

Although these assertions have been made without supporting proof, it has been considered necessary to the interpretation of the following facts that they be made.

Canada's tariff policy can be explained and understood only in the context of its historical development. The principal historical elements are as follows:

1. Internally, Canada is an economy in which unification and integration are difficult to achieve, and an economy subjected to

great strains, first because of the importance of the export industries and the underdevelopment of the manufacturing industries, and second because of the divergent interests of the various regions. The tariff has served as a *political* instrument (to increase population), and economic considerations have often occupied only a secondary place.

2. Externally, tariff policy has been dominated by the more or less close relations that Canada desired to maintain, or felt that it should maintain, at times with Great Britain, at other times with the United States. The attempts to arrange reciprocity treaties with the United States on the one hand and the British Preferences on the other are both expressions of these choices.

3. Since World War II, Canada has apparently been seeking to free itself from the exclusive attachments in which it has been led to favour one over the other.[1] To this end Canada is pursuing a rigorously multilateral and nondiscriminatory policy within the framework of GATT.

(a) Changes in the General Level of the Customs Tariff.

Table 15:14 is set up to show the changes that took place in the general level of the Canadian customs tariff between 1848 and 1962.[2] The period during which the tariff was highest was that of the 'National Policy' introduced by Sir John A. Macdonald in 1879, which consisted of a deliberate protection of the manufacturing industry for both political and economic reasons. The tariff reached its highest level in 1888 when the average rate of duties reached almost 32 per cent of the value of dutiable

---

1. The worst of it is that while favouring one (since 1900) we have had the other, since the British Preferences have not prevented trade from flowing in the direction of the United States.

2. In this field statistics unfortunately tend to be confusing and those of Table 15:14 are no exception. In general they undervalue the protection given, since, at its limit, the prohibitive duty disappears from the calculations; the import and the duty levied are equal to zero. A second deficiency is that the lowering of the percentages does not always mean less protection. If the duties are lowered on intermediate goods and maintained on selling final products, the effective protection of the enterprises concerned is increased (see p. 384).

imports and 22 per cent of the value of total imports (the difference between these two percentages representing the products admitted duty free). The range of products affected by the tariff increases was very wide, but the tariff was aimed primarily at creating a diversified manufacturing industry and encouraging the establishment of foreign enterprises in Canada. At that time the government could invoke the infant-industry argument already mentioned, and at first sight at least, the policy did produce the hoped-for results, judging by the diversification of the economy and the massive importation of capital that were the two essential characteristics of the period 1896-1914.

There was an over-all reduction of the customs tariff around 1900 as a result of the concession of preferential tariffs to England. Until the beginning of the depression of the 1930s the Canadian tariff was progressively lowered, though by small percentages. The depression then led to drastic increases in customs duties as it did in several other countries, each hoping to resolve its own unemployment problem at the expense of its neighbours. From around 1935 to 1937, however, Canada returned to almost the same tariff level that prevailed during the last years of the twenties.

Between 1939 and 1962 the Canadian tariff decreased by about 25 per cent (Table 15:14) as a result of concessions granted after the war within the framework of GATT; the rise in prices, which decreased the relative importance of specific duties,[1] and changes in the import structure have also reduced the tariff level. It is probable that as a result of this the actual amount of protection afforded Canadian producers has been reduced; but this is debatable. (See note 2 on page 376.)

(b) The British Preferences.

Contrary to a widely held opinion, the British preferential tariff has never exerted a profound influence on the Canadian econ-

---

1. The *ad valorem* duties are set as a percentage of the value of the products, the specific duties as an absolute amount (.08 cents per pound of butter, for example).

TABLE 15:14

Customs Tariffs Collected as a Percentage of Imports, selected years

	As a percentage of dutiable imports	As a percentage of total imports
1848	10.8	10.5
1849	16.3	14.8
1855	13.7	9.8
1859	18.9	13.2
1879	26.1	20.2
1888	31.8	22.0
1900	27.7	16.7
1929	24.4	15.8
1932	30.1	19.0
1939	24.2	13.8
1946	21.2	11.9
1955	18.2	10.2
1960	17.5	9.7
1962	18.2	10.1

SOURCES: John H. Young, *Canadian Commercial Policy*, Royal Commission on Canada's Economic Prospects, 1957. *Canada Yearbook*, *1963-64*. Dominion Bureau of Statistics, *National Accounts*, 1962.

omy except during the colonial period. At the beginning of the 1840s, Great Britain abolished the preferences that it had been granting to Canadian products, and it was only in 1932, when British markets had lost much of their importance for Canada, that they were reintroduced. Their abolition, at the time of the union of Upper and Lower Canada, had disastrous effects on the Canadian economy which were felt for a very long time. Canada had no other recourse than to abrogate, in 1847, the preferences that it had itself been granting to Great Britain; this decision resulted in 1849 in a rise in the Canadian tariff, as we can observe in Table 15:14. Fifty years later, in spite of a British refusal to grant reciprocal concessions, Canada again granted a preference to products of British origin by allowing a one-third reduction of the customs tariffs then in force. The effect on the tariff is shown by the 1900 figures in Table 15:14. This unilateral system of tariff preferences could not prevent British imports from dropping from 31 per cent of total imports in 1896 to 15 per cent in 1929 (then to 8 per cent in 1964, as Table 15:11 shows).

The Ottawa agreements of 1932 led to reciprocal preferences between Canada, Great Britain, and certain other Commonwealth countries. The preferences granted by Canada were much increased. These agreements were terminated in 1935, but two years later new agreements were concluded by which both the tariffs in force and the preference margins (rates) were markedly reduced. Since the war several special margins have been further reduced, but it is difficult to estimate whether on the whole the margins are higher or lower than they were during the 1920s.[1] The ratio of the duties levied on United Kingdom imports to the total imports from that country has been reduced more quickly, however, than the equivalent ratio in respect of the United States. In 1960, the percentages were 7.4 for the United Kingdom and 10.2 for the United States. In 1951, 1,450 of the 2,038 Canadian tariff items showed British preference duties lower than the 'most-favoured-nation' duties. The British Preferences, however, do not affect any more than 15 per cent of the total value of Canadian exports and 8 per cent of imports.

(c) The Attempts at Economic Co-operation with the United States.

After Great Britain abolished colonial preferences in the 1840s, Canada turned toward the United States to find new markets for its products. Negotiations began in 1846 but because of American indifference did not bear results until the Reciprocity Treaty of 1854.

Reciprocity consisted of abolishing 'reciprocally' the customs duties on certain agreed products. In today's terms we would say

1. John H. Young, *Canadian Commercial Policy*, Royal Commission on Canada's Economic Prospects, Ottawa, Queen's Printer, 1957, pp. 62 ff.

that the treaty set up a partial free trade association between the two countries. The list of products affected by the agreement was quite long for that time. It included a good number of important primary products such as wood, cereals, fish, animals, meats, butter, cheese, flour, and coal. The effect on the Canadian tariff level was quite marked (see Table 15:14, 1855), since the articles admitted duty free increased from 7 per cent to 29 per cent of total imports. In 1858, however, Canada increased the duties by 17½ per cent, and again by 20 per cent in 1859, on products that had not been included in the reciprocity treaty. These moves were very poorly received in the United States, and the treaty, which had never aroused any enthusiasm there in any case, was abrogated by that country in 1866. This first experiment, on the whole, was not a happy one. Not until 1934 was a new trade agreement adopted between the two countries.

In 1874 the two governments signed a new free trade agreement which on this occasion included manufactured products as well as primary products, but the American Senate did not take the trouble to ratify it. In later years a large segment of Canadian public opinion continued to favour economic co-operation with the United States, but in 1891 and in 1911, when the Liberal Party made free trade with the United States the major issue of its electoral campaigns, it was defeated. This question has never since been a central issue and the official attitude of the United States has remained what it was in 1874.[1]

Canada concluded bilateral trade agreements with the United States in 1935 and in 1938, but there was no intention of establishing preferential trade relations and certainly no discussion of free trade.

The question of lowering the customs tariff on both sides of the border keeps coming up with some urgency, however. The American tariff is relatively high; its structure is such as to encourage Canadian specialization in primary products and to hamper development of Canadian manufacturing industry. The

1. The historical sketch that we give here is based principally on John H. Young, *op. cit.*, chapters 3 and 4.

Canadian tariff has been constructed on a similar model, so that the two tariffs tend more or less to compensate for one another. It follows that a reciprocal lowering of customs duties would not necessarily plunge the country into ruin, whereas we might expect considerable gains because of the heavy volume of trade.[1] Whatever may be the answer to this controversial question, in our opinion it is worth while keeping this alternative in mind, if only out of concern for historical continuity!

(d) The General Agreement on Tariffs and Trade (GATT).

Since World War II, Canada has followed a commercial policy inspired by the principles of the General Agreement on Tariffs and Trade (GATT), and has applied the rules of procedure of that agreement. The agreement was signed in 1947 by twenty-three countries. Today seventy-two countries participate in it, either officially or unofficially. The Communist countries, except for Poland, do not take part. GATT calls for liberal policies in international trade. It aims at reduction of customs tariffs and removal of other obstacles to trade. In place of the bilateral agreements of the pre-war period it substitutes multilateral non-discriminatory negotiations, through which a concession granted to one country is automatically granted to all the other signatories of the agreement. Quantitative restrictions on imports are prohibited except in temporary balance-of-payments difficulties. Since the British Preference tariffs are contrary to the principles of GATT, the countries concerned have agreed not to increase them and to seek to bring about their progressive reduction.

Between 1947 and 1966, five international tariff-negotiating conferences were held under the auspices of GATT. The most important for Canada were those of 1947 and 1951. The list of Canadian concessions to other countries in 1947 comprised 1,050 items, of which 590 were reductions and 460 were adjustments of tariffs. At Annecy in 1949, eleven countries joined the agree-

---

1. On the customs policy of the United States, see I. Brecher and S. S. Reisman, *Canadian-American Economic Relations*, The Royal Commission on Canada's Economic Prospects, part 3.

ment and Canada's 1947 concessions were extended to them also. At Torquay in 1951, Canada and the United States agreed on additional customs reductions involving a total of 8,700 concessions and 55,000 adjustments of tariffs. Six further countries, including West Germany, joined GATT at this time. These three international conferences produced important and tangible results in respect of both reductions in customs tariffs and the general organization of international trade. The American tariff, for example, was lowered by about 50 per cent; this reduction was paralleled by more or less equivalent reductions on the part of the other countries. It is within this multilateral framework of GATT that Canada has been seeking to obtain a satisfactory trade adjustment with the United States.

The Geneva Conference of 1956 served primarily to re-establish the previous agreements, which had by then terminated. At the 1960-2 conference the European Economic Community presented its common external tariff for the first time. The E.E.C. and the United States agreed to reduce tariffs by 20 per cent on a list of 570 items. The common external tariff of the E.E.C. was probably lowered in total by less than 10 per cent. Canada obtained from the E.E.C. pledges and effective reductions affecting $250 million worth of Canadian exports annually, about half the Canadian exports to the E.E.C.

Then the United States began a large-scale campaign for the reduction of tariffs and the liberalization of international trade. By the Trade Expansion Act of 1962, Congress authorized the President to reduce all American customs tariffs up to a maximum of 50 per cent and to abolish a certain number completely, under certain conditions. An international conference on this matter was called in 1964 under the auspices of GATT in order to initiate the 'Kennedy Round' of negotiations.

It is on this conference that Canada's hopes rest at the time of writing. For it must be pointed out that since 1955 the fundamental principle of GATT in regard to nondiscrimination in international trade has been subjected to several attacks that seriously risk compromising the future of the agreement. Both the E.E.C. and the E.F.T.A. represent ideas contrary to this principle. Since it has not participated in these regional agreements, it is absolutely vital for Canada that the spirit of GATT continue to prevail, if it wishes to preserve its access to foreign markets.

2. THE PRESENT CUSTOMS TARIFF

The Customs Tariff Act[1] includes Canadian tariff regulations of a general nature and three lists of products. List A defines products and gives the duties relating to them, if any; list B enumerates products allowed a rebate of duties; list C gives products of which import is prohibited.

List C is short. Among the forbidden articles are counterfeit products; publications that are obscene or of a nature to foment sedition; aeroplanes, and second-hand automobiles.

Repayments of part of the duties (list B), called 'drawbacks', generally apply to parts or materials utilized in Canada in the manufacture of products for export. They may go as high as 99 per cent of the duty. The purpose of the drawbacks, which are very old and very widespread, is to avoid placing a deliberate burden on exporters' production costs through the imposition of tariffs on imported parts or materials. In certain cases rebates have also been granted for other purposes.

List A is composed of more than 2,000 tariff lines (items), and the descriptions of the products are extremely complex for the uninitiated. To each tariff line there correspond several duties: the British Preference duty, the most-favoured-nation duty, the GATT duty, and the General Tariff. The British Preference duty applies to the United Kingdom, to Commonwealth countries, and to territories under British control. In respect of five countries, special agreements add further to the number of duties (for example, on Australian and New Zealand butter). The most-favoured-nation tariff and the GATT tariff are the same in principle. Whenever they differ it is, with a few exceptions, the GATT tariff that is applied, the other being left in reserve, so to speak, only in case Canada might decide to with-

---

1. Customs Tariffs, R.S.C., chap. 44.

draw from GATT. The countries under the GATT tariff are the signatories of GATT and a few others, of which the most important is the U.S.S.R. When the GATT and the British Preference tariffs apply to the same country, the lower prevails. The General Tariff applies to countries that have not concluded any agreement with Canada. In practice this tariff is rarely applied. Exceptions aside and on the whole, the Canadian tariff may be reduced to two series of duties: the British Preference and the most-favoured-nation tariffs.

Apart from the various duties applying to different countries, there are often several duties on the same product or on the same class of products. Three main distinctions are used as a basis for these differences in treatment. The first is according to the anticipated use of the product. If a Canadian producer, protected by an import duty, imports parts or materials that go into the manufacture of his product, then he enjoys less protection if he pays a duty on these parts and more protection if he does not. Suppose that a commodity is made of raw materials imported duty free for half of the commodity's selling price, the other half being value added. A 10 per cent duty on the selling price gives the producer an effective protection of 20 per cent since only value added represents costs of his own. The use made of products therefore influences the level of effective protection. That is why tariffs on the intermediate products are often lower than on final products, thus increasing protection against foreign competition. It is estimated that the effective protection provided by the Canadian tariff is about twice as high as the nominal rate.[1]

A further distinction is made between imported products that are also manufactured in Canada and imported products that are not. It is evident that the latter will carry lower duties since protection is not being provided to any Canadian manufacturer.

An important provision of the Canadian tariff relates to the Canadian or British content of a product. Certain parts are admitted duty free or at a reduced rate, if the final product is

1. C. L. Barber, 'Canadian Tariff Policy', *Canadian Journal of Economics and Political Science*, November 1955, pp. 513-30.

manufactured in Canada or in the Commonwealth. This regulation developed from the necessity of defining a British product for purposes of applying the British Preference duties. Today these provisions have their greatest effect on the automobile industry.[1]

It is not possible in one or two sentences to indicate either what the level of the Canadian tariff is or what degree of effective protection is enjoyed by Canadian industries. Nor would several pages be enough, since it is very difficult in any case to arrive at any accurate conclusion. In the study we have mainly followed, the author picked out some hundred 'key duties' in order to give a more general picture. The non-weighted average of these 'key duties' (most-favoured-nation *ad valorem*), including the zero rates, is 19.55 per cent.[2]

In recent years several observers have expressed the opinion that Canada's customs policy should be subjected to a searching re-examination because of the persistence of deficits on trade and current account in the balance of payments, and because of Canada's excessive dependence on the United States.

The possibilities of any change in the policy pursued since the war under the auspices of GATT are very limited. Since most authors have rejected an increase in protectionism as a solution, the question resolves itself into searching for various ways of lowering the customs tariff. First is the possibility of a unilateral decrease which would not require the consent of any other country: this may be justified in theory, but it would be costly in practice, so that it has no chance of being adopted. The other possibilities are that Canada might enter a free trade zone in

---

1. Trade is greatly affected by the way in which the customs tariff is applied as well as by the restrictions that are not covered by the tariff. We shall not discuss these problems here. But a useful reference on the subject is G. A. Elliott, *Tariff Procedures and Trade Barriers*, University of Toronto Press, 1955.

2. Young, *op. cit.*, pp. 126-8. The changes that have taken place in these rates have been verified with the aid of the 1963 schedules. The changes primarily concern iron and steel and textile products. It has not been possible to discern any clear tendency indicating a rise or a fall.

association with either the E.E.C., the E.F.T.A. countries, or the United States. At first sight a rapprochement with one of the European groups would appear to offer more advantage from several points of view than one with the United States, but reflection soon suggests two major and perhaps insurmountable disadvantages. Canada's trade with Europe represents only a small proportion of its total trade, so that reducing tariffs with Europe would not have the necessary impact on the Canadian economy. Experience with the British Preference tariffs leaves no room for doubt on this point. Secondly, the European solution provides no remedy for the trading obstacles and the losses resulting from the Canadian and American tariffs on mutual trade exchanges, which represent two-thirds of Canada's total external trade.

A free trade association with the United States would have the advantage of not disturbing trade patterns that have become established (the barriers erected on both sides notwithstanding) as a result of a favourable geographical location. Consideration of this solution, however, leads to the raising of profound political difficulties that bring into question Canada's very existence. An economic association between two entities politically and economically as unequal as Canada and the United States would inevitably have grave political repercussions.

This brings us back to GATT. Canada's best policy would appear to be to strive for a general reduction of tariffs within the framework of GATT in such a way that the groupings into regional blocks, if they do become consolidated, will nevertheless permit Canadian products access to the great world markets under the least disadvantageous conditions possible.

SUGGESTED READINGS

H. G. JOHNSON: *Canada in a Changing World Economy*, University of Toronto Press, 1962.
   Description and comments on the post-war world economy.

H. G. JOHNSON: *The Canadian Quandary: Economic Problems and Policies*, Toronto, McGraw-Hill, 1963.

J. H. YOUNG: *Canadian Commercial Policy*, Royal Commission on Canada's Economic Prospects, Ottawa, Queen's Printer, 1957.
A study of the tariff and other instruments of Canadian commercial policy. The author makes a strong case for free trade.

O. J. MC DIARMID: *Commercial Policy in the Canadian Economy*, Cambridge, Mass., Harvard University Press, 1946.
The record of commercial policy, especially during the period 1867-1939, is examined.

T. N. BREWIS: 'International Economic Relations', chapter 12 in Brewis, English, Scott, and Jewett, *Canadian Economic Policy*, Toronto, Macmillan, 1961.
An introductory text to Canada's economic relations with the rest of the world.

W. A. MACKINTOSH: *The Economic Background of Dominion-Provincial Relations*, a study prepared for the Royal Commission on Dominion-Provincial Relations, Ottawa, King's Printer, 1939.
A review of Canada's economic history, with particular attention to the national economic policies that have influenced it.

F. MASSON AND J. B. WHITELY: *Barriers to Trade Between Canada and the United States*, National Planning Association (U.S.A.) and Private Planning Association of Canada, 1961.
A discussion of various aspects of commercial trade barriers between the two countries. This volume is part of a series of reports on Canada–United States relations prepared for the Canadian-American Committee. Other reports deal with wheat surpluses, oil, natural gas, Soviet economic power, and composition of trade, as they affect the two countries' relations.

CANADIAN-AMERICAN COMMITTEE: *A Possible Plan for a Canada –U.S. Free Trade Area*, National Planning Association

(U.S.A.) and Private Planning Association of Canada, Staff Report, 1965, p. 68.

D. W. SLATER: *Canada's Imports*, Royal Commission on Canada's Economic Prospects, Ottawa, Queen's Printer, 1957.

R. V. ANDERSON: *The Future of Canada's Export Trade,* Royal Commission on Canada's Economic Prospects, Ottawa, Queen's Printer, 1957.

M. C. KEMP: *The Demand for Canadian Imports, 1926-55*, University of Toronto Press, 1962.
An analytical and empirical survey of Canada's imports during that period.

H. C. EASTMAN: 'The Canadian Tariff and the Efficiency of the Canadian Economy', *American Economic Review*, May 1964.

J. H. DALES: 'The Cost of Protectionism with High International Mobility of Factors', *Canadian Journal of Economics and Political Science*, November 1964, pp. 512-26.
An original and important paper.

G. A. ELLIOTT: *Tariff Procedures and Trade Barriers*, University of Toronto Press, 1955.
This study illustrates the procedural costs of government regulation to importers; the protective effects of the procedures described are emphasized.

G. BLAKE: *Customs Administration in Canada*, University of Toronto Press, 1957.
In examining Canada's commercial policy, the author gives attention to the implementing acts as well as to the enabling acts.

CHAPTER

16

THE BALANCE OF PAYMENTS
AND THE EXCHANGE RATE

The trade in commodities, which was the subject of the preceding chapter, makes up only a part of a country's external trade. It is now time to present the over-all picture with the help of the balance of international payments.

A. Principal Concepts

The balance of international payments is a document of economic accounting that records all the transactions carried out in a given period of time between one country and the rest of the world. The transactions concerned are not only international transactions of the State, but also those of every one of the country's residents, individual and corporate. The balance of payments provides the detail of the *external account* that appears in the national accounts (see p. 20).

1. RECEIPTS AND PAYMENTS

As in every accounting system, a distinction is made first of all between receipts and payments: in this case between the goods and services sold to foreigners and those acquired from them. In the Canadian balance of payments, receipts are indicated by a plus sign, payments by a minus sign.

Since transactions with foreign countries are varied and complex, it is often difficult to know at first sight whether a particular

TABLE 16:1

**Simplified Statement of the Balance of Payments,
Canada 1964 (preliminary)**

	Balance in millions of dollars
A. CURRENT ACCOUNT	
1. Merchandise trade	700
2. Non-merchandise trade	−1153
3. Current-account balance	−453
B. NET LONG-TERM CAPITAL MOVEMENTS	
4. Direct investment	75
5. Transactions on stocks and bonds	619
6. Government transactions	53
7. Other	4
8. Total	751
C. NET SHORT-TERM CAPITAL MOVEMENTS	
9. Total	65
D. CHANGES IN RESERVES AND INTERNATIONAL MONETARY FUND POSITION	−363*
Total net capital movements (B+C+D)	453

*A minus sign indicates an increase in reserves.
SOURCE: Bank of Canada, *Statistical Summary*.

operation should be classed among the receipts or the payments.
The general rule consists in placing among the receipts (or on
the credit side) transactions that lead to a demand by a foreign
country for Canadian dollars, and among the payments (or on
the debit side) those that lead to a supply of Canadian dollars to
a foreign country.

An import of perfume obviously represents a payment
because, in order to pay for it, we will supply Canadian dollars
to the foreign country. But a payment also occurs when the
government buys gold or American dollars, or when a bank buys

a foreign bond. An increase in the gold stock in Canada, an increase in reserves of foreign currencies, an increase in foreign securities held in Canada – all these are equivalent to exports of Canadian dollars and so are included on the debit side of the balance of payments. Conversely, if exports of commodities clearly represent a receipt, so also do borrowing abroad, selling common stock abroad, and giving gold away.

2. CURRENT TRANSACTIONS

Transactions are divided according to their nature into two conventional and well-known categories: current transactions and capital movements. Current transactions include first of all the exports and imports of commodities, the difference between the two being the *trade balance*; they also include service exchanges sometimes called invisible items of trade, such as shipping and insurance charges, interest and dividends, travel expenditures. The balance resulting from the current receipts and expenditures is called *the balance on current account*. In several respects this figure is the most significant of all. A positive balance (or surplus) indicates that total sales of goods and services to foreign countries have exceeded total purchases; a negative balance (or deficit) indicates the contrary. A positive balance consequently represents a loan to foreign countries and a negative one a borrowing from foreign countries. This consequence is necessary and automatic; it follows from the rule that whatever is not paid for represents a debt.

We may also consider a positive balance on current account as a saving (in terms of the national currency) that the country has realized. It can be invested in foreign enterprises, it can serve outside the country for the purchase of securities, or to repay debts, or to buy gold and foreign exchange.

Whatever use may be made of the current-account surplus, and whatever the objective may be, the surplus is always equivalent to an investment or a loan by the country that benefits from it, and to an indebtedness on the part of the other country. Table 16:1 shows that in 1964 Canada incurred a deficit of $453 million on its current transactions: this is the amount of debt it contracted with other countries in that year.

3. CAPITAL MOVEMENTS

The transactions for which a current-account surplus can be used, of which examples were given above, belong to the category of capital movements. *These transactions can be classified as long-term capital movements, short-term capital movements, and changes in official holdings of gold and foreign exchange.* The distinction between long-term capital and short-term capital rests on the fact that decisions regarding one or the other category of capital depend to a large degree on different circumstances and factors. Moreover, a change in economic policy produces immediate consequences on short-term capital movements; long-term capital flows are much less volatile, and will be altered only over a period of time.

Movements of gold and foreign exchange come under the jurisdiction of the Department of Finance. They consist of the variations in the official holdings of gold and foreign exchange as shown in the assets of the Exchange Fund Account.[1]

One of the movements of long-term capital is *direct investment*. In the strict theoretical sense, direct investment is an international transfer of capital aimed at the acquisition of real assets such as factories, machinery, or land. In practice, it includes capital flows involving 'the controlling, affiliated, or principal owners' of foreign-controlled companies.[2] Direct investment can easily be distinguished from *securities transactions*, or portfolio

1. Canada's position in the International Monetary Fund is included in this item. This ambiguous expression refers to the I.M.F. holdings of Canadian dollars. When these holdings go up, the increase obviously represents a non-resident demand for Canadian dollars and so it is given a plus sign in balance-of-payments terms. When the I.M.F. holdings of Canadian dollars go down, as in 1964, the decrease must be a minus-sign item in the Canadian balance-of-payments (Table 16:1). It may be useful to add that it is for the same reason that an increase in gold reserves is indicated by a minus sign in Table 16:1.

2. Dominion Bureau of Statistics, *The Canadian Balance of International Payments, 1961 and 1962, and International Investment Position*, p. 97.

investments, which are holdings of government or private bonds and stocks 'where these holdings are not sufficiently concentrated to constitute control'.[1] *Government transactions* consist of inter-governmental loans and repayments and Canada's subscriptions to international organizations. These are the main categories of long-term capital movements.

The short-term capital movements are not broken down in Table 16:1; this category includes resident holdings of foreign bank balances, non-resident holdings of Canadian dollars and other assets, short-term borrowings of business firms, and the balancing item representing the difference between the current account and the capital account (capital account $= B + C + D$).

4. ACCOUNTING *v.* ECONOMIC EQUILIBRIUM

The accounting conventions listed in section 2 ensure an exact balancing of plus and minus signs between the total of the net capital movements and the current-account balance. To compensate for the deficit of $453 million in the current account (indicated by the minus sign), the net capital movement, by definition, must show an indebtness of $453 million (indicated by a plus sign). It is in this conventional or 'accounting' sense that a balance of payments is always in equilibrium. The conventions that we use here, however, represent an underlying reality, for the accounting system does not distort the facts: it records and reflects them. A mechanism exists that automatically adjusts the capital movements to the surplus or deficit of the current account. This balancing mechanism must allow for the fact that the decisions to invest or to lend are largely independent (but not absolutely) of the decisions to exchange goods or services: the American investor who buys stock in a Canadian company, thus causing an inflow of capital, does not bother to find out if the current-account balance will show a deficit sufficient to compensate for his transfer of capital. Moreover, the compensating mechanism must come into play not only between

1. *Ibid.*

Canada and all foreign countries at the same time, but also between Canada and each individual country, for if Canada borrows from England, obviously England is the sole lender in this case. A surplus with one country can be used to pay for the deficit with another, but in the account with each individual country as in the over-all account, the capital movements must be equal to the current-account balance. In fact, the rule applies to every single transaction, so that for every export of goods or services there is a corresponding import of capital.

The compensating mechanism operates because all transactions are expressed in or translated into one currency, the Canadian dollar. Whatever the nature of the transactions, they are all registered at the same table at the same casino. An export puts dollars on the table, a loan to a foreign country takes off dollars. That a compensating mechanism does exist is attributable to the fact that everyone is, so to speak, buying or selling the same product, the Canadian dollar.

Let us now see how a particular transaction will cause its counterpart to appear. Suppose, to take a simplified case, that a Canadian importer wishes to buy a commodity from an American producer. Assume the value of the commodity is $100. The American will accept Canadian dollars if he in turn intends to buy a Canadian product, or if he plans a Canadian holiday. The export of the Canadian good or service will be the positive counterpart of the initial import, and trade will be in balance. But if the American wishes to spend his money at home he may request American dollars from his Canadian customer. The importer might then buy American dollars from the Exchange Fund, and complete the transaction. The import will have caused a deficit of $100 to appear in the current-account balance. The Canadian holdings of American dollars will have been lowered by $100, and so the capital movement will have been positive: the balance of payments is in equilibrium.

SCHEMA 1:

A. *Current transactions*	
Import	$- \$100$
B. *Capital movements*	
Decrease in the Canadian holdings of American dollars	$+ \$100$

In practice the American exporter probably will not request payment in American dollars because he knows that his fellow countrymen wish to invest in Canada. In this case he will sell his Canadian dollars to American investors and we can say, for the sake of simplicity, that a direct investment of $100 will then correspond to the initial Canadian import.

SCHEMA 2:

A. *Current transactions*	
Import	$- \$100$
B. *Capital movements*	
Direct investment	$+ \$100$

There is no reason, obviously, why a direct investment (in a Canadian oil well, for instance) should be exactly equal to the initial import of $100. These two transactions have no relation to each other. Let us suppose that the American investment in Canada actually amounts to $200, but only the 100 Canadian dollars are in circulation in the United States; it will be necessary for the American investor to buy the required sum. The Exchange Fund will thus acquire American funds to the value of 100 Canadian dollars. The balance of payments will be as follows:

SCHEMA 3:

A. *Current transactions*		
Import		— $100
B. *Capital movements*		
Direct investment in Canada		+ $200
Rise in the Canadian holdings of American dollars		— $100

These examples illustrate how a balance of payments is always in 'balance'.

The sceptical reader may say, however, 'This isn't possible! If the balance of payments was always in equilibrium, why did Europe take ten years to overcome the dollar crisis after the war? Why was Canada obliged to borrow a billion dollars in June 1962? Why is the United States in difficulties with its balance of payments?'

Let us clear this up at once, to avoid confusion. The balance of payments is always in equilibrium, but certain types of adjustments are spontaneous and realized with no attendant hardship while others are forced or undesirable. Schema 2 is an automatic adjustment in that no intervention of the Exchange Fund is required. Schema 1 and Schema 3 represent situations in which the decisions of citizens to engage in trade and to invest force the Exchange Fund to take action. Assuming that these interventions are not deliberate and that they do not necessarily agree with the objectives of the government's economic policy, the adjustment of Schema 2 is preferable to those of Schemas 1 and 3. By merely reading the balance of payments, however, it is not possible to distinguish the desirable adjustments from the undesirable. Only an examination of the over-all economic conditions allows us to do this. For example, Schema 1 would represent a satisfactory situation if the reserves of foreign currency were excessive and an undesirable situation if the reserves were inadequate. Indeed, at the limit, Schema 1 might prove impossible in the sense that if no reserve of foreign currency was available at all, the import could not have taken place. When difficulties arise, governments have to reduce imports in various ways because no means of payment can be found – because in our terms no counterpart can be made to appear. Similarly Schemas 2 and 3 may present serious disadvantages if it is considered that there should be no further increase of foreign investment in the country.

Using as a basis the distinction between an automatic adjustment and a forced adjustment, certain countries use the term *balance-of-payments surplus or deficit* to indicate changes in the movements of short-term capital (or of certain categories thereof) and in the official holdings of gold and foreign currency. It is in this light, for example, that we must interpret the information widely publicized in recent years concerning the balance-of-payments deficit of the United States. This deficit is calculated on the basis of gold exports plus the increase in short-term debts to foreign countries. If Canada's balance of payments were analysed according to this very arbitrary convention, it would record a surplus of $298 million in 1964 ($65 million minus $363 million, Table 16:1).

5. THE EXCHANGE FUND ACCOUNT

Where may foreign currencies be purchased? In Schema 2 the investors were buying dollars available in the market, and in the other two cases we introduced the Exchange Fund Account. A brief explanation of these two sources of currency follows.

In most countries a market exists for the purchase and sale of foreign currencies. In Canada this trading is done through the banks. Nine times out of ten, the customer's bank already has the desired currency available, so that the foreign-exchange trading amounts to no more than accounting transfers within that bank. The exchange market proper consists of the *interbank trading* for which the two brokers (one brokerage house in Montreal and another in Toronto) of the Canadian Bankers'

Association are the exclusive agents. Only the chartered banks and the Bank of Canada have direct access to the market. Transactions totalled $3.5 billion in 1961. Each transaction is for at least $100,000. The foreign currencies already available within the country, currencies received by exporters, tourist operators, and others, finally end up in the banks and their abundance in relation to the demand fixes their price.

When there is an excess demand or an excess supply of foreign currencies, the Exchange Fund Account appears on the stage.

The Exchange Fund Account is a special account of the Department of Finance. It records the official holdings of gold and foreign exchange. Until 1939, the gold reserves served to guarantee the bank-notes in circulation; now their purpose is to control fluctuations in the exchange rate and to finance residual external debts. The account comes under the authority of the Minister of Finance, and the executive agent is the Bank of Canada. Foreign currencies are bought by advances in Canadian dollars drawn from the Consolidated Revenue of the federal government.[1] The balance sheet appears in Table 16:2.

When the Exchange Fund Account makes purchases, it does so in the local market if foreign currencies are available there. If not, it applies to the foreign central banks. Whether the account is a buyer or seller of foreign currencies in the local market will, of course, depend on the state of the balance of payments.

It is important to bear in mind from this section not only the principal concepts used in connection with the balance of payments, but also the networks through which the exporters and importers, the banks, and the public authorities come into contact in the money market and by their dealings determine the

---

1. These advances to the Exchange Fund Account are the bridge between the external and the internal monetary markets. It is through this connection that the movements of gold and foreign currencies influence the internal money supply, depending on the method of financing chosen by the government. This liaison is one of the most fundamental in the functioning of the monetary mechanisms.

TABLE 16:2

Exchange Fund Account, Canada 1964 (year-end), millions of Canadian dollars

Assets		Liabilities	
U.S. Government short-term securities	1,680.6	Advances outstanding	2,737.0
Gold	1,108.9	Earnings on investments not transferred	
U.S. dollar deposits	25.3	to the Consolidated Revenue Fund	63.6
Canadian dollars	1.3		
Revaluation account	−31.7		
Total	2,800.6	Total	2,800.6

NOTE: The revaluation account mainly reflects the revaluation, at successive year-ends, of the gold and foreign exchange held in the Exchange Fund Account on the basis of variations of market exchange rates. When the Canadian dollar depreciates, a surplus is shown.

SOURCES: Bank of Canada, *Statistical Summary, Supplement, 1964.*

level of what we shall later call the exchange rate of the currency.

B. Recent Developments in the Balance of Payments

It is high time to stop introducing the characters and look at the performance. What have been the developments in Canada in recent years?

1. CURRENT TRANSACTIONS

Current transactions showed surpluses from 1939 until 1950, and deficits after 1950. These deficits progressively increased and reached the fantastic sum of $1.5 billion in 1959 (22 per cent of current receipts and 18 per cent of current expenditures). After 1959 the deficit began to decrease until, in 1964, it was less than $500 million. The deficit accumulated from 1950 to 1962 reached $10.76 billion, an annual average of $820 million.

It is not primarily the trade balance that explains the deficits on the current account. We shall therefore briefly examine the transactions in services (non-merchandise transactions).[1] Except for the export of gold, which is not, strictly speaking, a service transaction, all the items contribute to the total deficit. Travel expenditures are related primarily to the tourist industry and the transactions are mainly with the United States. From 1962 to 1964, however, a surplus was recorded with the United States and a deficit with other countries. In 1964, the surplus with the United States was $106 million and the deficit with all other countries was $158 million. This series of surpluses with the United States, of which the 1962 surplus was the first in ten years, resulted in large part from the depreciation of the Canadian dollar since April 1961. The interest and dividends paid out to foreign countries contribute most to the total deficit. They have represented about 10 per cent of the current-account receipts and 2 per cent of the gross national product since the end of the war. This means that in absolute figures they have

---

1. For a useful reference see John Popkin, *Non-Merchandise Transactions between Canada and the U.S.*, Montreal, Canadian-American Committee, 1963.

TABLE 16:3

Net Current Transactions with Foreign Countries, Canada 1951-64, millions of dollars

	1951	1956	1959	1962	1964
1. Merchandise trade	−147	−728	−422	177	700
2. Travel	−6	−161	−207	−43	−52
3. Interest and dividends	−335	−381	−489	−592	−673
4. Freight and shipping	−3	−45	−105	−86	−61
5. Inheritance and migrants' funds	7	−16	−56	−51	−25
6. Gold production available for export	150	150	148	155	144
7. All other current transactions	−183	−185	−373	−434	−486
8. Total non-merchandise trade (total of 2-7)	−370	−638	−1,082	−1,051	−1,153
9. Current-account balance	−517	−1,366	−1,504	−874	−453

SOURCES: 1951 to 1959: Dominion Bureau of Statistics, *The Canadian Balance of International Payments, 1960.* 1962 and 1964: Bank of Canada, *Statistical Summary,* April 1965.

been constantly increasing. These payments are obviously explained by Canadian borrowings and by foreign investments in Canada; we shall return to them later. Passing over the next three items in Table 16:4 as not requiring special comment, we come to the miscellaneous transactions. These may be broken down in the following way:

All Other Transactions, 1964, millions of dollars

	Balance
Commercial, industrial, and financial services	− 240
Official contributions	− 68
Other government transactions	− 44
Personal or institutional remittances	− 64
Investment income and other items	− 70
Total	− 486

The commercial, industrial, and financial services are an addi-

TABLE 16:4

Non-Merchandise Transactions with Foreign Countries, Canada 1964, millions of dollars

	Receipts	*Payments*	*Balance*
1. Travel	661	713	−52
2. Interest and dividends	287	960	−673
3. Freight and shipping	642	703	−61
4. Inheritances and migrants' funds	166	191	−25
5. Gold production available for export	144	—	144
6. All other transactions	468	954	−486
7. Total	2,368	3,521	−1,153

SOURCE: Bank of Canada, *Statistical Summary*, April 1965.

tional aspect of the presence of foreign enterprises in Canada and of the very close bonds existing between Canada and the United States. A good number of these services reflect, in fact, the exchanges between the American parent companies and their Canadian subsidiaries or branches.

As to the geographical distribution of the total current transactions, we show the heaviest deficits with the United States. Our transactions with other countries have traditionally shown a surplus. For a long time our surpluses with Europe were sufficient to finance our deficits with the United States. This useful triangle was definitely broken in 1950. From 1950 to 1962, Canadian surpluses with other countries almost stabilized at $300 million, whereas deficits with the United States exceeded $1 billion. In 1963 and 1964, both the deficit with the United States and the surplus with other countries increased considerably. In 1964 they stood respectively at $1,659 million and $1,206 million.

2. CAPITAL MOVEMENTS

Since net capital inflows are equal in total to the deficits incurred on the current account (see p. 393), it is clear that capital inflows have been very large since 1950 (particularly between 1956 and 1960).

Almost half of the new net foreign capital since 1950 has taken the form of *direct investment*. Between 1956 and 1962, foreigners invested annually more than $500 million in Canada and Canadians invested about $80 million abroad. During 1963 and 1964, Canadians annually invested $100 million abroad and non-residents reduced their direct investment to $200 million annually. More than two-thirds of the direct foreign investment came from the United States.

Transactions in portfolio securities are a second important source of foreign funds and give rise to a greater number of financial operations than one might think from the size of the net balances (see Table 16:5). Securities are classed as Canadian and foreign. Trading in Canadian securities is heavier than that in foreign (Table 16:6). A distinction is also made between

TABLE 16:5

Net Capital Movements, Canada 1956-64, millions of dollars

	1956	1959	1962	1964
1. Direct investment	479	470	386	75
2. Transactions on stocks and bonds	727	617	291	619
3. Government transactions	48	−23	107	53
4. Resident holdings of foreign bank balances and other short-term funds	−215	−120	93	−499
5. Non-resident holdings of Canadian short-term assets	−24	13	−13	9
6. Other capital movements	384	477	165	559
7. Changes in reserves and International Monetary Fund position	−33	70	−155	−363
8. Total	1,366	1,504	874	453

SOURCES: See Table 16:3

transactions in outstanding securities and transactions in new issues. Among these transactions, the main sources of foreign capital are *new Canadian issues* sold abroad (principally in the United States). Table 16:6(1b) shows that in 1964 new Canadian securities were sold abroad to the tidy sum of $1,053 million. After retirements are deducted, the net capital import on this item alone is $696 million. The main initiative in this category of investment does not come from abroad but from Canadians, often from governments. From 1952 to 1960 two-thirds of the Canadian securities issues sold abroad were government bonds – mainly provincial and municipal. On the other hand, trade in Canadian *outstanding securities* reached between $2 billion and $3 billion in recent years, but the net balance of the flows was relatively small. Lastly, Canadians spent $582 million on *foreign securities* in 1964 (particularly stocks) and sold $525 million, creating a negative balance of $57 million on this item.

Returning to Table 16:5, we come next to 'Government transactions'. Government transactions cover intergovernmental loans, subscriptions to the capital of international agencies, and loans or advances related to the financing of Canadian exports.

Canadians' bank balances in foreign currencies and their other holdings of short-term funds constitute one of the most important items among the short-term capital flows. These holdings are very sensitive to economic conditions; they represent floating capital *par excellence*. Thus, when there was speculation against the Canadian dollar during the second quarter of 1962, these balances in foreign currencies increased by $245 million, and by the end of the following quarter they had decreased by $257 million. (The purchase of foreign currencies is obviously equivalent to the sale of Canadian dollars and vice versa). The fluctuations were thus $500 million in six months. The net change in 1964 was again 'unusually' large: it was $500 million. Total resident holdings of bank balances were estimated at about $1.5 billion at the end of 1964.

TABLE 16:6

Transactions in Securities with Foreign Countries, 1964, millions of dollars

	Sales abroad	Purchases from abroad	Balance
1. CANADIAN SECURITIES			
(a) Outstanding			
bonds and debentures	227	150	77
stocks, common and preferred	535	632	−97
total (1a)	762	782	−20
(b) New issues			
government securities	643	—	643
private securities	393	—	393
common and preferred stocks	17	—	17
(c) Retirements (all categories)	—	357	−357
total (1b) + (1c)	1,053	357	696
total (1a) + (1b) + (1c)	1,815	1,139	676
2. FOREIGN SECURITIES			
(a) Outstanding			
bonds and debentures	71	70	1
common and preferred stocks	444	485	−41
total (2a)	515	555	−40
(b) New issues and retirements	10	27	−17
total (2a) + (2b)	525	582	−57
total (1) + (2)	2,340	1,721	619

SOURCE: Dominion Bureau of Statistics, *Sales and Purchases of Securities between Canada and Other Countries, December, 1964*, and *Review of Security*

The item 'Non-resident holdings of Canadian short-term assets' (dollars and Treasury bills) is similar in nature to the previous one, but the fluctuations were less pronounced. These holdings amounted to approximately $550 million at the end of 1964.

'Other capital movements' include non-resident holdings of commercial paper and of finance company securities, changes in loans and accounts receivable and payable, and the balancing item between direct estimates of current and capital account.

It should be noted that resident holdings of foreign short-term assets and non-resident holdings of Canadian short-term assets represent funds of considerable size compared with the official holdings of gold and foreign exchange which at year-end 1964 were $2.8 billion (Table 16:2, p. 399). In 1961, the 'reserves' scarcely exceeded $2 billion. From 1951 to 1960 no attempt was made to increase them; it now appears this should have been done in view of the great amount of short-term funds on the market. On the contrary, since the exchange rate was free at that time, the Exchange Fund during this period acted only to ease the short-term fluctuations of the external payments, and it was deemed sufficient to maintain the reserves at the $1.8 billion level they had held since 1951. When the exchange rate is fixed, however, as it has been since 1962, it is essential that the reserves be adequate to handle potential threats to the currency.

What conclusions may be drawn from this brief examination of Canada's balance of payments?

1. Current expenditures abroad generally vary in the same direction as the gross national product, increasing during periods of expansion, decreasing during contractions. They did not decrease, however, from 1957 to 1961, and as a result the deficit on current account remained, despite internal economic stagnation.

2. This deficit was made possible and was financed by an

influx of foreign capital in the form of direct investment and by the sale of securities abroad.

3. Capital imports lead to an increase in productive capacity (in the absence of domestic disinvestment) which in turn generally leads to an increase in exports (or a decrease in imports) and to a reduction of the deficit on current account, if there is one. Since in this case the direct investment was largely channelled into the exploitation of natural resources – an exploitation of high capital intensity – the effect on exports was slow to manifest itself. On the other hand, the major part of capital imports resulting from the sale of securities was absorbed by the financing of government services; these capital imports have served to make up for the inadequacy of domestic savings. Here again the positive effect on the balance of payments has been negligible.

4. It is generally admitted that the balance-of-payments situation has deteriorated disastrously between 1955 and 1959, and that the federal government should have acted by 1957-8 to reduce the importation of capital and the deficit on current account by increasing substantially the supply of money, an action which would have lowered interest rates.

C. Foreign Capital

In the same way that a distinction is made between a corporation's operating account and its statement of assets and liabilities, there is a distinction between accounts indicating international flows and accounts indicating the country's international investment position (chapter 1). In Canada's economic relations with foreign countries, the balance of payments records the flows and a 'balance of international indebtedness' records total assets held abroad and total liabilities to other countries. Suppose a net capital inflow in the amount of $100 during the year: it is indicated in the balance of payments. The statement of Canada's balance of international indebtedness, on the other hand, indicates the total liabilities at the beginning of the year as, let us say, $50. If we add the net flow during the year to the total liabilities at the beginning of the year we obtain the total liabilities at the end of the year: $50 + $100 = $150.[1]

Table 16:7 is a summary of Canada's external balance sheet. In 1962, Canadians had $10 billion in foreign assets and $29 billion in foreign debts – a net external indebtedness of almost $19 billion.

This indebtedness increased considerably between 1951 and 1962 and in fact, until 1961, increased much more rapidly than the gross national product. It increased from 24 per cent of the G.N.P. in 1951 to 47 per cent in 1960, reached almost 50 per cent in 1961, and then fell back to 45.8 per cent in 1962. An indebtedness of this proportion is not new in Canada since the indebtedness during the years 1926 to 1930 was about 50 per cent.[2] What is surprising is that we should have returned to this figure in an economically advanced country which should have available an abundant supply of domestic savings. The servicing (that is, the cost) of this debt is represented by the interest and dividend payments shown in Table 16:3, and amounts to about 10 per cent of the external receipts on current account or 2 per cent of the G.N.P. Three-quarters of the foreign long-term investment in Canada comes from the United States.

The importance of foreign capital in the Canadian economy becomes still more apparent if it is compared with total investment and if its concentration in certain industrial sectors is taken into account. Tables 16:8 and 16:9 give the information necessary to make these comparisons.

---

1. The non-distributed profits of foreign enterprises in Canada do not give rise to an import of capital but are added to the external indebtedness. The same pertains to the non-distributed profits of Canadian enterprises abroad. Apart from this item, one can obtain the variations in the statement of external assets and liabilities of the year from the figures of the balance of payments for that year.

2. I. Brecher and S. S. Reisman, *Canada–United States Economic Relations*, Royal Commission on Canada's Economic Prospects, 1957, Part 2, pp. 85-165.

TABLE 16:7

Canadian Balance of International Indebtedness, billions of dollars

	1951	1956	1960	1962
1. ASSETS				
(a) Direct investments abroad	1.2	1.9	2.5	2.8
(b) Portfolio investments	0.6	1.0	1.3	1.7
(c) Government of Canada loans, subscriptions, and holdings of gold and foreign exchange	4.1	3.9	3.8	5.1
(d) Short-term assets	0.3	1.0	1.7	0.7
Total gross assets	6.3	7.7	9.3	10.3
2. LIABILITIES				
(a) Direct investments in Canada	4.5	8.9	12.9	14.5
(b) Non-resident other long-term investments	4.9	6.6	9.4	10.2
(c) Short-term liabilities	1.8	2.1	3.8	4.1
Total gross indebtedness	11.3	17.7	26.1	28.8
3. NET INTERNATIONAL INDEBTEDNESS (2−1)	5.0	10.0	16.9	18.6
4. NET INTERNATIONAL INDEBTEDNESS AS A PERCENTAGE OF THE G.N.P.	24	33	47	45.8

NOTE: Apparent errors are due to rounding.

SOURCES: 1951-60: Dominion Bureau of Statistics, *The Canadian Balance of International Payments, 1961 and 1962, and International Investment Position.* 1962: Bank of Canada, *Statistical Summary,* 1964.

TABLE 16:8

Direct Foreign Financing of Total Public and Private Investment, 1946-62, percentages

	Gross capital formation	Net capital formation
1946-1949	19	24
1950-1955	25	33
1956-1960	33	45
1961-1962	32	46

During the period 1956-60, and again in 1961 and 1962, investments in Canada greatly exceeded the domestic savings available for this purpose. Table 16:8 indicates that 45 per cent of net investment in 1956-60 was financed by foreign savings and 46 per cent in 1961-2.[1] This proportion was almost double the 1946-9 figure. A more thorough analysis would show that this development was mainly due neither to much higher investments nor to a fall in private savings, but to heavy budgetary deficits. Without the inflow of foreign savings, Canadian investments from 1956 to 1962 would have been reduced by almost half in each year.

Table 16:9 provides a breakdown of long-term foreign capital and shows what share it represents in the total amount of invested capital and outstanding securities. Of the $23.6 billion[2] of long-term foreign capital in Canada at the end of 1961, 14.6

---

1. Net domestic savings came to more than 55 per cent of investments (64 per cent between 1956 and 1960, and 71 per cent during 1961 and 1962) but part of these funds were exported. This is why we use the expression 'savings available for this purpose' in the preceding sentence.

2. If 1961 were shown in Table 16:7, the figure $23.6 billion would be lines 2a and 2b for that year.

TABLE 16:9

Long-term Foreign Capital in Canada, 1961

	As a percentage of total foreign capital	As a percentage of total amounts outstanding in Canada
1. GOVERNMENT SECURITIES	*14.6*	
Dominion	2.8	3.5
Provincial	7.4	21.2
Municipal	4.4	25.6

		As a percentage of total capital
2. INDUSTRIES	*61.9*	
Manufacturing	27.3	54
Petroleum and natural gas	17.1	60
Other mining and smelting	8.9	62
Railways	5.8	25
Other public utilities	2.8	13
3. MERCHANDISING, FINANCIAL, OTHER ENTERPRISES, AND MISCELLANEOUS INVESTMENTS	*23.5*	
Total	100	

NOTE: The U.S. share in foreign capital, for the above industries, is as follows: 79 per cent, 85 per cent, 87 per cent, 37 per cent and 77 per cent.

SOURCE: Dominion Bureau of Statistics, *The Canadian Balance of International Payments, 1961 and 1962, and International Investment Position.*

per cent was invested in government securities and 8.6 per cent in railways and other public utilities. The distribution of the remainder is indicated in the table.

Particular attention is directed to the second column, which shows that 21 per cent of provincial and 26 per cent of municipal securities, but only 3.5 per cent of federal securities, were held abroad in 1961. The foreign share in ownership of Canadian industry appears in the bottom part of the column: 54 per cent of all manufacturing industry, 60 per cent of the oil industry, and 62 per cent of the mining industry (particularly non-ferrous metals).[1] The most progressive and dynamic manufacturing industries belong to non-residents: for example, automobiles, electrical apparatus, synthetic chemical products, heavy equipment. And with few exceptions, the foreign firms within these industries are the most important. *With the exception of the chartered banks and the railroads, the major decision-making centres within the Canadian economy are for all practical purposes foreign centres.*[2]

It is not surprising that a growing number of observers are worried about this Trojan horse stationed at every strategic control point. The extent and the scale of foreign control becomes ever more disturbing, in spite of the economic advantages, even if it is impossible to prove by any performance test that it harms the public interest. At any rate, there are so many arguments, economic as well as non-economic, on both sides of the question of foreign capital that one would be well advised to avoid sweeping judgments.

It is undeniable that foreign capital has speeded up Canada's economic growth. Indeed it is difficult to see how it could have been done without at certain periods. But it does appear that in secondary industry the production units have focused too exclusively on the domestic market at the expense of the export market, and that this has probably increased Canadian balance-of-payments difficulties and increased the need for still more reliance on foreign capital. The limited scope of this book prevents more thorough discussion of this rather common opinion,

---

1. As it is not necessary to acquire 100 per cent of the equity to gain control of an enterprise, the statistics on foreign control differ from the statistics on ownership. Foreign control was as follows in 1961: manufacturing industry, 59 per cent; petroleum and natural gas, 69 per cent; extraction, smelting, and refining, 59 per cent; railways, 2 per cent; other public services, 5 per cent.

2. Appendix B of the book already cited, by I. Brecher and S. S. Reisman, contains an instructive list of several foreign enterprises.

but let us not forget that foreign capital in Canada has always been invited by Canadian policy and is undoubtedly a result of such policy. Very little will be achieved therefore by a direct attack on foreign investment, or by imposing controls. If correctives are needed, then they should be in those policies that make capital imports too profitable – that is, the tariff, fiscal, and monetary policies.

D. The Exchange Rate of the Dollar

It has not been easy to discuss the balance of payments at such length without introducing the concept of the exchange rate. It is rather like explaining a complicated game while studiously avoiding mention of one of the principal rules.

The exchange rate is the price at which one currency is exchanged for another. If the Canadian dollar is exchanged for four Swiss francs, the exchange rate of the dollar is 4, that is

$$\frac{1 \text{ dollar}}{1 \text{ Swiss franc}} = 4$$

The price of the dollar is here expressed in Swiss francs (one dollar is worth four Swiss francs).

Inversely we can write:

$$\frac{1 \text{ Swiss franc}}{1 \text{ dollar}} = 0.25$$

Here the price of the Swiss franc is expressed in Canadian dollars (one Swiss franc is worth $0.25). Since each currency has its price, the Canadian dollar has as many exchange rates as there are foreign currencies (and it has in addition an exchange rate with gold) Thus the par value of the Canadian dollar has been 92.5 American cents from May 2, 1962, to the time of writing; it has been about 4.5 French francs, and so forth.

1. BALANCE OF PAYMENTS AND THE EXCHANGE RATES

Like all other prices, the exchange rate of the national currency (in terms of foreign currencies) rises if demand increases and falls if supply increases. Demand for Canadian dollars is made up of all items in the balance of payments bearing the plus sign: exports of goods and services, direct investment in Canada, borrowings from non-residents, and the like. Supply of Canadian dollars is made up of all items in the balance of payments bearing the minus sign: imports of goods and services, direct investment abroad, loans to foreign countries, and the like. It follows that the exchange rate varies under the influence of the factors affecting the items in the balance of payments. A rise in the price of commodities, by reducing exports and increasing imports, causes the exchange rate to fall; a rise in interest rates, by attracting foreign capital, tends to raise it; an increase in national income, which is usually reflected by an increase in imports, sends it down.

In the section beginning on page 393 (Accounting *v.* Economic Equilibrium) it is explained that the balance of payments is always in equilibrium. The concept of the exchange rate allows us to consider the matter from another aspect. If the supply and demand curves for the product (the Canadian dollar) have a normal shape, and if the price fluctuates freely, there is always a price level at which supply and demand are equal. When a deficit on current transactions causes the exchange rate to drop, foreign products and services become more expensive at home and Canadian products become cheaper abroad. Consequently imports decrease and exports increase. A fall in the exchange rate tends to correct the initial deficit in the current-account transactions. There is a similar tendency in capital movements.

It follows that the balance of payments is not only always in equilibrium in the accounting sense of the term (the purchases of some are the sales of others), but it also tends towards equilibrium in the economic sense. This means, for example, that no country will indefinitely show a surplus or show a deficit with other countries. Such a condition can only be temporary because of the mechanisms of adjustment inherent in the exchange system. ('Temporary' here is being used in a theoretical sense.

In practice the temporary can last for a hundred years, as the Canadian experience shows.)

At times, however, these mechanisms do not take effect quickly enough, and the State intervenes. This is nothing exceptional, since the government already intervenes in several other markets, for example agriculture and housing. The government may establish a system of fixed parities (a price control) and may then be forced to adopt complementary measures in order to regulate the supply and demand affecting the exchange rate – that is, in order to gain direct control over the balance of payments. *When the government pegs the exchange rate of the currency we have a fixed-exchange-rate system; when the rate varies in response to market forces we have a fluctuating-exchange-rate system.*[1] 'Exchange control' refers to direct government interventions in respect of imports and exports.

2. SOME NEWS ITEMS

Canada is one of the few countries to have experienced both the fluctuating – and the fixed-exchange-rate systems since the war. In conformity with the statutes of the International Monetary Fund, of which Canada is a member, the exchange rate of the Canadian dollar was not freed at the end of the war. In December 1946 its value was fixed at 100 American cents. As a result of the depreciation of the pound sterling, the Canadian dollar was depreciated in September 1949 to 90.9 cents U.S. The restrictions imposed at that time, combined with other circumstances favourable to capital formation, caused the Canadian dollar to rise during the succeeding year. As it was not practicable to resort to frequent changes of parity, the government abandoned the fixed-exchange-rate system in September

---

1. These concepts now enable us to understand that the Canadian dollar, as an expression of the over-all economic development of Canada compared with foreign countries, may be exchanged at par with the American dollar only through some accident. Once the monetary unit has been defined (this was done in 1858), there is no reason, apart from a sentimental one, why this particular exchange rate should be preferred to some other.

1950 and let the dollar fluctuate according to market pressures. In spite of the growing deficits that Canada was to show in its current transactions, the dollar became firm soon after it was freed, reached par in March 1952, and remained constantly above par until 1961.

The Canadian dollar maintained such high levels because of the massive importation of long-term capital. Until 1956 there was no concern about the rise in the exchange rate or about the capital imports. On the contrary, the appreciation of the dollar was regarded as proof that the adjustments and adaptations were working in the right direction. In 1956 and 1957 the advisers and the members of the Royal Commission on Canada's Economic Prospects (the Gordon Commission) paid considerable attention to the question of foreign capital, but they did so from a long-term point of view, in which the advantages for the Canadian economy easily compensated for the temporary disadvantages. Later, persistence of unemployment led to increasingly unfavourable comment on the foreign investments that were allowing Canadians to 'live beyond their means' (as James Coyne, Governor of the Bank of Canada, put it). Bitter controversy ensued.

At the end of 1960 the government adopted the first measure that directly affected capital imports: an increase in the withholding tax on dividends. Then it announced that the Exchange Fund would acquire American currency in order to lower the exchange rate of the Canadian dollar. In the first half of 1961 the Fund purchased $156 million to this end. These measures, combined with a decrease in Canadian borrowings from abroad, caused the dollar to weaken in a very marked manner in the spring of 1961. As the graph below shows, it dropped by almost five points between April and July. In spite of the lowering of interest rates, which discouraged the entry of short-term capital in the second half of the year, the exchange rate seemed on the point of rising again in October. Once again the Exchange Fund resisted this tendency by buying foreign currency in the net amount of $186 million. But in fact the market had by then become irregular and unstable. The exchange rate began to fall again. In January 1962 it stood at 95.7 cents American.

Canadian Dollar in United States Cents, average noon rates

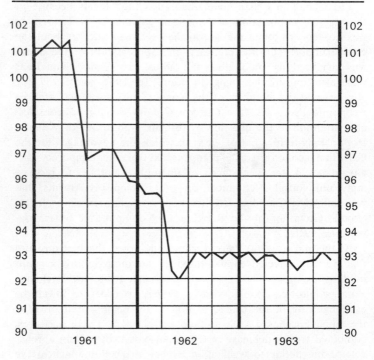

SOURCE: Budgetary documents, p. 49, House of Commons Debates, June 13, 1963.

If the exchange rate could have been maintained at this level without serious difficulty most Canadians would have been satisfied, for the rate of 95 cents American had been the objective of the government throughout 1961. Thus, at that time its efforts seemed to have been reasonably successful. Unfortunately, however, foreign capital stopped entering Canada in the first quarter of 1962, so that the current-transactions deficit had to be financed out of the gold and foreign exchange holdings of the Exchange Fund. These reserves dropped by $364 million. The second quarter was one of complete collapse. To the current-transactions deficit ($362 million) a tremendous flight of capital was added: a net exit of $14 million in long-term capital and $217 million in short-term capital. The Exchange Fund thus had to finance almost $600 million. On June 24 the Fund was down to half its usual holdings, not counting considerable forward commitments still to be honoured.

By the end of April it had become evident that the export of capital was leading to the collapse of the exchange rate. On May 2 the government therefore decided to lower the exchange rate to 92.5 cents American and to fix it at this level between limits of 1 per cent each way. This rate represented a slight devaluation in relation to the dollar's actual worth at the end of April. It ended the system of fluctuating exchange rates that had been in operation since 1950. One might have expected that this action of the government in lowering the price of the dollar and in affirming its will to maintain the new rate would have been sufficient to block the flight of capital. At the end of May, however, capital funds resumed their flight to the border; the downward pressures became almost an avalanche following the uncertain result of the federal election of June 18. On June 24 the government had to adopt stringent emergency measures to replenish the reserves of the Exchange Fund and to halt speculation against the dollar. Briefly, these measures consisted of borrowing more than $1 billion in foreign currencies, raising interest rates, decreasing government expenditures, and imposing supplementary duties on imports. A very appreciable improvement immediately took place in the capital movements: in the third quarter the return of capital was just as spectacular as its previous flight had been precipitate.

Between June 1962 and the time of writing, no change has been made in the exchange rate system. As to the review of recent developments, it need only be recalled that the story has been carried up to the end of 1964 in the section of this chapter beginning on page 400.

SUGGESTED READINGS

DOMINION BUREAU OF STATISTICS: *The Canadian Balance of International Payments, 1926 to 1948*, Ottawa, King's Printer, 1949.
A factual and analytical presentation of the characteristics and structure of the Canadian balance of payments. A follow-up was published in 1953: *The Canadian Balance of International Payments in the Post-war Years, 1946-1952*.

BANK OF CANADA: Annual Reports of the Governor to the Minister of Finance.

I. BRECHER AND S. S. REISMAN: *Canada–United States Economic Relations*, Royal Commission on Canada's Economic Prospects, Ottawa, Queen's Printer, 1957.
Part II is concerned with non-resident ownership and control of Canadian industry, with special reference to U.S. investment.

IRVING BRECHER: *Capital Flows between Canada and the United States*, Canadian-American Committee, Montreal, 1965, p. 138.

R. J. WONNACOTT: *Canadian-American Dependence*, Amsterdam, 1961.
This study is an attempt to bring recent developments in quantitative economic analysis to bear on the problem of Canadian economic dependence on the U.S.

P. WONNACOTT: *The Canadian Dollar, 1948-1958*, University of Toronto Press, 1960.
An analysis of the effects of a freely fluctuating exchange rate on international trade and domestic monetary conditions.

S. A. SHEPERD: *Foreign Exchange in Canada: An Outline*, University of Toronto Press, 1953.
A description of foreign exchange operations in Canada under a fluctuating exchange-rate system. The following three articles also deal with the same topic.

H. C. EASTMAN AND S. STYKOLT: 'Exchange Stabilization in Canada, 1950-54', *Canadian Journal of Economics and Political Science*, May 1956. Also 'Exchange Stabilization Once Again', *ibid.*, May 1958.

R. R. RHOMBERG: 'Canada's Foreign Exchange Market: A Quarterly Model', International Monetary Fund *Staff Papers*, April 1960.

T. L. POWRIE: 'Short-term Capital Movements and the Flexible Canadian Exchange Rate', *Canadian Journal of Economics and Political Science*, February 1964.

A. E. SAFARIAN: *Foreign Ownership of Canadian Industry*, Toronto, McGraw-Hill, 1966.

J. VINER: *Canada's Balance of International Indebtedness, 1900-1913*, Cambridge, Mass., Harvard University Press, 1954.
A study of the interrelations between cyclical fluctuations and international capital flows. A classic book.

INDEX